WITH THOSE EYES

WITH THOSE EYES

by
Michèle Morgan
with the collaboration of Marcelle Routier

Translated from the French by
Oliver Coburn

W. H. ALLEN · LONDON
A Howard & Wyndham Company
1978

Printed and bound in Great Britain by
Butler & Tanner Ltd
Frome and London
for the publishers W. H. Allen & Co. Ltd
44 Hill Street, London W1X 8LB

ISBN 0 491 02185 2

PUBLISHER'S NOTE

Oliver Coburn died at the age of sixty shortly after completing the
translation of this book. He was a man of great talent, ebullience, wit
and charm, a tireless worker and, above all, a true philanthropist.
Those who knew him had no better friend.

Contents

		page
1.	*The prediction*	1
2.	*'You'll make an actress'*	14
3.	*The First Chance*	30
4.	*Triumph with Raimu*	49
5.	*Setback with Boyer*	63
6.	Quai des Brumes	72
7.	*Romance amidst Rumours of War*	88
8.	*End of the Romance*	108
9.	*The Promised Land*	115
10.	*Sunset Boulevard*	127
11.	*Joan of Paris*	148
12.	*Orchids for Miss Morgan*	158
13.	*Mr and Mrs Marshall and Baby*	166
14.	*The Return*	181
15.	La Symphonie Pastorale	192
16.	The Fallen Idol	205
17.	*Fabiola—and Divorce Proceedings*	213
18.	*Remarriage, Light and Shade*	230
19.	*The Tunnel*	248
20.	Les Orgueilleux	255
21.	*Diversion beneath the Olive Trees*	270
22.	*Separations*	286
23.	*The End of the Tunnel*	297

Illustrations

(*between pages 104 and 105*)

Aged two and a half at Cayeux-sur-Mer (Photo: G. Huette).
The Family.
Dance lesson at Dieppe.
At the René Simon Drama School.
The first film.
With Jean Gabin at her house-warming party.
A scene from *Remorques*.
The start of the war-time journey to Hollywood.

(*between pages 168 and 169*)

The welcome from Ginger Rogers and her mother (Photo: J. Miehle—RKO Radio).
An RKO publicity photograph (Photo: E. Bachray—RKO Radio).
Bill Marshall.
Mike (Photo: P. Eustice).
A scene from *La symphonie pastorale*.
Michèle with her brother Paul and agent Olga Horstig.
The second marriage (Photo: Night photo).
La belle que voilà with Gérard Oury.

(*between pages 232 and 233*)

The last film with Jean Gabin.
Micheline Bonnet ('La Miche') (Photo: Paris Match).

Maxine with Charles Boyer.
Michel Deville's *Benjamin*.
The *Légion d'Honneur* (Photo: Bureau Parisien).
The second meeting with Charlie Chaplin.
'With those eyes ...' (Photo: Bleekman)

I   *The Prediction*

My childhood, no doubt, was commonplace enough; but for
me in retrospect it still has a quality far from ordinary.

For one thing, I was born into a family I still think very
special: good-natured, warm-hearted, easily amused, much
given, in fact, to crazy laughter for no good reason. The un-
initiated do not realise how extremely beneficial to the soul
such laughter can be.

Moreover, I believe it is a gift granted only to the pure
in heart, and all my family possessed hearts of unusual purity.
That is to say, we could well be called naïve and innocent;
we saw no evil, because it was so alien to us.

We lived in a small flat on the third floor of a house
in the rue de l'Église at Neuilly. One evening my mother
was bathing me in the kitchen, in the old zinc bath with
a gas heater underneath it. I was three. There was a cheerful noise in the steam-filled room as she washed me all
over and I splashed about. Then we heard Papa's voice
calling impatiently in the passage: 'Georgette, where are
you?'

'In the kitchen,' Maman replied, 'giving the little one her
bath.'

Papa framed himself at the door. 'I can't wait to tell you.
Marcel has just read Simone's horoscope for me.' (Marcel was
one of his office colleagues.)

Maman was giving me a vigorous rub down. 'Oh yes?'
she said absently.

'Listen to this: Simone's destiny will be ex-cep-tion-al.' He
took me from Maman, and hugged me passionately. His big
gingery moustache pricked me. He called me: 'My darling!
My first baby!' I was a little scared of his passionate hugs,

which were inclined to choke me. He held me up high, very high. At the end of his arms, I kicked.

'Put the famous lady down, you'll make her sick.'

Unperturbed by Maman's somewhat prosaic reaction, he continued lyrically: 'She *will* be famous, too. That's if war gives her the chance.'

It was only 1923, but Papa was a far-sighted man. He had been through the '14–'18 war, and when he looked at Germany in its convulsions caused by defeat and the Treaty of Versailles, he guessed, rightly, that we were only enjoying an interim peace.

The whole evening he expatiated on my future: being born under the sign of Pisces, with various other astrological data taken into account, I was to make a career in the arts, where I should be brilliantly, exceptionally successful. The next day he informed the whole family of my destiny, and it seems they all accepted the information as gospel truth.

They went on accepting it, and so did my parents. They were practising Catholics, so I find it very strange that they set such store by this prediction. At that time people did not learn about their characters and their futures in the horoscopes provided by their daily paper. Only a few initiates, which did not include my parents, believed in astrology.

We were middle-class, even lower-middle-class; and as I grew older, it would have made more sense for my parents to impress on their dreamy little girl the need to work hard at school, which, as everyone knew, was the surest road to success. But they were less concerned about that, since they were buoyed up by 'the prediction', a lodestar on the family horizon. It was not a gamble on the future; it was a certainty, mysterious and inevitable.

In other ways they had their feet well on the ground, but I bless them for this eccentricity of belief, which—to say the least—made for a most encouraging background.

Seven years passed. For me they are years recalled mainly through sights, sounds and smells. The provincial streets of a forgotten Neuilly, furrowed by a rattling tram with its bell, ding-ding-ding, which woke me in the mornings. Every day Maman, wedded to principles of natural living, revolutionary at that time, would take me for a walk in the Bois de Boulogne; the best air was surely to be found in the square of pines on the corner of the avenue de Madrid and the rue de la Ferme! On Thursdays, when we didn't have school, I rode my scooter there. On other days, coming out of school, I was content to race around the nurses, generally English, in grey cloaks and caps, and the well-behaved children sitting in coach-built prams; the 1900 style, dancing on its springs, did not return till later. I was a tomboy, to Maman's despair, and loved climbing trees, but with those pines it just couldn't be done.

In the autumn the Bois had a slightly bitter-sweet smell; but whatever the season, these outings retain the taste and scent of the bananas I ate. 'Chocolate is binding and bad for the liver.' I was fed on a strict diet, before it became the fashion, with plenty of cream cheese and curdled milk. Yoghurt was exotic and not to be found in the Maggi Dairy, to which sturdy cart-horses still brought milk in iron cans. 'This will give you a good skin,' Maman insisted; and it could well be part of the secret of my complexion.

On Wednesdays the house reeked of haddock from the ground floor up. There was no lift; I climbed the stairs four at a time. Mme Degon would be there (the daily dressmaker—a forgotten profession); it was her day. Maman and she would have sewing sessions, everything was done at home. I loved haddock and I loved Mme Degon. One Wednesday I remember going up the stairs very slowly, even more slowly as I came to the last flight. That morning, leaving for the primary school in the rue des Poissonniers, I had taken twenty sous from Maman's purse to buy some chewing-gum and a stick of liquorice from Mme Erard's shop at the corner. I was afraid I might get a good smack if she had noticed. I rang, and observed that she was wearing her frosty face. I was for it. She *had* seen. She saw everything.

'Simone, go and wash your hands and come to table.'

'Yes, Maman.'

Mme Degon and Papa were already seated. Their faces were those of a jury which has just brought in a verdict of guilty. On the sideboard stood a chocolate cake from the pâtisserie, my favourite. It was quite a rarity with us; for reasons of health and economy, if we had cakes at all, they were usually of semolina or rice. Silence reigned while Maman cut the cake. Then: 'Simone, you can't have any dessert, you know why.'

It was infuriating, and what was more, I should have to confess everything to the priest.

The Sunday chicken I used to eat *chez* Grandmother and Grandfather Payot in the rue de Sablonville was crisply roasted and crunched deliciously between my teeth—it must have been extra special for me to have remembered the taste. At that time, anyhow, frozen chickens had not been invented, and hens did not lay in batteries. On the edges of Neuilly there were some farms and market gardens which sold big chubby lettuces in the village market; small red apples (they seem to have disappeared today, as if those apple trees had ceased to exist); and eggs in baskets, like nests, overflowing with straw.

I have no regrets for those days; I like the present and live in it completely. But I have retained a gentle nostalgia for them, and for a happy childhood, full of simple marvels. When I talk about them to my grand-daughter, Samantha, I feel I am talking to her of a period as old-fashioned as my grandparents' days were for us.

How could she grasp that at her age, seven, I knew of the existence of lifts but had never used one, that it was a memorable event the first time we took a taxi? I found it sensational, much more comfortable than the Métro, where you had to go up and down those steps. Samantha's granny is a lady she sometimes watches on the television screen. What about *my* grandparents?

The Payots were typical of the ordinary people of Paris, those of the faubourg Saint-Antoine, of the alleys of Saint-Germain, the small craftsmen and journeymen who were gradually disappearing. I was greatly impressed by Grandfather, so handsome and distinguished, and attributed his severity to mixed origins, smatterings of which I had picked up during overheard conversations. His mother, whose birth,

4

it was whispered, remained mysterious, had been brought up by his stepmother—a romantic and unhappy childhood. His father, a member of the Paris Commune of 1871, fought at the gates of Paris, and Grandfather, aged ten, had stayed in hiding down in a cellar; a benevolent and heroic woman living near them waited for nightfall to pass him through the ventilator a chunk of bread which he devoured greedily. Perhaps that was the origin of the traditional sentence we heard so often: 'Finish your bread before you leave the table.'

All I knew about the war of 1870 was the bronze balloon firmly anchored at the Porte des Ternes, where Gambetta saluted Paris before flying beyond its walls under Prussian siege.

As to my grandmother's story, that too was quite romantic. The daughter of a small paint-seller, she had an easy start in life, but then her father died, leaving her mother and her without means. 'We were without a sou, dear—imagine that!' Petted and pampered, having everything I needed, I was quite incapable of imagining anything so horrid, but my heart constricted. And like all children being told a story, I would say: 'Go on.'

'To make a living, Maman and I started sewing privately for fine ladies. Small pleats with such fine small stitches they couldn't be seen. Those pleats were all the rage ...'

There was more unhappiness to come. Her sister died of T.B.; her brother, an artist who painted on china, 'took to the bottle', as it used to be called.

With her needle still active, Grandmother sewed delightful dresses for my dolls, and Grandfather made a wardrobe for them. The Payots had run a haberdasher's, not making much money. Now they were retired.

Maman's mother, Granny Roussel, was tiny, the shape of three little apples, with a charming cat's nose, palest blonde hair, and a skin as pink as a baby's which she brushed lightly with rice-powder from her powder-puff. She talked of very different people from those I heard about from Grandmother Payot. Hers were middle-class, lawyers or army captains. Part of her family was Walloon, another part had gone in exile to England. They had nobler destinies, but had less appeal for me.

This tiny Granny used to appear on Wednesday evenings. Wednesday was quite a special day—and the day before Thursday, so I could go to bed later. Directly she was inside the flat, Granny would open her bag and bring out as a surprise her usual packet of Petit-Beurres. I can't see those biscuits even now without finding myself back in our flat, hearing our voices and laughter, punctuated by mouse-like nibblings.

When I was ill, and I didn't miss out on any of the usual illnesses—measles, scarlet fever, whooping cough, mumps—it was Granny Roussel who would sit at the foot of my bed and play with me.

Then there were the uncles and aunts. Papa's younger brother, Uncle Edouard—who would later be called Teddy—was in love with Maman's younger sister, Yvonne. What a beauty she was, with that radiant smile, her eyes slanting towards the temples, and a classical nose, perhaps a little long; that was no doubt why, at the bank where she worked, she was nicknamed 'the Jewess'. Maman often said she was like a ray of sunshine, and it was true.

Uncle Edouard was fifteen years older than her and to me must have seemed a great age. He was the most handsome man I knew. Besides being so attractive, he had all the trappings of prestige, including that of uniform. He and Papa had both been at Verdun, but for some reason he stayed on for a time in the army. When I heard someone say: 'He's a hero—several times mentioned in despatches', although I didn't know exactly what this meant, I felt myself basking in his glory, and I loved him. How I loved him!

Anyhow I was going to marry him, he had promised to wait for me. So it was two fiancées who on certain evenings went to see him at the Military Academy. I found that the sky-blue of his uniform matched his eyes, and I always hoped he would ride out on a horse in true martial fashion.

Alas, he married my aunt, a tragic day. I fled into Maman's room and wept for love. It was no joke being five years old and betrayed.

I wept; and noticing myself in the wardrobe mirror, I thought I looked quite good in little Granny Roussel's boa and cloche hat.

Uncle René, Maman's brother, had been gassed in the war, and I used often to overhear things like: 'Poor René's in a mess again. You can't wonder, with him being gassed. The effects will be with him for life.'

He and his wife lived at Sainte-Antoine on the Marne. We had a half-term holiday starting on Shrove Tuesday, and I generally went to spend it with them in the country. It was daffodil time. With my aunt and cousin Geneviève, we would go and pick daffodils in the woods, where there was a smell of humus and spring in the air. From a distance you could see the 'ruffs' of the bare trees in bloom beneath the pale, still shy, sun of winter's end. We returned with red cheeks and wet noses to my uncle's neat, well-arranged house, our arms filled with bunches of a splendid glaring yellow.

Is it still like this? Since then I have only seen daffodils in bunches, like Easter eggs offered on roadsides by people selling wild flowers. I have often thought that they can't leave many for the children of today to pick.

Other important events, surrounded by mystery, turned my universe upside down: the birth of my brothers and my sister. I don't remember anything about Paul's birth, I was really too small—only three. But with Pierre it was different.

One morning Maman, who had certainly grown a bit large, went away, leaving the house in the care of Granny Roussel, which was nice, and us—my brother Paul and me—in the care of Mme Louise, the charlady. We nearly sent her round the bend. One morning Granny announced to us: 'Maman will be coming back with a little brother.'

The little brother in Maman's arms was something rather wrinkled-looking, a pinky-mauve in colour.

'I say, Maman, is it true he was born in a cabbage?'
'Of course, dear, just as you were born in a rose.'
I imagined Maman in a kitchen garden walking down paths with cabbages and roses on either side, from which baby boys' and girls' heads emerged, choosing my little brother. But why him more than any other?

'Maman, why did you pick him?'

'Because he was mine.'

What a splendid answer! It plunged me into embarrassment. Did he have a label on him? Had he been made on commission? Later on, when I was grown up, I would go and choose one, too.

At twelve and a half, if you please, though completely ignorant as to how babies were produced, I did know that Maman carried them inside her. On this particular point I was not a precocious child, and the mystery did not bother me. Still, I made up my mind one morning to find out more about it; I must say Granny Roussel unwittingly pushed me into it. 'You're not curious enough,' she would often tell me. This time I was going to be. While Maman was having her bath, I put my eye to the keyhole. A horrifying sight! Instead of her tummy Maman had a huge balloon. How ugly it looked! That disillusion was not my only punishment. Little Granny caught me looking and gave me a resounding slap— the only one I ever received from her. Surprised and shaken by this violence, which I found unfair, I actually slapped her back. Disgraceful; but I was by no means a passive child.

Did I tell them at school what I had seen through the keyhole? I don't remember. I had certainly had some sex education but found it rather disgusting, which was a pity though I don't think it had any deep traumatic effect. Today a little girl puts her ear against Maman's stomach to 'listen' to her little brother or sister and it no longer seems wrong: quite the contrary.

Time passed. I left the primary and went to secondary school. I was above all preoccupied with gymnastics and rhythmic dancing; it was the rage just then. In a little Greek tunic, a girdle round my waist, I threw my arms gracefully towards the sky and brought my forehead down towards my raised knee. I did not show the same zeal over the rest of my schooling, although when younger I had been a good pupil. The mistress complained that my mind was elsewhere: 'Scatter-brained during class, dreamy during study time.' It was all too true. The breaks served as a scene for my imitations of Anny Ondra, Gaby Morlay and many others. My friends split their sides laughing, and I found it quite funny myself. My best-kept and most up-to-date exercise books were those in which I stuck the photos of the actresses of the time. How beautiful they were, these ladies of the cinema! It had nothing to do with an irresistible vocation—so many little girls have indulged in the same sort of thing—but showed my unfortunate tendency to become enthusiastic over everything except my studies.

In principle, the Sunday afternoon cinema to which my parents took me was supposed to reward my diligence at school. Luckily this condition was not taken very seriously or my cinematic education would have been most incomplete. At tea-time, when we got home, my cousin José came to see the family. His prestige as a tennis-player had long eclipsed Uncle Teddy's. In whites, with racquet under his arm, very free and easy, his dashing air dazzled me. He was very dark and his hair, sleeked by brilliantine, made a shining crown. 'Hullo, little cousin!' His lips rested on my cheeks and I died of love for him. His Christian name alone had the languors of a tango, while his surname, Obaldia, was so wonderfully exotic. It was not José, however, but his younger brother, René, who was to make that name well known, as a writer of plays and poetry.

I didn't expect life to change much, although Papa began talking more and more frequently about an uncertain future. He was very politically conscious, but Maman was uninterested in politics and his talk was well above our heads. For my brothers and me, politicians were silly old fogeys, so my poor father discoursed on the League of Nations, Poincaré's stabilisation of the franc, the Briand–Kellogg Pact and the Wall Street crash—before an audience of children who found it boring and Maman who found it irritating.

Gradually, however, the atmosphere at home did change. Papa was now repeatedly using that terrible, all-embracing word 'crisis'. Every day some business would go under. Even Maman became worried. 'So long as he doesn't lose his job— we'll be in a fine mess if he does.'

For twenty years Papa had worked in the perfume industry. His firm, Godet Perfumes, though less substantial than Coty or Houbigant, was next to them in importance. Speaking several languages, he was head of the foreign orders department. The firm exported a great deal, and in the prevailing economic circumstances his key position suddenly looked precarious. 'With the crisis, the Americans aren't ordering any more perfumes. Forget the Germans, they're completely broke. Soon I wonder what use I'll be at all.'

He didn't have long to wonder. One evening in 1930, several months later, he came home saying: 'That's it. The firm is closing its doors. I'm unemployed.'

A dismal-sounding word. A black-hued word, evoking long files of men and women waiting for something under a sooty sky and, of course, in the rain. Where did I get this realistic vision? I don't know; perhaps from a photograph in a paper or a scene in the newsreels at the cinema.

First consequence: no question that year of going on holiday.

Oh, those journeys on holiday! Paul and I weren't too happy when we left, because we would rather have gone to stay with my aunt and uncle at Riva Bella. But we always went to the Alps, which Papa loved; it didn't excite us. Another thing was that, as my parents hadn't much money, they rented cottages without many amenities, so we had to drag along with us a sort of gypsy caravan: sheets, bedding, all sorts of utensils, buckets and saucepans. In addition Maman brought an old canvas umbrella-stand containing walking-sticks, alpenstock and ice-axes for Papa, and umbrellas in case of rain.

So we staggered off—Papa, Maman, Paul and I, and little Granny—all loaded like mules, counting and recounting our packages at each stop. Crossing the station was an adventure in itself. 'Stop!' Maman would order, 'we've lost little Granny!' We put down our baggage and scrutinised the crowd. Little Granny was so tiny. 'There she is!' cried Papa. 'I can see our sticks. Over there, behind the fat gentleman! She's seen us, she's coming towards us.' That umbrella-stand was providential, the handles of the sticks served as a periscope amidst the hordes of travellers.

A second ordeal was stowing our baggage in the racks of

the third-class compartment we would be occupying as far as Grenoble. Before we had been sitting there ten minutes, we children would be clamouring for our picnic of sausage, ham, hard-boiled eggs, Gruyère, bananas, oranges and bread and butter. The trains were not electrified, and we insisted on sitting by the windows, so that Maman was scared all the time that we would get smuts in our eyes. It was a relief for her when we eventually dropped off to sleep under the slightly eerie blue lights.

I was a boisterous child, always on the go. I had memorable fights with Paul, rolling down the grassy slopes of the mountain. But it seems to me there must have been a lot of rain because Maman took as 'work' a big table-cloth for at least twelve places, which she and Granny embroidered tenaciously. They needed to: ten years' holidays were required before they finished it. Recently I saw this masterpiece again in Maman's cupboard; I don't think it was ever unfolded.

Papa meanwhile was having a wonderful time striding over the mountains; and this part of the Alps eventually held no more secrets for him.

However, back to his unemployment. Small ads were scanned avidly but usually produced only new gloom. 'Nothing this morning,' he would say, putting down *Le Petit Parisien*. 'Nothing!' he would sigh, returning from an interview. 'Nothing in the post, either,' Maman would answer his unspoken question.

I don't know whether that day had been particularly wretched, but the door bell ringing made us all start.

It was Uncle Teddy. He immediately revived our spirits. He had left the army for some years now, and had become a traveller for a sugar firm. These last weeks he had been travelling all over the west of France. Standing in front of our dining-room table, he summed up the situation in his powerful voice: 'Listen, Louis, we must face facts. You're not finding work. So we must do something.'

He and Papa and Maman sat down round the table for a serious discussion.

'Do something?' echoed Papa. 'But what?'

'You must look around for something outside your own trade. We're in the midst of a crisis, agreed, but people are still eating, Louis. For that they even make sacrifices. I bring back my order-books filled. Food is the only business still working.'

'So?'

'I may have found something for us by an extraordinary stroke of luck. I just happened to be talking to a customer, who told me that at Dieppe, in the rue de la Barre, there's a grocery for sale in a very good position. We mustn't miss it. Have you any savings?'

'Yes, forty thousand francs.'

Twenty years of careful saving. But Uncle Teddy rubbed his chin doubtfully. 'I'm afraid that may not be enough. But here's what I propose to you. I've had enough of commercial travelling. So we'll buy the grocery business between us and run it together.'

Papa as a grocer! I found the idea astonishing and, frankly, not very exciting. But we weren't there yet. The sellers were greedy. Well, after all, you had to make the most of it, it wasn't every day you had the opportunity of selling your business to someone who didn't know anything about it. Well baited, my father and uncle trembled at the thought of this marvellous scheme slipping away before their eyes. What could be done? How were they to make up the rest of the amount needed?

'What about my jewellery and silver?' Maman suggested shyly. 'That might give you enough.'

Granny gave her curb-bracelet of massive gold, her rings and Napoleon III brooch; Papa his tie-pin and Uncle Teddy his cuff-links. Maman polished her silver, which made up a good weight. Armed with the treasure of the Roussels, Uncle Teddy set off for Dieppe.

The wait began. How far would he succeed? Would the amount be enough? What suspense! Then quite soon, the door-bell rang, and Uncle Teddy appeared, pale as death, looking as if he were about to have a heart attack. Maman and Aunt Yvette dashed over to him, Papa gave him some brandy. Tragically he murmured: 'They've taken everything!'

This was greeted by cries of horror.

'Yes,' he went on. 'I had to stop at the office, and left the car outside the door. When I came down a few minutes later, the boot was wide open. Oh, I realised at once ...'

It was a bad shock, but Papa was still determined not to pass up this wonderful opportunity: he borrowed the money needed. At some cost the grocery in the rue de la Barre, Dieppe, was ours at last!

Dieppe was quite a pleasant place for a girl in her early teens. The town, especially the boulevard du Maréchal Foch running along the sea front, had an Anglo-Norman charm. less 'pretty-pretty' than Deauville, more English, with its gardens, stone balustrades and well-aligned lamp-posts, its Victorian hotels, boarding-houses and villas.

When Easter came, the English sent us ferry-boats full of boys and girls in navy-blue blazers and school ties, with pink skins, blue eyes and fair hair. It wasn't that the boys interested me particularly at thirteen or fourteen; but like the swallows they heralded fine days, the reopening of the Casino and the hotels and villas by the pier. Dieppe, in fact, came to life again.

For the winter months were indeed a bit dismal, though redeemed for me and my friends by the cinema and by classes in dancing and gym. At these I learnt splendid tricks like handstands, doing the splits, entrechats and pirouettes, all things which were bound to be very useful to me in my future life. Having read it in one of my favourite magazines, *Ciné-Miroir*, I thought American actors and actresses were all accomplished athletes. I trained with enthusiasm, for my main objective had not changed. I was ten, I think, when I first answered the question, 'What are you going to do when you grow up?' with the statement: 'I'm going to be a film star.'

Dancing and contortions were a great pleasure to me and, as my teacher reminded me, I had it in my blood. At a time when women were little inclined to cultivate their bodies, in the '14–'18 war, Maman as a young married woman did Swedish drill every morning in front of an open window, winter and summer, which might almost have been considered 'daring'. Long cycle rides were a familiar pastime for her and in her circle they said: 'She's very athletic.'

My enthusiasm was also maintained by my two admiring friends, Tanine and Suzanne. Every year, at the end of our dancing class, our teacher produced a little ballet to show off our talents. I remember particularly one which took place at the Casino, no less. I performed with little wings on my back, disporting myself attractively, throwing multi-coloured balloons, light as bubbles, while Tanine and Suzanne revolved gracefully round me. This delightful masterpiece was called 'The Dance of the Dragonflies' and it got me a mention in the local paper. My first notice!

The three of us were inseparable off-stage as well. Tanine was a colonel's grand-daughter. She had qualities I admired because I wasn't sure I possessed them myself: class, natural elegance, boldness. She was more 'up-to-date' than I was— the vogue phrase—and she nursed a romantic secret passion, which I found equally enviable. Suzanne, a brunette with light eyes, was the daughter of a big local baker. I don't know if it was to prepare her for that honourable trade, but on Thursday mornings she would go delivering bread, and Tanine and I would accompany her. They were marvellous bakers' rounds, during which we chattered like magpies, laughed like lunatics, and indulged our critical faculties when we happened to meet boys.

These began to be one of the poles of interest in our conversations, though I was only thirteen and can't really speak of our senses being awakened. The realms of love were still ethereal and sentimental: the holding of hands, eyes gazing into eyes, a few innocent kisses much talked about afterwards. We told each other of 'shameful' things that took place among grown-ups. Some woman had 'sinned' or 'let herself go'. We preferred the latter term, and our envy was mitigated by fear. There was no such thing as the Pill.

It is over thirty years since we went on our bakers' rounds to the fine villas in the streets of Dieppe; and we are still inseparable. Tanine, whose sureness of taste had enchanted me, has become a cinema costume designer; she has created most of my film costumes. Suzanne, who works in the Ministry of Sport, acts as my secretary out of affection for me. The continuity of our faithful friendship gives me a comforting feeling; thanks to this lasting bond, I bask in a climate of confidence which is indispensable to me.

As to our other main recreation, Dieppe had two cinemas which showed films all year round, and which we frequented most Thursdays and Sundays. They fed my intoxication, they were the holy places of my passion. I can't recall much of their interior; it was not the walls of the temple which concerned me but the altar—the screen. Although I saw all the films going, I didn't find them all spell-binding; only the ones with Greta Garbo had that quality. I knew everything about her, everything I could read in the papers. I appreciated the discretion of her private life, and envied the romantic mystery surrounding her. At that time journalists still respected the private lives of stars, but they revealed a fair number of idylls, described in very discreet terms. Stars had engagements rather than affairs, and the engagements generally led to weddings, enough material for gossip columns to savour. But the divine Garbo was not a party to any of this, although she breathed love and passion; she was all ice and all fire.

Her beauty impressed me so much that I did not even dare to try copying her. As for the others, I would stand in front of my wardrobe mirror and transform myself into Anny Ondra, Katharine Hepburn, Joan Crawford, and other Hollywood luminaries. I would take up their special poses, my eyes would become deep like theirs, I made up my mouth as they did, very full, the fashion being for sensual lips. I played a love scene with Clark Gable. I put my soul into a long kiss on the mouth. I knew little about the secrets of such kisses; those exchanged with my first boy friends had given me only a very vague idea of them.

The only time I dared to copy *Her*—Garbo—was through a new outfit. I cajoled Maman into making me a costume in imitation black Persian lamb. Straight calf-length skirt, three-quarter-length coat, Russian blouse in natural satin: I wore it crowned with the imitation fur cap which I had seen on Garbo in *Anna Karenina*. I found myself 'divine', but Aunt Yvonne did not agree. 'What's this dog's dinner!' she exclaimed. 'All right for fancy dress, but you don't get yourself up like that at thirteen for any other reason.'

My admiration was not merely superficial. How could anyone be in turn Mata Hari, 'the mysterious lady' and Queen Christina? I felt she embodied these women so completely, went so deep into their minds, that their actions, their loves, became hers. That was what it meant to be a great actress, to be a star, and that was what I envied much more than the furs and jewellery and cars and villas, which were only the small change of a star's glory. How was this transformation brought about? You had to learn the trade, and work at it, of course, but you also needed to have a gift, a talent, and how could you know if you had it? Could it be seen in a girl of my age?

We lived above the shop, and my room was covered with the photos of my beloved stars, most of them cut out of *Ciné-Miroir*, a well-named magazine from my point of view: I admired my reflection in the faces of others, I became these women of my dreams.

Immersed in thoughts of future fame and Hollywood, my inevitable destiny, I let school work suffer badly, except for French literature, painting, and English—which was an indispensable language for a future Hollywood star. Papa, who attached importance to an all-round education, was very disappointed with my reports. But I was learning all sorts of useful information, like the fact that Bette Davis adored grapefruit cocktails and fair men, and I was recollecting in tranquillity the delightful disturbance to my equilibrium caused by Jacques Dupont taking my hand in the intimacy of the dark cinema, and his cheek brushing mine, while some heroine swooned on the screen. How could I at the same time be expected to master the rules of transitive verbs or the secrets of algebraical equations?

Suzanne, Tanine and I were now in a regular gang of boys and girls who went about together, to the cinema, for walks, for bathes. Jacques was in the gang, but I didn't think I was in love with him. I was in *love* with Gary Cooper, yes, and with Fernand Gravey. After seeing the latter in *Passionément*, I dared to write to him that I loved him 'passionately'—a marvellous gesture, bold yet without danger.

During the summer especially, I had a heady sense of entering the life of young grown-ups, who made dates, got engaged, got married, deceived each other, quarrelled, made it up again.

Our winter boy-friends paled by the side of those brought to us by the summer holidays: sons of the rich wool merchants of the Nord in swagger British plus-fours, sophisticated young Parisians in pink silk ties and enormous 'bags', who pitied me for my exile, since in their eyes Paris was the only city with bright enough lights. They were wasting their pity. I knew I wouldn't be here for ever. Between the nice extensive beach and the *thé-dansants* at the Casino, I was a contented fifteen-year-old who enjoyed life to the full.

But however pleasant my existence, and however self-centred the young, I should have had to be blind not to see that the shop was in a bad state. Starting with the man who sold it to them, everyone had taken advantage of my father and uncle who were, after all, not professional grocers. The suppliers and travellers cheated them over weights, deliveries and invoices, and happily palmed off on them anything unwanted elsewhere. Papa and Uncle struggled on, but it soon became obvious that the business could not support six people; so Uncle, having found a small agency, set off again on the roads of Normandy.

Maman worked in the shop more than ever, and against great odds. I remember her coming up the stairs to my room complaining that most of the stock was unsaleable, all the food in the tins had gone bad, the coffee was stale, and she couldn't even find a decent tin of beans for our lunch. It didn't help, either, that Papa was always turning the shop into a forum for political discussion. I used to laugh at this habit, but Maman didn't find it at all funny.

'Monsieur Roussel,' some dignified lady in a black hat would say, still smiling, 'I sent my maid to fetch a litre of oil, but you gave her vinegar.'

The stock of oil had run out, and Papa hadn't the money

to replace it. 'Madame, we are waiting for it. But this vinegar is excellent, pure quality, they won't be making it any more like this. I cannot recommend you too strongly to lay in stocks. With events taking the turn they are, you'll thank me afterwards.'

'What events?'

'War, madame, war.' Like a prophet he waved his arms, taking the stuffed sauerkraut and Toulouse stew as witness.

The lady lost her smile, and Papa a customer.

It was increasingly seldom that we had the product asked for; and when we did have it, it was often the customer, with political opinions opposed to Papa's, who did not please *him*. 'Monsieur, I'm not selling my sugar to a Bolshevik!'

The ex-customer went out, banging the door, leaving the bell still clanging. It had stopped well before my father had finished his diatribe: 'But for the Communists, Hitler would never have come to power, never, and one day you'll see them make an alliance with the Germans to attack *us*. Everyone gives in to the Boche all the way, and leaves us exposed. The revision of the Treaty of Versailles, the evacuation of the Ruhr, and so on. With Hitler there'll be war within ten years. And this government of nitwits tries to get a new union of the Left!'

A customer might struggle in vain to escape, but Papa would not release his prey until he had had his full say. Then the wretched man would depart, vowing never to set foot in the shop again.

'Louis,' Maman tried to reason with him, 'leave the customers in peace. They don't come here to listen to your views on politics. Anyhow, you frighten them with your talk of war.'

'Stupidity makes me boil, I can't stop myself telling them what a mess this wretched government is making. After all, Georgette, you must admit I'm right when I say ...'—and he would be off again.

The business continued to suffer, though he was certainly right in his main prophecy.

Summer was coming to an end. There were fewer husbands arriving by train on Saturdays in their dark suits and hats,

absently kissing their wives on the platform. In another fortnight, Dieppe would have put on its winter face, the villas
would close their shutters all along the boulevard de Verdun.
The big hotels were preparing for their annual closure or
going into semi-hibernation. The bright-coloured tents
would disappear, the cabins would be padlocked. And I
should be returning to school—how sad.

Still, life was quite good that morning, sun-bathing in the
warm sand between a green-striped tent and a prize sand-
castle from one of the last beach competitions. Also, there
was a man looking at me. A man with blue eyes. His stare
was embarrassing but flattering. When you are fifteen, a
man's interest makes you grow up in a very pleasant way.
Anyhow, there was no danger. I knew he was married with
children. A guarantee of safety!

I was with Eric, one of my boy-friends—English-sounding
names were popular in the Nord. The peppermint drink he
had offered me on the terrace of the Casino bar was a pretty
green, which went well with the red of the geraniums and
harmonised with the turquoise of the sea. What a pleasing
picture—a Manet. But I wasn't concerned with aesthetics just
then; the gentleman was still looking at me, and even made
a little sign to me with his head.

'You know him?' Eric asked suspiciously.

'Yes, what's that to you?'

'You go with old men now?'

'Is that your business?' He irritated me, I wondered what
I could have seen in him.

'Oh well, don't worry about me, go and say hullo to him.'

This was enough to make my pride collapse. At the mere
thought, to my fury, I felt myself blushing to the roots of
my hair. However, the gentleman with such blue eyes rose
in a nonchalant way, and greeted me as he passed our table.
'Morning.'

Our relationship had started. When he had gone the peppermint tasted stale and sickly, and Eric's charms had faded
altogether.

The next day I went to the *thé-dansant* at the Casino, rather
hoping he would be there. He was, and invited me to dance.

I wasn't capable of appreciating what a skilful dancer he was, but I knew that his arms held my body in a very different way from that of my usual partners. I felt it, and was at once attracted and unnerved.

'Do you know you're beautiful?' he asked me.

How delightful!

'With those eyes you ought to become an actress.'

It was the first time I had heard this splendid remark. 'I'll have to get my School Certificate first,' I answered with due sobriety.

'Oh well, when you've finished your studies, come and see me in Paris if you still want to be an actress. I can introduce you to two or three people who may be useful to you. I can even arrange for you to meet Georges Rigaud.'

The star of René Clair's *Quatorze juillet*!

'Oh yes, he's a friend of mine.'

In the glide of a tango under the orange light, a golden opportunity had presented itself. I must catch it in flight, not let it escape; but how?

Marc—let's call him that—went on in his deep, warm voice: 'What a shame we've met so late. My holiday is just finishing. I'm going back to Paris.'

'When?'

'At the end of the week. But I won't go without giving you my 'phone number.'

Under a week! I had the rest of the week to act. Ought I to wait another year? A few minutes before, the thought of that year had left me indifferent; now it seemed intolerable.

How sad the shop seemed to me that evening, with its subdued lighting, its iron curtain half drawn, its dark wood and half-filled shelves like a scene in a German film. Papa was sitting behind the pay-desk doing his accounts; he suddenly looked much older. My brothers and sisters and I were automatically fishing in a half-full bottle of sweets.

Papa looked up. 'Stop, children. I can't afford to buy any more ... Where are you going?' he asked me.

'To the promenade to meet some friends.'

'Don't come back later than nine.'

Accompanied by my brother Paul, I went out, very upset: nothing to buy sweets with, we had reached that point. It was more serious than I had thought; well, to be honest, I hadn't thought about it all that much. If only I could help them! This resolve gave me a sudden exaltation of spirit. There was a breeze that evening, my hair shivered in the wind. I was resolute, invincible. I was Joan of Arc, a fine part for Garbo. I would have to think about that. I saw her playing to her judges. Tears filled my eyes. She was on the stake, her beautiful, wonderful face gradually blurring in the smoke.

'Do look out, Simone, you almost got me run over,' cried Paul.

Where was I? Oh yes, Joan of Arc. How splendid to feel ready for any sacrifice to save my family! That was where my dishonesty began. The first and only sacrifice I envisaged wasn't one at all, but a really delightful solution: I would become a film star and make pots of money. I could already see between my fingers a sheaf of notes which I was handing my father ...

'Simone, stop!' Paul clutched my arm. 'Look at the poster. There's a photographic competition for pretty faces on the beach tomorrow.'

Luck was definitely on my side. This morning Marc, tomorrow the competition.

To be photogenic: that was, in a way, the first visa for Hollywood. And I won second prize. This was less dazzling for me than the photographer's words: 'You ought to become an actress.'

Twice in forty-eight hours. It was enough to turn one's head. Thoughts raced through my brain. If I talked about it to my family, who might have remembered 'the prediction', they would say: 'We'll see.' For me there was nothing more to see. I would go to Paris, an opportunity such as I had found would not occur again. This was among the fervent arguments I developed before Maman, who was undecided but anxious. For the moment that was all I asked of her.

The next day Marc was alone on the beach; his wife and

children had gone back by train, he would be going by car with the luggage. What he didn't yet know was that I should be with the luggage.

How incredibly innocent I was! I simply asked him if he could possibly take me to Paris, put me down at my god-mother's house, and ... introduce me to Georges Rigaud. Who could have refused such a request? Not Marc, who was quite fond of girls. Indeed, for all I knew, he might be a wicked wolf licking his chops at the thought of devouring this sun-tanned Red Riding Hood.

Completely unaware of the risks I might be running, I per-suaded Maman—as naïve as I—to let me go off in Marc's car—without revealing my plans to my father, of course.

'You realise, Maman, directly I've seen this producer—he's one of the biggest there are—I'll come back. I'll be home in three days.'

'Is it very wise?'

'But look, Maman, I'm in no real danger. He's a married man, he's got children.'

I was in no danger, to be sure, but I hadn't forgotten the warmth of his hand on my waist, the slightly worrying insis-tence of his stare. Inexperienced but no fool, I made the suggestion: 'Suppose I take Paul with me? He's twelve.'

So next morning, with my little brother in one hand and my case in the other, I was at my rendezvous with fortune.

The idea of a little brother as protector was quite a sensible one since Marc, without showing the slightest chagrin—he was a man who knew how to wait—left me on the pavement in front of my godmother's house with baggage and little brother.

Judged by today's standards, the beginning of this adventure sounds barely credible. What followed sounds equally improbable.

I was in Paris. Paris had the sweet smell of tarmac, petrol and glory. I took a deep breath, and if I had known Rastignac, I would have paraphrased him: the film world is mine!

Meanwhile, more modestly and with less assurance, I con-fronted Godmother, who, stupefied to find me and Paul out-side her door, demanded: 'Where have you come from?'

'Dieppe.'

'And your parents?'

'Well, you see ...' I came out with the whole story.

Godmother took a positive attitude: I've no room. I'll drive you to your grandparents, they'll be able to put you up.'

Poor Payot grandparents, what a shock and what a responsibility for them! They welcomed us, and immediately dispatched a telegram to my father, with the message: PAUL AND SIMONE SAFELY ARRIVED WHAT DO WE DO WITH THEM?

The reaction was thunderous. Maman, retrospectively appalled, did not dare admit the truth to Papa. After a scene which I cannot think of today without laughing, in which he inveighed against his wife's irresponsibility, the culpable weakness of all mothers, the decadence of a society contaminated by socialism, the decline in morality, the folly of the young, and many other evils in the same logical chain, my father ended, of course, by giving in to his wife and granting me a reprieve: 'The girl must be back in three days, or I'll go and fetch her myself.' This was a threat to be taken seriously; impulsive and quick-tempered, Papa was quite capable of carrying it out.

Three days: an eternity during which I hadn't a minute to lose. A wonderful sequence of unlikely things happened. I didn't have to wait anywhere, the people were all there, all available, all friendly and efficient—as if they had already booked me a place in their day.

As promised, Marc introduced me to Georges Rigaud, who gave me a note of introduction to the impresario Jean Devalde. Affable and smiling, Devalde gave me a letter for the director Yvan Noé, then shooting *Mademoiselle Mozart* with Danielle Darrieux. And this went on.

We were back in Neuilly. I passed through the gate of the Neuilly Studios. I couldn't make a nostalgic pilgrimage there today, for like many others they have disappeared.

'Monsieur Yvan Noé, please.'

The doorman, with his braided cap and grey moustache, looked in some surprise at the schoolgirl. 'What do you want with him, young lady?'

'I want to see Monsieur Yvan Noé. I have a letter of introduction to him.'

His paternal air turned to suspicion. 'Does he know about it?'

'I don't know. But Monsieur Jean Devalde should have told him I was coming.'

There were ten endless minutes before the door of the studios opened, my first steps into fairyland. It was grey and dusty, with a terrific bustle in the corridors, like the coming and going on Métro platforms. Suddenly I found myself in a windowless office, facing a young assistant producer overwhelmed by telephone calls. My letter was in his hand, its envelope opened. A dismaying fact dawned on me: M. Noé hadn't read the letter.

The assistant producer had no time to waste. 'Mademoiselle,' he said to me, 'at the moment M. Noé is shooting an important scene so he can't see you. Come back tomorrow when we need extras. Have you an evening dress? It's a night-club setting.'

'Yes,' I said enthusiastically. 'In white organdie.'

It was the first thing I had put in my case. He couldn't have realised what innocence such a dress represented for he told me: 'Right, tomorrow morning at half-past seven, in the make-up rooms.'

This is how my first appearance in films came about. As biographical accounts were to accurately report: 'In 1935 Michèle Morgan made her film début in *Mademoiselle Mozart*.'

Tomorrow I was to start my career in films, but my time in Paris was up tonight. I convinced my grandparents, and they sent my father a telegram asking for a further reprieve for five days. He accepted this.

The ease with which these developments occurred, their logical sequence, seemed to me completely natural. It was how all the glorious débuts were summed up in my favourite magazines. She was asked to be an extra, and was noticed by Thingummy or So-and-So. I was on the road. How could I doubt it was a royal road?

★　　★　　★

It is hard for me, when so many years of films superimpose their images on my memory, to rediscover the freshness of that youngster, in her little organdie dress made by Maman, who was there at 6 a.m., waiting for the gates of the studios in the Boulevard du Château to open.

I must have been an unusual sight in this maidenly attire. Neuilly slowly came awake. It was going to be a glorious day; the sun was already lighting up some red leaves on the trees. Paris was enjoying an early autumn. The birds chirped, the sparrows fought in the dust. A workman passed on his bicycle; I fancied he turned his head. There were only a few cars to disturb the suburban calm.

That exceptional morning, in which I realised my life's dream and for the first time appeared on a film set, has left behind in my memory a smell: the smell of studios, a compound of fresh paint, wood shavings, sawdust, glue, make-up, dust, and painted canvases overheated by lights with a reek like hot rubber.

At that time you were made up with great foundation sticks of Leichner, and it was taken off with vaseline. The light was intense, for the quality of film in those days was very inferior. My make-up, three millimetres thick, gave me the feeling that I was wearing a mask which stopped my skin breathing; I was afraid it would crack at the slightest movement of my face. Also, I did not recognise myself in the mirror. Where had I been to get those dark rings round the eyes, that blood-stained mouth?

Not daring even to smile, I went on the set in my 'first communion' dress, as the stunned assistant producer had just called it, and at once found myself sitting by—Danielle Darrieux herself. Cinema was as magical as I had imagined it. It had transported me close to one of my favourite actresses. More beautiful than in her photographs. But her make-up was not plastered on, it was quite light; silky eyelashes darkened her eyes, her mouth retained its moulded delicacy. Why this difference? For a long time it seemed unfair, a sort of segregation; then I realised that you could not give individual lighting to fifty or a hundred people, so colours and lights had to be unified.

It took a long time to arrange those lights. 'Close-up of Mademoiselle Darrieux!' someone shouted. Danielle was in position; she waited, motionless. It seemed to me terribly slow. Finally an assistant shouted: 'Quiet, we're shooting!' A cameraman wheeled up his camera. My heart beat faster, as if it were me they were taking. Danielle's eyes became deeper, a sort of distant self-questioning look. I decided she could only be questioning herself about love.

'Cut!' cried Yvan Noé.

He went and sat down near her. At last I had a view of him. I had imagined him a true patriarchal Noah. Now I found him almost ordinary, despite his green eyes slanting towards the temples and his tallness. He was talking in a low voice. Danielle Darrieux listened attentively.

The ritual started again from scratch. The silence on the set was what might be called 'religious'.

'Cut. Good.'

I sighed with relief. She had done it satisfactorily. Not so. Yvan Noé assured her she could do better. They started again. This close-up, for no apparent sequence, in which she did not even speak, was shot four times till it was perfect.

I had just been given my first lesson in filming, and was aware of it.

I listened and looked, living those moments so intensely that I jumped on hearing, quite close, the voice of Yvan Noé. 'Well, do you like filming?'

'Oh yes, sir.'

'How old are you?'

'Fifteen, sir.' And at top speed, blushing under my make-up, I confessed everything to him: how I had left Dieppe, my desire to learn about films, my ambition to become a great actress. He told me later: 'Even more than your pleasant face, it was your spontaneity, your freshness, which attracted my attention. I was more used as a rule to cheeky youngsters, ready for anything, than to your innocence.'

He smiled at me. His eyes had an amused glint. 'You know you will have to work hard if you want to go in for this profession seriously.'

'I know.'

This moment, both very short and very long, was over. Yvan Noé was leaving me to arrange the next shots; then he changed his mind. 'Well, go and see René Simon. Tell him I sent you.'

Now he had said everything. No, there was still more. 'Ring me up as soon as you have your appointment. I will try to come with you.'

My naïvety was so great that I was not even astonished by this offer. It wasn't the Métro I took to return to my grandparents, but a pink cloud. I was in a hurry to open my bag in front of them and show them my first pay: for coming close to Danielle Darrieux, talking to Yvan Noé, and 'appearing' in a nightclub, I had earned a hundred francs. What a profession!

A year later, after remaining without work for long months, I also said: 'What a profession!' But in a quite different, much more professional tone.

René Simon's drama school! If you had ever opened a film magazine, if you had read anything at all about show business—and I certainly had, more than most—you could not help knowing the unique and privileged position this school occupied in the profession. It was reputed to be a nursery for young hopefuls. Theatre and film impresarios, producers and directors attended its performances. Some older stars, looking for young partners, also made conspicuous appearances, which of course drew much comment. To be accepted for the school was as indispensable as to attend the military school at Saint-Cyr in order to become a general. That was how I imagined it, and my picture was little exaggerated.

So, with Yvan Noé as escort, I came to the school which I regarded as the ante-chamber of success. There things moved quickly. René Simon was a brown-haired man, intense, nervy, and on this occasion terse, who possessed the authority of a Louis Jouvet without his height. He gave me a scene from *Les femmes savantes* to study. 'Ring me up when you've learnt it.'

The reprieve from my father expired in three days. 'Could I come the day after tomorrow?'

Surprised by such haste, he raised his eyebrows. 'If you like.'

'Well, are you pleased?' Yvan Noé asked me as he said goodbye.

'Oh yes, sir, thank you. Thank you so much for coming with me.'

My thanks indeed were heartfelt, but in retrospect I can't sufficiently express my gratitude for his disinterested kindness: he even promised to find me bit parts to play in the next few months, and kept his word.

Two days later, very erect in front of René Simon, not omitting a word, not stopping except to draw breath, I recited my scene, and obtained from him what could be called an undoubted success—in laughter. Sitting behind a girl producer-trainee, he slapped his thighs joyfully and could not control his mirth.

Stunned and mortified, I stayed there, incapable of movement. My whole world was crumbling.

'Wait!' he cried. 'Let's have a look at you.'

He lit the two spots framing his desk and had me turn around in their light. As I waited to hear the worst, he said to me, still laughing: 'Right, you can come to the school. I believe you'll make an actress.'

The First Chance

Back home to Dieppe, where you can imagine the scene.
'Hullo, it's me, I've made it!' 'Bravo, my girl, come into my
arms!' It would be pleasant but untrue to describe my return
along these lines. On the contrary, I was greeted with the
reaction not uncommonly met by the young when they tell
their parents they are hoping for a career on the stage or in
films.

'No daughter of mine will go into films!' yelled my father
in a paroxysm of rage.

Wedged between the wall and the corner of our Henri II
sideboard (which had moved with us), I could not escape
from him. I let myself slide to the ground. With a powerful
grip he hauled me up again. His blows rained on me somewhat erratically. Intended as punishment, their main effect
was to make me laugh; the scene struck me as irresistibly
funny. Luckily my father took my mirth for the sobs of
repentance. 'Abandoned girl!' he was ranting. 'You'll make
your family shed tears of blood! You'll come to a bad end,
you will—in the gutter!' In those days erring boys were
promised the scaffold, girls the gutter.

Maman bravely intervened: 'I forbid you to lay hands on
the girl again. You're hurting her!'

In a few minutes poor Papa was overcome by remorse
and smothering me with kisses. We were used to his
violent tempers, generally in proportion to the anxiety
we had caused him; and this time I had no doubt gone too
far. But even when his fury was appeased, he still declared
with dismaying authority: 'You will finish at school first.
That will enable you to enter a good, safe, respectable
trade.'

'But I don't want a future like that, or a safe trade. I want to be an actress.'

'In two or three years,' he continued firmly, 'I'll see if you can go to your Monsieur René Simon's place.'

Long before that he would have completely forgotten me. 'No, Papa, I'm not going back to school.'

'Yes, you are, and next week at that. Back to school with your brothers and sisters, like everybody else.'

It was all over. The shock made me really cry this time. My despair didn't last long, but it was salutary for me to have felt it. You can't make a career in films without being able to overcome despondency—a lesson I should later have to learn many times over.

The more likely it seemed that I should have to give up my plans for the moment, the more exceptional the prospects appeared. So without straining myself at all, I could give Maman a dazzling account of my stay in Paris, my meetings, my début in *Mademoiselle Mozart*. I was admittedly a little over-sanguine in describing my audition with René Simon: to listen to me, he might have been practically waiting for me at the station every day.

Dear Maman, with her pretty face, the severe mouth softened by that tender smile and eyes—how ready she was to believe me! 'All right,' she said, 'I'll talk to your father. You know what he's like. He gets carried away, but he's only thinking of your own good.'

Unfortunately, our ideas of 'my good' did not tally. Maman was very convincing, but he answered all her arguments with: 'No, I shall not give in!'

This was a very different reception from the one I had imagined for the returning 'prodigal daughter'. Still, it was no good agonising over that. I had to win my objective. In the arsenal of means of pressure available to me, I chose the hunger strike. Shut up in my room, I carried it out very conscientiously—for the first hours. Towards midnight, feeling a hollow in the stomach so painful that it stopped me going to sleep, I decided that a small tin of sardines couldn't really be considered as a meal. Next day, in the same spirit, Maman secretly brought me up some fruit and a brioche.

As the secret of these lapses was very well kept, Papa became extremely worried, fearing I might starve to death. I had discovered the mysteries of make-up and gave myself some fine rings round the eyes. He entered into negotiations. 'And how would you live? Where would you find the money to pay for your classes with this Monsieur René Simon?'

'By doing my job. Yvan Noé promised he would find me parts in his films.'

'Where would you live?'

'With the grandparents.'

'Don't count on it. At your age you're too great a responsibility for them . . . You see,' he said triumphantly, 'it just isn't possible.'

This time I seemed to have reached the end. But, no. Everything happened as if it really *had* been fated. Oh splendid prediction, things would have been very different without you! My career was no longer a vocation, it was part of my predestined future.

My parents duly informed Aunt Yvonne and Uncle Teddy of the course of events. Far from supporting my father in his doubts, they went to the opposite extreme—what had happened strengthened their belief in the prediction which had been made twelve years before. So that I could become an 'artiste', they were actually prepared to move house— back to Paris. My uncle found a different job, my aunt returned to her old position in the bank; and three weeks later there we were—them, my cousin Renée, their daughter, and me—living again in Neuilly, back in our village.

To think that there are people who don't believe in miracles! They don't know what they're missing. The French word *chance* means both 'chance' and 'luck'. My first chance, in the second sense, was certainly in having the family I did.

'Be careful, my darling, and look after yourself,' Papa told me as we said goodbye. Two little cliché phrases. Until you have had children yourself, and have had to say goodbye to them some morning or evening, you cannot know the tenderness they contain and also the confession of powerlessness they represent: you cannot protect your child from the world, the child must be left to be careful and look after itself.

That morning, in the Métro on the Nation line, my real life was beginning. I was very conscious of the fact. 'Today I'm having my first day at drama school.'

Sudden dismay: I had forgotten the name of my station. Opposite me, with his nose studiously stuck in a book, there was a young man, or perhaps only a boy. He was quite attractive and also looked an approachable sort of person, so I ventured to say: 'Excuse me ...'

He raised his head and looked at me with curiosity. He had fine chestnut brown eyes, with heavy lashes.

'Do you know where I have to get out for the boulevard Garibaldi?'

His eyes were now full of life but still shy. 'Sèvres-Lecourbe. I'm getting out there too.' He plunged back into his book.

As I headed for the boulevard Garibaldi, I had the feeling I was being followed, perhaps by the boy? Paris was not Dieppe, I knew that. I increased my pace and gave a discreet glance behind me. Yes, I was right, it was the boy from the Métro. What did he think he was up to? As we reached the building, he caught me up. I went through the main gate, and so did he. He's got some cheek, I thought. I rang, and heard his breathing behind me. The door opened. I deliberately paused before going in. He had started moving, and bumped into me.

'Can't you look where you're going?' I protested.

'Sorry,' he explained in confusion. 'I thought you were going in—so, er, I didn't put the brakes on soon enough.'

I laughed, as much at his bewildered air as at my suspicions. My 'shadow' was also a drama student. He was sixteen, and later achieved fame as François Périer.

I went in.

I knew the lecture hall, of course, I had seen it already: a big room, very high-ceilinged, with rows of benches.

Today it was swarming with boys and girls, perhaps about thirty—there seemed an awful lot of them. I envied their free, relaxed air. They formed groups, broke away, joined other groups, bustling about, laughing and talking. I wished I could be laughing with them, and had their self-assurance. I didn't realise that appearances are deceptive, that in learning to act they were already putting on an act; that I, too, when it was nearly time for me to 'go on', should be gripped by this fever which makes you talk and laugh louder, live at a higher level. For the moment I was feeling at a lower level than usual. In this setting I felt like a foreign body. The boy I had come in with must be very amusing—the girls round him were laughing a lot. And I had thought him shy! How deceptive things were here. Everything was an illusion, and you created it on that kind of stage framed by dangling curtains. No scenery, everything in the imagination. The accessories, a table and three chairs, would stand as required for a drawing-room, the Forest of Brocéliande, Macbeth's castle, or the bed-room in a farce. Shakespeare and Feydeau were equally at home there. As to the absence of any kind of window or door, this gave rise to peculiar interchanges such as:

'Your door!'

'What door, sir?'

'The one you came in by.'

'What about it?'

'You're leaving it open, you fool. For God's sake, shut it.'

The student shut the imaginary door.

No one would laugh, for the places where you act, even at drama school, are magical; and those who don't feel cold when the imaginary window is opened on a winter day will never be touched by the grace of inspiration.

The hubbub and chatter all round me, which seemed to dull my brain, was in itself part of the theatrical atmosphere. I was surrounded by people talking and breathing theatre, and talking theatre 'shop' too. I wished I could understand and assimilate everything at a stroke, that I could be like them.

Meanwhile, taking refuge near the door, I felt extremely awkward, very much the new girl. What did I do next?

Present myself before René Simon, knock at his office door? My anxieties were quickly swept away. Just then he came in and recognised me. 'Ah, it's you. Today you can watch the others. There's no better way of learning. It's amazing the progress you make by seeing what not to do. As you were the last to join the class, go and sit there at the back.'

The last bench was to be my place, and I would stay there. It gave me a feeling of safety: without anyone behind me, with my back to the wall. I listened and watched, which kept me very busy. I was far from grasping all the nuances of what I heard. Some of the language used at the school was quite esoteric to me, but I heard a lot of laughter and my brain was seething in an effort to understand everything. During the two hours of the class I must have seen all the students, the good ones and the less good.

François Périer, witty and amusing, was one of the most brilliant; but René Simon took him as an example to launch into a tirade on how disastrous it can be to possess talent if things come too easily; how it can stop your working in depth; and how, when you have realised the dangers, the damage may be done and take years to undo. This was a warning I retained in my memory.

It was natural that I should be impressed by Jacqueline Porel, Réjane's grand-daughter. 'The Master', as I learnt to refer to him, did not forget to remind her that her grand-father's talent should not prevent her from developing her own. She certainly did have her own talent. Her fine little nose and sharp chin greatly enhanced the delivery of her lines and the precision of her diction.

But the student who left me gaping with admiration most of all that day was Denise Bosc, daughter of Henri Bosc, a well-known actor I had often seen on the screen. Denise, a brunette, seemed to me a born tragedienne who achieved her tragic effects with an ease I envied, without lavish gestures or shouting. The tears which flowed over her face were lacerating tears that couldn't be restrained. To weep like that at will must be a wonderful thing.

My admiration was not quite unreserved, however. Now and then I instinctively caught a gesture that was not in place, an intonation that sounded false. When 'the Master' criticised them, I felt satisfaction, but when he let them pass I lost my confidence. Was I wrong, or was he? It did not occur to me that indifference might be the worst and most cruel of criticisms.

For days I felt overwhelmed, like a stone washed over by the waves, unaware that they were polishing me. It isn't easy to become a good round pebble, and it will probably be painful while it's happening. Not that this satisfying analogy occurred to me at the time. For the moment I just suffered.

Everything in our tuition surprised me. In my ignorance, and my experience of recitation solely from school, I expected to learn lines by heart and then deliver them with the right intonations, facial expressions, and gestures. I felt well equipped to express all the emotions: grief, anger, joy, jealousy and love. Love above all. I was ready for languorous poses, passionate dialogue, and even film kisses in close-up!

I expected to be instructed in dancing and singing and to have to practise various gymnastic activities, preparing myself for Hollywood, my lighthouse, my sun on the horizon. Instead, with complete seriousness, René Simon gave me tongue-twisters for exercises in diction, like: 'A combien sont ces six saucissons-çi? Ces six saucissons-çi sont six sous.' I started saying them in the morning at Aunt Yvonne's while doing the housework, sweeping, with and without a pencil between my teeth, interspersed with great long passionate speeches from Racine which I had physical difficulty in articulating.

The flavour of René Simon's school is almost impossible to communicate to those who did not experience it. What was so special about it—so unique, as its former students would say? The chief factor, obviously, was the Master's own personality, which we found an education in itself. He had flat but rebellious hair, penetrating eyes, wore polo-neck jerseys long before they became fashionable and trousers that always looked as if they might be about to slip down. He would lash us with scathing words, enlarge on the glories and obligations of the actor's profession and accuse us of only wanting to know the former. (While waiting for those heights, by the way, most of us adopted the habit of making white coffee and a roll or sandwich our main meal.)

'From inside you!' he would yell. 'You don't act a part by making faces. It doesn't happen here in your brain.' (He slapped his forehead.) 'Intellectual actors are shit. It's here. here!' (With hands spread out, he tapped his stomach.) 'In the guts, and you've got to bring it out of them. That's what guts are for, to make you feel!'

It wasn't only guts we needed to have. All the boys were periodically called miserable eunuchs, and some of us girls were stupid little virgins who hadn't ever been 'fucked'. He was always ready to call an agricultural implement a bloody shovel, and the first time I heard his robust language I was so dumbfounded I forgot to be shocked. It was incredible. Circumlocutions were banned here; only the four-letter words were permitted.

For him, the state of virginity was bound to act as a severe brake on the development of femininity, and without that there was no salvation for an actress. 'You poor creature!' he would exclaim in tones of ironical pity. 'Is it really possible you've never made love? Then how do you hope to express it?' To be frank, this was a reproach he could level at very few of us; and as a result I became a prime target for his pitying scorn. He made no allowance for my age.

At least I was immune from the opposite criticism, which was applied to students of both sexes. Accused of being shagged out, some wretched boy or girl would be sent home with the words: 'At least respect your training, even if you don't respect yourself.'

Self-respect: all René Simon's moral and philosophic teaching was contained in the phrase 'respect for yourself and others', the others being an audience. For he did not only inculcate the rudiments of our art and play Pygmalion with some of us; he taught us a way of living, an actor's way, which for him was incomparable to any other.

I think he was very fond of us, though this assessment only came to me later. At the time I felt blocked. I knew what he was asking of me, what he expected of me, but when I was on that damned stage, it seemed as if someone else had taken my place: an awkward creature with a choking voice and dangling arms ending in hands that were as clumsy as feet. I could have wept at how hopeless I felt. What finished me was the Master's indulgence. He was patient, grumbling kindly: 'All right, all right—not bad. You've everything to learn, but it's coming.'

Then one day, at the height of my despair, it came. I felt light, liberated, like a bird which ventures successfully on its first flight.

'Good! We're there. You've been quick, in fact. Three months is quite good going.' (I'd been sure I was being terribly slow.) 'Now you've stopped gabbling your words, and we can understand what you're saying, we can really get down to it and work in depth.'

This ended his indulgence towards me, his faint praise, 'Yes, all right—not too bad, carry on.' I learnt to dread, more than before, the moment when he would shout from his place, without turning his head: 'Over to you, Simone', and then announce in a voice at once resigned and blasé: 'Go ahead, I'm listening.'

I would plunge into my lines, often wishing I could close my eyes so as to avoid his gaze. Then the critique would start. 'Simone, your voice. Ar-ti-cu-late!' He would leap to his feet, bound up onto the stage, and place his small, expressive hands on my stomach. 'And breathe with that. Otherwise you'll be out of breath. You need a lot of breath for Racine.'

Racine was not the only writer to make demands on one's breathing; so did Corneille, Molière, Marivaux and La Fontaine. When I could cope more or less adequately with the rigours of the classical authors, Simon launched me onto the romantics. Victor Hugo proved a real test of breathing and trying to perform de Musset was a hazardous business.

One day I was doing a scene with François Périer in the de Musset play, *On ne badine pas avec l'amour*. He was playing Perdican, I was Camille. She says: 'I look forward to dancing at your wedding'—at first sight a simple enough statement.

Calmly and precisely René Simon dissected it for me. 'It contains all the emotions, or almost all of them. Chagrin, jeal-

ousy, love, despair, pride, even a modicum of hope. Everything except resignation. Now go back on it.'

I did so.

'No, you're giving it me as if you were saying, 'The roast
veal has got burnt.' Again!'

I started: 'I look forward ...'

'No, you're not announcing a disaster to me. You want
pride merging into chagrin. Start again a few lines back. That
will help carry you through.'

I certainly needed help to be carried through that passage.

'Good God, this isn't a Corsican vendetta, you're not
avenging the family's honour. You love Perdican and you're
going to lose him.'

I had fourteen more tries, François counted them; and each
time my tormentor found a different image. I passed from
Messalina to a wronged village maiden without ever finding
Camille. By the end I was almost in tears.

'Look, I'll show you!' Then the real performance began.
The Master climbed up on the stage, turned round, and—
became Camille. It was miraculous. No more polo-neck
collar or trousers slipping at the waist; here was Camille as
he, and no doubt de Musset also, intended her, proud and
passionate.

There were sometimes even more violent reactions to our
efforts. 'Get that into your head!' he would yell. 'This will
help you to remember it!' 'This' was a hard slap with no play-
acting restraint about it. Most of us received such a slap from
time to time, and the astonishing thing to me in retrospect
is that nobody ever felt it to be humiliating. He had the knack
of making even that seem fair criticism.

Very soon I felt a new identity in his school. I was part of
an élite. But although, on the stage especially, my relations
with the other students were spontaneous and direct, when
school finished I lost touch with them.

For one thing they were very different from the boys and
girls I had gone about with in Dieppe. Here I was the baby,
only fifteen. I watched them develop almost with the eyes
of a little girl watching grown-ups. They had a tumultuous

emotional life: a succession of overlapping flirtations and love affairs, with partners changing in the middle of scenes; tragic dramas which, luckily, were decidedly histrionic.

Every day they were concentrating on becoming other people, expressing passions, living through dramatic situations heightened by fine language. They could not help being affected by all that. Putting themselves into the skins of adults, and unusual adults too, they grew up faster. At the end of the day's class, when they separated from these characters of drama, it was natural enough that they had to go dramatising themselves to avoid terrible withdrawal symptoms—and often over-dramatised in the process.

A few years later, the whole atmosphere was very well caught by Marc Allégret as director, and André Cayatte and Henri Jeanson as scriptwriters, in their film *Entrée des artistes*. It was René Simon's school in its peak period that served as their model. The film came out in 1938, a few months after *Quai des brumes*, and I remember feeling when I saw it that all that was an age ago. Although only three years had gone by, I looked at this comparatively recent past with the affectionate eyes and indulgent laughter of someone contemplating her salad days.

One reason why I felt less close to my fellow students was that we hadn't really a common language. Theirs was the theatre, and mine was already the cinema. They were anxious to tread the boards, while I dreamed only of studio sets and the camera lens.

Gaston Baty, Dullin, Marcel Herrand, Georges Pitoeff, however famous, were not the breath of life to me. I wanted to absorb the auras of René Clair, Marc Allégret, Marcel Carné, L'Herbier. I think I was the only one of my contemporaries at the school who was mainly interested in the cinema.

I have several times been offered parts in plays, and still am. I have read some manuscripts I liked very much and even found tempting. But I haven't crossed the line. The stage is not my medium, its constraints do not suit me. I am inhibited by the thought of acting every day, and twice a day when there is a matinée: having to use the same gestures, the same intonations for the same situations, surrounded by the same faces. I have too independent a character, too strong a need for freedom, to feel pleasure in this form of discipline.

Probably no drama school would have been as good for me in this respect as René Simon's. Though a man of the theatre, he knew the demands of the screen. His taste for true-to-life acting, for simplicity in means of expression, made him castigate all intonations or gestures that were even slightly forced. What would have passed all right on the stage, because of the distance between actor and audience, he immediately saw as hamming. His eye had the precision of a camera taking a close-up.

As time passed, my relations with my fellow students still remained superficial. I was at the age when one is completely self-centred. The blossoming period, when we open out to the world, comes later; it takes quite a few years to achieve some detachment from oneself.

Besides, it was a form of isolation which suited me. I was 'my own man' (or girl), I had time to think, an activity I prefer to carry out without pressure from others or even myself, without being distracted by the outside world.

I did, however, have a brief involvement with someone else, which had a disproportionate influence on my career—in that it gave me part of the name I am known by.

'Tell me,' said René Simon one day, 'are you going to use your own name as a stage name?'

I was taken by surprise and didn't know what to answer. I thought my name sounded quite good.

'Right, you haven't decided yet. There are plenty of more urgent things.'

There was a young man called Albert at the school who had begun to attract me. He was not a dazzling actor but I found him a very nice boy. He was working on Othello and Don Juan, certainly from inclination, and something of the latter character remained with him: he *was* slightly seductive—but no dandy (a species I couldn't stand)—nor a lady-killer (that sort merely made me laugh). The only trouble was that he showed no great interest in me, or anyhow not enough for my taste. One day as we were leaving, he remarked to me, with the passionate, hopeless look of those who dream of an impossible love: 'A pity I don't know any Michèles. I'd so much like to have a mistress called Michèle.'

The next day, before starting on my lines, I told René Simon in a deep theatrical voice: 'Sir, I have found my stage name: Michèle Roussel.'

When we left, it was quite clear the message had been received. Putting a furtive hand round my waist, Albert said: 'Michèle—we're going to a film. I'm taking you.'

The film was not bad, but his arm round my shoulder, his hand seeking mine—what a triumph! Some walks hand in hand by the Seine, two or three port and brandies at a bar with rosewood walls, deep armchairs and subdued lighting, all convinced me that I was now in love.

So one afternoon, when Albert said quite cunningly, 'Come on, we'll go and have tea at my parents,' I accepted. I thought he was so fond of me he wanted to introduce me to his Papa and Maman. But they were not there. I was really only half surprised when I saw the empty flat and their imposing double bed. 'Come on,' he said, 'don't be scared, I won't touch you, I swear.'

On this unknown bed I was a bit cold, a bit hot, vaguely alarmed. I wanted everything to be nice and harmonious, that it should go well, that I should be able to satisfy him. He stretched out at my side, and told me in a slightly trembling voice, 'Michèle, I only want to sleep right by you, very close to you.'

How many women have heard this statement, made to give us confidence but never fulfilled!

Albert took me in his arms. It was strange, this unknown body, its warmth mingling with mine; strange and perhaps rather disturbing.

He had rested his cheek in the hollow of my shoulder. This gentleness and patience, when I had been apprehensively expecting a fierce lover, was at first reassuring. But then nothing happened. Albert's head became very heavy, his peaceful breathing was now regular: he was asleep. I might have been furious, disillusioned. In fact I felt very much like laughing, seeing myself by the side of this peaceful boy, whose face in sleep was as innocent as a baby. But I was far too young to find that touching. Disenchanted, I closed the door on Albert and on the love I might have had.

Twenty years later this incident had a sequel. In mid-winter, on the sunlit highlands of Montana-Vermala I was striding along on a walk—walking is one of my favourite forms of recreation—when a tall gentleman with a moustache, wearing a fur cap, came dashing up to me. 'Michèle, don't you recognise me?'

I looked at him, searching in my memory, then it suddenly came to me. 'Albert!'

Yes, it was him all right. In a stupor I watched him bring his face close to mine, as if we shared a guilty secret, and heard a heavy voice murmuring to me: 'Michèle, you remember!'

We can't have shared the same memory. For him, if he remembered his sleep, it could only have been a good 'shagged' sleep following an afternoon of love-making with a Michèle who was not yet Morgan. If she had remained Roussel, would he have transposed the image in the same way?

Still, he left me more than a memory: a Christian name. I believe in the influence of Christian names on behaviour, and have often thought that Michèle imposed on me a *persona* different in some ways from what Simone's would have been: a slight reserve, an apparent coldness. A Simone found it easier to get the giggles, was allowed to be less reserved, more spontaneous. I may be wrong, but that's how I feel. The person one becomes, I believe, is partly one's own creation. This is even more the case, probably, with an actress. She is never completely free to be only herself. Would Simone have done her hair, made up, dressed like Michèle? Would she have had the same attitudes? Would even her thoughts have been identical? And because of the differences there might be, would she have been offered the same roles?

I have often found myself thinking of the women to whom I have lent my face, my gestures, my voice; women who in return have obliged me for a certain period to live and think like them, to undergo their destiny. Perhaps when you identify yourself with a personality in this way, although it doesn't seem to have anything in common with you, except that the producer's imagination has seen your face in hers, you have accepted that personality because in your subconscious there is a small character trait bringing you close to her. Where is the respectable lady who hasn't dreamed some nights of being a courtesan? We actresses are offered this opportunity in our work.

The year ended. I had learnt a lot but was by no means self-confident.

When I was a little girl of six, I remember on my birthday having marvelled at the progress of what I called 'my brain'. This year, I said to myself then, I know many more things than last year. If I go on like this, there'll be no stopping me.

Now too, I knew more things, just enough to show me that I knew very little. I had also realised some things which didn't make the picture look very rosy: to live in this profession while learning the trade wasn't as easy as I had imagined in Dieppe.

Integrated into my environment, which was already a professional one, surrounded by girls and boys who all had looks, personality and talent, whose prospects were no more certain than mine, I began to realise the truth of the Biblical saying adapted to this field: 'Many are called but few are chosen.'

Yvan Noé kept his promise, but he wasn't working all the time; so I took part in the great hunt for 'shop windows'. We students exchanged tips on the films being shot and the plays in production. Here too there were a great many mirages. 'He's looking for someone to play a small part.' You set off on a dream and came down to earth in reality: one day's work as an extra, though even that quarter of a loaf was better than no bread.

I learnt also to dance attendance on impresarios. Their secretaries, friendly or otherwise, would take my photograph and address, and give me a variant of the time-honoured response: 'Don't call us, we'll call you'—'We'll let you know when we have something for you.' I was no longer enough of a novice to cherish illusions over the prospects. Not one of the producers who, I won't say 'saw' me but registered my presence, exclaimed: 'Come in, Mademoiselle. You're the girl I've been looking for all my life.'

Demoralising though these visits were, I persevered, feeling sure that in this or some other way I should succeed. I had faith.

Faith was a useful commodity for others besides me. At Uncle Teddy's, life was not without its difficulties. Maman sent us the remains of the grocery stock: packets of noodles, rice and tinned food, often unusable, complemented—I have never understood why—by various liqueurs which in contrast were perfectly saleable: Benedictine, Chartreuse, Cointreau, etc. When Uncle Teddy told our neighbours, 'Do have a liqueur,' the display of such munificence gained us an unexpected respect. 'No, really, take your pick,' he would say, putting them at their ease. 'You see, my brother's always sending them from Normandy. He has a business there.' Restraining laughter with some difficulty, I could see them imagining my father as some high-class wine merchant.

Like all my fellow students, I relied on luck. With a very few exceptions, we had come into this calling through a lucky chance. So it is not surprising that, like most artistes, we were superstitious. When you are expecting everything of chance, you cannot help scanning the signs of destiny and sometimes dreading them.

When I met Nicole Ferrier, I hadn't thrown salt over my shoulder or had a black cat crossing my path. I arrived at the school one day as usual and noticed a new girl. I liked her straightaway and found her just right, reserved but smiling; charming, dressed in dark colours, but what style— although I can't say I fully appreciated that point yet. A girl's elegance, obviously, was noticed at the school, but let's say I didn't then possess very good taste, having learnt it largely through Hollywood—and the Hollywood of the magazines, at that. I discovered English tweed, flannel and cashmere. I didn't know the predilection of her uncle, Jean Gabin, for these materials. She didn't talk about her relationship, by the way, nor did it have much interest for me at the time. (He was also uncle of the more famous Jean Gabin whom I was to meet a couple of years later.) No, I liked Nicole for her qualities of kindness, sensitivity and modesty. We talked about love, marriage, fashion, and our profession, that inexhaustible subject. The wretched thing slipped into every discussion. You weren't even free to love outside it, and of course it sometimes put the men in your life into your arms.

One afternoon Nicole complained to me: 'There's no happy mean in this profession. Either you're left with nothing to do for a month, or everything happens at once. Tomorrow I've got a small part with my uncle in *La belle équipe*. Two cues, you know—I can't miss that. This morning I was called to be an extra in *Le mioche*, and I can't let that slip by either. How about your going in my place?'

Everything went well. Léonide Moguy was a calm director with no gestures or unnecessary shouting; he gave clear orders, rolling his 'r's' attractively. He was on the short side, with a huge forehead. I found him very pleasant, and was soon to find him even more so.

'Mademoiselle, would you come up here?'

'Me?'

'Yes, you.'

I walked forward. With his eye riveted to the camera's viewfinder, he was defining the field. I felt forgotten. But the cinema is a great teacher of patience. I waited, and eventually he returned to me: 'Could you speak a line?'

'Several, if need be.'

'Good. That's fine. Come over this way.'

I followed him. The set represented a dormitory at a girls' boarding-school.

'I want you to go up to the window like this, put your head out, and say: "Look, Prosper has gone to bed." '

What promotion: from an extra, I had become a principal. That's to say, I had a speaking part. It was a big difference. You created more of an impact, your image stayed longer on the screen and would get you noticed, or so everyone thought. I have to admit, however, that my 'Prosper has gone to bed' made no impression whatever.

At lunch in the studio canteen, I found myself placed near

Jeanne Vita, the film's script girl. At these tables where I had never sat before, I felt out of my element. The others were older than me and talked of people I didn't know, films I hadn't seen or they had been in. They laughed, and I didn't understand the jokes. I listened in silence. Unable to fix on a subject, my attention wandered and I began day-dreaming, always a favourite pastime of mine.

'What's your name?' Jeanne Vita suddenly asked me.

'Michèle Roussel.'

She looked at me thoughtfully. 'You have a very interesting face.'

At that moment I would have preferred her to say that my 'Prosper has gone to bed' had been noticed. What stupid ideas one can have at that age!

'Well, if I see anything for you, I'll let you know. Give me your address.'

Another few months passed. I was once more living with my parents, whose Dieppe adventure was over. Having settled accounts and shut up shop, they had returned to Paris rather poorer; Papa had obtained various loans, and there were repayments to be made monthly. He had, however, found a job in the foreign department of St James' Rum. My brothers and sister were pursuing their studies, the family was united again. Far from saving it from poverty, as it had been my ambition to do, I only managed with difficulty to pay my way at drama school. All that did not stop us being happy.

Still, there were days when I would have liked things to change. One evening, sitting in the Métro with my nose in a book which I was not reading, I went over my disappointments since my one line in *La mioche*, which had given me such a thrill. I always seemed to arrive too late or too soon, I was too tall or too short, also too young; it would have been difficult for anyone to tell me I was too old. In short, I wasn't finding any work.

'Evening, Simone, you look rather glum. What's the trouble?'

'Oh, Marcel, it's you! How glad I am to meet you!'

It was my father's former colleague, the astrologer. At that moment I was quite sure he was the man I needed. My future was collapsing, so was my faith, too; he would put everything to rights. His appearance between Barbes-Rochechouart and Havre-Caumartin could only be prophetic, as it had been when I was three years old and he had revealed my destiny.

The remarkable thing is that I was confidently expecting another favourable prediction from him. As a matter of fact, I have continued to consult him over the years, and he has accurately foretold all the decisive events in my life.

Marcel asked me for news of Papa, whom he still missed as a colleague, of Maman, my brothers, the whole family. The stations were passing. He might get off at the next station without my having asked the question which was tormenting me. At last he turned his attention to *me*.

There was no time to lose in unnecessary talk. I gave him a brief account of my situation, ending with the question: 'You told Papa that I should become famous. Will it be much longer?' There! I had got it out.

He did not smile at my impatience. He asked me my date of birth, brought out a booklet he always carried around with him, consulted it, and murmured enigmatic things like 'Aquarius in the ascendant, Mercury passing through the 5th House'—I can't guarantee those were the exact terms used. Then he calmly assured me: 'In about six months you will have your first chance.'

If I wanted to embroider a bit, I would say that I felt despairing or joyful that morning or had some special sort of feeling. In fact, I don't remember my frame of mind. The morning started with Maman opening the door of the little room that served as my bedroom and shouting: 'Simone, hurry up, the telephone—it's for you.' I dashed, full of hope, to the telephone over at Mlle Sapin's, our neighbour and landlady. Perhaps somebody wanted an extra.

'Mademoiselle, I am Marc Allégret's assistant. He would like to see you as soon as possible. We've had your name from our script girl, Jeanne Vita, and your 'phone number from René Simon. He wants you to do a screen-test for a part in *Gribouille*, M. Raimu's next film.'

Names like Allégret and Raimu left me spluttering. In a minute or two, after replacing the receiver, I found my voice again to tell Maman all about it very volubly, and no doubt incoherently, ending with: 'And you know what he said to me? 6 a.m. tomorrow on the Champs-Elysées!'

I had a sleepless night, of course. Almost every actor has had one of these before a fateful occasion, before he 'goes over the top' on D Day, the invasion of some new stage or film territory.

Sitting in the production office next morning, I waited for the door to open on Marc Allégret. 'Mademoiselle . . .' he would say, and what after that?

'Morning, Michèle.'

It was Jeanne Vita. How angelic of her. Really a marvellous woman. She did not leave me time to thank her, or even to kiss her. 'You see,' she said, 'I didn't forget you. M. Allégret was looking for someone and I remembered your face.

Here's the text of your scene for the test. Learn it and be at the studio at ten on Tuesday.'

'Oh, thank you, thank you!'

'Don't get too excited. There'll be other girls going for a test at the same time as you. Plenty of them are hoping for that part.'

What part? I didn't dare ask her.

'Good luck, Michèle.'

I had two days to learn it. I cut the school, I stayed shut up in my room and worked on my monologue as René Simon had trained me: 'First get a good grasp of the character and the situation, then express it from the heart with simplicity.' There were two pages of Marcel Achard's script, thirty lines to give a good account of myself as a girl called Nathalie. I had to make a guess at her character and the situation: I was accused of an offence, so what did I have to be— sincere, pathetic, in distress? All that at once? The more the hours passed, the less sure I became. I felt horribly lost, very much alone.

Every actor knows this loneliness on first reading his part. It is like that of the writer facing a blank page on the typewriter, or the artist before an empty canvas.

I increased my own anxiety by pouring out all my doubts—and even more, my hopes—on my mother. 'You see, Maman, Marc Allégret is terribly important to me. He's considered a "discoverer" of young stars. Before meeting him and playing in *Lac aux dames* under his direction, Simone Simon was unknown. Jean-Pierre Aumont, too. Like me today. And that film launched them, so one film is enough. Then she made a second with him, *Les beaux jours*. Since then she's been a star. I could never have a better chance.'

Prudently, Maman tried to prepare me for a setback: 'Of course, darling, but if you didn't get the part, it would only prove you weren't the right person for it.'

Not the right person? But I had to be. Already I was planning to arrive at the studio with hair-do and make-up like this Nathalie, dressed like her. However little I had learnt about acting, I knew you had to transform yourself completely into a different character, down to the smallest details.

Despite this excellent principle, I am none too sure whether, had I possessed an ample wardrobe, I would have put on suitable clothes, or whether I might have fallen into the trap of trying to make myself the prettiest of them all. I don't think I would, first because I have never believed I was that, and second because my 'excesses' in costume were always very moderate: I was afraid of 'making myself a guy', as we said in those days. In any case there was no decision of that sort for me to make that morning. The only 'reasonable' thing I had to wear was a light grey suit, bought with my pay as an extra. I gazed at the suit, saw it for the first time. How sad and tired it looked on the back of the chair, my little off-the-peg suit. Ready-to-wear clothes were far from being what they are today, a bit of luxury brought within everyone's range. They were inferior in cloth and finish, though comparatively well cut. If you couldn't afford your own tailor or dress-maker, this did at least allow you to follow the fashion.

Maman saw to it that I looked attractive, even if very simply dressed. It was easier to be satisfied with what I had because I wasn't brought up to compete in the way I dressed. Adolescent girls of my class were by their very age used to a certain modesty, good taste and good form. 'When you are a woman, you will be able to wear that' was a respected criterion.

I was wearing my little suit, although it looked so wrong in the morning light. Perhaps I ought to have taken it to the cleaners? With this fear added to the others, I entered the studio less sure of myself than ever. It was a place I knew, but it too looked very different that morning. The atmosphere prevailing in the dressing-rooms and corridors was one of ruthless competition: about ten candidates stared at each other furtively, cunningly or boldly according to their respective characters; two or three were accompanied by their mothers whose eyes, when not murderous, were full of pity for these poor ugly ducklings who dared match themselves against their daughter. It was the only moment of amusement I got, and it did not last long. Walking on to the set brought all my anxieties back.

I waited in a corner of the studio with my 'rivals'. The first name was called; we were being taken in alphabetical order, so I should probably be the last. Good or bad? Perhaps good—on the René Simon principle, I should have time to see what not to do.

They passed in front of the camera one by one. For the first time I took notice of Marc Allégret. He was good-looking, kind, and above all impassive; he accorded to each girl the same polite interest. In the harsh lights my rivals looked very different, and on the whole, I thought, at a disadvantage. This change would also apply to me, no doubt. Some of them were really very easy on the eye, though. But when I listened to them, I felt I was in luck. Most could have done with training from René Simon.

The tests were going through very fast; the minutes seemed to be speeding by at a terrifying rate. Soon there were only three girls left, then two—and I was trembling, hot all over, sweating, my throat constricted, my heart thumping. I wished it were all over, no matter how, just so long as the torture stopped: my first bout of real stage-fright.

'Mademoiselle Roussel! Test 2, first take.'

The clapper-board descended like a guillotine. I went on. I did what I could, as well as possible. I heard him say: 'Thank you, mademoiselle.'

There, it was finished. Those minutes, those seconds, were irremediably fixed on the film. Nothing could alter them now.

Shirva, Marc Allégret's assistant, was Indian. He gave me a kind smile and with a courteous gesture showed me the door. 'We'll have seen the rushes in forty-eight hours, and we'll ring you to give you the result, favourable or otherwise.'

Favourable or otherwise? Was this preferential treatment; or would he make eleven telephone calls, only one of them favourable? Anyhow the die was cast; if only it was a lucky throw! In my heart of hearts I felt it hadn't gone too badly. But I spent another horrible night.

Much later I realised that everything had served me well: my little suit, which could have been the heroine's, my hair-do, my make-up, and above all, my actual emotional state. This could also have been hers. It made an impression of sincerity.

At the time, I suffered all the throes of suspense. From eight o'clock in the morning I listened for the ring of Mlle Sapin's 'phone. Each time it rang, I prepared to dash over there. Luckily she didn't receive many calls. After all, that 'We'll ring you' was merely a standard saying. It didn't mean they would really do it.

The third day I thought they must have already let the winner know, and it was all over for me. Not so. The call came, and I heard Shirva's voice—recognisable by his way of slurring the French 'r's', so painful to foreigners.

'Mademoiselle 'Oussel, Marc Allégret and Marcel Achard would like to see you. They are waiting for you at Fontainebleau. I'll be coming with our producer André Daven, who will be driving you there.'

I hung up and closed my eyes, savouring the moment.

I don't remember what was going through my mind as I got into the producer's car in my little grey suit; I no longer felt any inferiority complex about that. I know I was quite calm, and although André Daven was worth more than a glance, I scarcely noticed his elegance, charming smile and dark eyes.

He drove very fast, but that didn't worry me. Although I was interested in what was going on around me, the remarks he and Shirva exchanged did not reach me. Sitting comfortably in the back of the car, I studied the next scene I was to do at the school. Good sense or innocence? Whichever it was, I had managed, in modern phrase, 'to keep my cool.'

Later on, Daven expressed his astonishment. 'I shall always remember you that first time, Michèle. I was doing eighty and you didn't seem to notice. Not the slightest sign of emotion. You had your nose in your little book, completely withdrawn.'

I have always had the faculty of concentration in difficult circumstances; but my reaction to fast driving has changed since then!

★　　★　　★

53

I knew nothing of the next test I was to undergo. Would it be the final one? My first impression of Marcel Achard was his pair of enormous horn-rimmed spectacles, round as portholes, balanced on a small bit of nose. He was the author, after all; suppose he said no? I didn't worry too much about it. There was a mischievous glint in his eyes, but he looked a straightforward sort of man, and he had an air of serene good naturedness which I found reassuring.

Marc Allégret might have his eyes narrowed professionally, but he didn't scare me either. For one thing his good looks appealed to me, and for another he knew how to smile. That was very important for me.

Seen from outside, the scene must have been rather funny. They had been waiting for me in a garden. There I stood in front of these three men. They examined me, with questioning eyebrows and critical eyes, like a connoisseur who has discovered an *objet d'art* in the back room of an antique shop and has it brought to his home to see if it fits his future décor. Was I really the one they were looking for?

Evidently I was. André Daven started. 'Well, we've seen your screen test and we found it pretty good.'

Marc Allégret went further. 'We're thinking of you for the part of Nathalie.' As I showed no apparent reaction, he added: 'It's the chief part.'

This time there could be no further doubt. They had chosen me.

'However,' Allégret went on, 'we cannot take any final decision without M. Raimu's agreement. He is going to have a look at your test.'

Afterwards we had lunch, but I was oblivious to it, a prey to two conflicting emotions, joy and anxiety.

The 'however' was a substantial one: Raimu's agreement. He was legendary, his fame was such that I couldn't imagine little me having any contact with him.

I was naturally very excited and keyed up when I got back to the school. I was the youngest student; nothing had ever happened to me before. I made the most of it, but had my enthusiasm damped down by René Simon, who went into a brilliant improvisation on the theme of 'Monsieur Raimu':

'Raimu, my dear girl, is a mountain. He's the Himalayas. Whether you see him from the front or the rear, he's always motionless and always colossal, and when he speaks, it's a roll of thunder—and such storms! His fury is like a hurricane—he's been known to kick the scenery to pieces. But what an actor! And what a lesson you'll be given!'

I didn't fancy having lessons from a cyclone. Then my fellow students, not without malice, embroidered on the theme. I hadn't expected them to be so well informed about Raimu. It began with that comment so reassuring for a beginner about to act in her first film with him: 'Oh, *he's* only interested in the theatre.'

'You know what he told Pagnol when Pagnol asked him to play in *Marius*? "Your talking picture business is an attraction for Luna Park. It's got no depth to it—and I have."'

'It's going to be no joke for you. It seems he refuses to shoot a scene more than once.'

I began sweating, and they proceeded to elaborate: 'No time wasted. He says film dialogue ought to be like a telegram, the essential words, without punctuation. And as he insists on his rules and his words, he'll reduce it to "good morning" and "good evening"—and perhaps he'll only let *you* say "morning" and "evening".'

In more serious and kindly vein René Simon took me aside before I left. 'I'm glad for you, you know.'

'Can he really want a beginner like me?'

He looked at me hard, then declared: 'If I were he, I'd take that risk.'

He did take it. Daven rang me up the next morning. 'Victory, Michèle. Raimu agrees.'

I heard the voice of Marcel, our astrologer: 'In six months you will have your first chance.' It was six months almost to the day.

There was a family party that evening, never to be forgotten, with everyone letting their imaginations run riot, Maman and Aunt Yvonne promising me a star's life. Teddy could already see my portrait on the façade of the Gaumont Palace. 'A hundred times larger than life, and underneath it: Michèle Roussel!' It may have been this euphoric vision of my name in giant letters which suddenly made me realise something. 'That name's impossible. It's no good.'

My name and theirs, no good? They were almost choking with indignation. 'And what have you got against your father's name?' Maman demanded with dignity.

'It's not international. I need a name which could sound American.'

This lofty answer left them speechless.

The next day, passing the Place de la Concorde, I noticed a sign saying 'Banque Morgan'. There was my new surname! It was displayed on that façade in gold letters. I repeated to myself *sotto voce*: Michèle Morgan, Michèle Morgan. It sounded good, I thought it would be easy to pronounce and for the Americans already familiar to their ear.

When I got their reaction a long time afterwards, it was unexpected. On my arrival in Hollywood, the journalists asked me: 'What is your real name, Miss Morgan?'

'Simone Roussel.'

'Wonderful! So romantic. You had an absolutely delightful name—why did you change it? Morgan for us is like Smith in England or Dupont in France.'

The shooting of *Gribouille* was to start, and I had still not met Raimu. 'Don't worry, you'll meet him on the set.' I would have preferred somewhere less forbidding than the place for his histrionic outbursts.

In some forty years of films I think I have only once had the scene which starts the film shot on the first day; in fact, it is quite common to start with the end. But that once was for *Gribouille*: we started at the beginning. The first shot was of Nathalie, me, in court. There I was, in the hall of the Law Courts, enclosed on three sides, with its dark, austere, weathered wood, waiting to be tried. The impression of having judgement passed on me was real enough: I was once more overcome by stage fright.

I now knew the story of *Gribouille*, a girl of sixteen, my own age, is alone in life. By accident, she kills her lover. At the trial she is acquitted, and one of the jurymen, Raimu, takes her in because she looks such a poor waif and gives her shelter. His son falls in love with her. Wanting to save her, this simpleton juryman turns out to have put her back in the same situation—and the whole thing starts over again.

In a minute or two, I should be standing in the dock and Raimu would be in the jury. It would be a moment of intense emotion for me, my 'future' was beginning! He was there, close to the camera, silent, his hands behind his back, contemplating the scenery. Was he preparing himself for entering the jury-box, becoming a juror; or was he thinking of something else? Suppose whatever it was displeased him, suppose he suddenly smashed the court into a thousand pieces? No, he wasn't doing that. He raised his right eyebrow, turned his head, and moved across with heavy steps, taking possession of his territory like an elephant.

'Come over, Michèle, we'll introduce you.'

This was it. In front of Raimu I felt very small, so small that I had the impression he was leaning towards me. It was an illusion, though, for I am not all that short, five foot six.

The thick black eyebrows came down on chestnut brown eyes, half covered by the pupils, which softened their sharpness. Deep and magisterial, the inimitable voice spoke: 'What a nice girl, but how shy! Good morning, mademoiselle.'

Transformed by his intonations, those simple words in Raimu's mouth became lines from Pagnol. And he had held out his hand to me. I was no longer afraid of the ogre. I liked him.

In fact, I never saw anything of the impossible, despotic, unpleasant, temperamental Raimu. I worked with a placid, good-natured man who had a wonderful presence. If I was specially favoured, all the better—because the shooting of *Gribouille* had its bad times for me.

It was lucky for me that we started in the court. Shut up for over four days in this almost enclosed setting, I had time to experience Nathalie's pain and fear, to get to know and share her torments. I did not have to force myself to take part in the trial. Choking, indignant and crushed, I listened to the public prosecutor—Jacques Baumer—in his red gown, with his accusing finger, cover me with opprobrium. Here indeed was the law prosecuting a criminal. What a pathetic creature he made of me! As the trial went on, I could see this image in the eyes of Juror No. 8, Raimu. They were on me all the time, stern, attentive, for a moment or two paternal. His gaze radiated such true feeling that it helped me to be Nathalie, the stray kitten he was going to take into his house.

For the moment, everything between us took place at a distance. But when we were face to face and I had to engage in a dialogue with him, I was afraid it all might change.

What had I in common with this Nathalie? An appearance chosen by her creators. But I was a happy, protected teenager, pampered by my family, who had never known anything but the sheltered surroundings of the middle classes. I had to get into this part by guesswork and imagination; there were no memories of anything near her experience to help me. To have continued to express accurately the feelings and emotions of that lonely child, my guesses would have had to be very lucky indeed.

The first time Marc Allégret said to me: 'No, Michèle, not like that . . . Make an effort'—as if I weren't making one—'Don't give us the chore of having to start again'—I felt an unpleasant sense of guilt. At the school you could start again several times and be shouted at; it didn't matter. But here a whole bunch of technicians and actors depended on you. You became responsible for lost time, and you realised at once that 'time is money'.

I looked up uneasily at Raimu the thunderbolt. Would he explode? The black eyebrows were not stormy, the face was still placid.

Patiently—too patiently for my taste, it was already the patience of exasperation—Allégret explained the scene to me again. 'You're intimidated, you understand, not terrorised; anxious but not in a panic. You must also pay more attention to where the camera is. That doesn't mean you have to look at it, but as it has to see you, don't get out of its range all the time.' His sensitive hands flew into the air, indicating the limits of the lens. 'Stay natural, don't be rigid.'

It was hopeless having so many things to do and think about at once. I was in the situation of a learner-driver at the wheel of a Bugatti: he must think simultaneously of his feet, his hands, his car, the lights. He is not asked as well, however, to simulate joy or sorrow, spontaneously and with simplicity.

I felt tied up inside, and the last recommendation finished me. 'Don't forget what I've told you, and everything will be all right. O.K. Start shooting.'

It was not all right at all. The scene was repeated.

'No, you're saying it wrong,' sighed Allégret.

We started again.

'She's going out of frame,' muttered the cameraman.

I dared not even look at Raimu—but I was doing him an injustice, he could not have behaved better. At each new take, as if the thing were quite natural, he resumed his position and spoke his lines again, always with the same perfection.

'But it's so easy,' Allégret was saying in baffled surprise. 'All you have to do is . . .'

He was interrupted by Raimu's voice, usually so resonant, which suddenly became gentle as he referred to me: 'The girl . . . isn't old enough yet to know. You have to be quite old to hit the bull's eye first go. And anyone who boasts he never misses it is a liar, a great big liar.'

The 'great big liar' became so enormous in his mouth with its southern accent that I relaxed and laughed. At that Raimu looked down at me in a fatherly way, and winked at me. 'But she's laughing, our little girl has dared to laugh.'

Those few words were said so expressively, with such redolence of his native Toulon countryside. He was to repeat them two years later, in 1938, in Berlin at the time of the Munich Agreement. We were in different productions, both at the UFA studios; and one evening, returning to our hotel, I heard Raimu's big voice thundering: 'It's the end. What are we doing here, I ask? What do we look like? Like the cowards we are.'

He proudly declared he was going to his consulate to get himself repatriated. He was magnificent, his voice rumbled and rolled and swelled, then softened when he noticed me. 'I didn't see you, and here you are. But how beautiful you've grown!'

Then, without a break, his anger returned to its Olympic heights. It was so perfect that I burst out laughing; and he said in a wondering voice: 'She's laughing, the little girl's laughing!'

An astonishing man!

It was an exceptional piece of luck for me to be with Raimu in my first film: the naturalness and simplicity of his acting, the life he gave to his character, made it so realistic that I could thoroughly believe in it. This was essential for me, and in itself took me over half-way into my own part. As a result the scenes with 'Monsieur Raimu' which I had dreaded so much became the easiest.

I was reminded constantly of the difference between what you learn in a drama school, however good, and what you learn at real work. Here you had no time to be carried through by your lines; there was no scene long enough to put you into the mood, prepare the build-up of emotions. You were in the thick of it straightaway. For technical reasons, the plan for splitting up sequences does not always follow the chronological order. It makes you weep, get in a rage, or swoon, before you've been able to explain why. This entails a concentration which at sixteen I found hard to maintain.

I have always felt sure that if I hadn't had that magnificent actor Raimu playing opposite me, I shouldn't have achieved the success I had in *Gribouille*. For it really was a success, enough to turn one's head; though I just about managed to keep mine.

My family was in raptures, and I suspected them of making decidedly roundabout journeys so as to walk past the Madeleine Cinema where I was 'displayed', as large as Uncle Teddy had imagined.

I was modestly happy, but can't claim great merit for the modesty. The fact was that I did not yet feel the success was really mine. In a way, I never have come to feel that. I have continued to possess the faculty of 'standing outside myself', contemplating this 'star' without forgetting that she is only Simone Roussel, a girl like many others, able to laugh at herself and enjoy herself. That is no doubt why journalists have never accused me of becoming 'big-headed'.

At the première of *Gribouille* I could hardly credit that the clamour and excitement was about me. I was bewildered by all the people in the hall of the Madeleine who thronged to clasp my hand when they hadn't had anything to do with me two hours before. In my long turquoise satin dress, made for me by Maman, I was surrounded by dinner-jackets, fabulous evening dresses, furs and jewellery. It was all brilliance, sparkle and chatter, which left me rather dazed. Success certainly had its intoxicating moments. 'Look, Marlene Dietrich has come!' She was some way away from me, but I caught a glimpse of her languorous figure as I had always dreamed of it. *There* was a real star, Hollywood in France.

The flood of compliments showed no signs of drying up. I was swamped in them. 'Delightful, and so natural . . . extraordinary eyes, such freshness . . . real personality.'

That evening I watched myself being born again. I have to admit it was an unforgettable night.

I was happy, as I have said, but not carried away. All that was very fine, too fine perhaps. Something I had wanted with all my heart and soul had just started, but now I had to follow it up. I heard René Simon's voice: 'Distrust flashes in the pan. They give a good bright flame, but they don't keep you warm for long. It's better to have fuel for a real fire.' The fuel was talent, the real fire my career. I didn't know what to think about my interpretation of the part. Some sequences satisfied me. In fact, I found them very good, a blend of talent and natural grace; at other moments, I found myself clumsy and was very disappointed. So what of the future?

Long afterwards, I had the opportunity of seeing *Gribouille* again and I decided that my judgment at the time, though very much an instinctive one, was sound. My scenes were of uneven quality, and not always in character; but clearly, although my features still had a childish look about them, I had shown presence and personality. This was undoubtedly why André Daven offered me a contract giving him exclusive rights. 'For if you're left alone,' he said, 'you'll go and accept anything.'

This was true enough. I was dazzled by the figure I had been paid: twelve thousand francs, an enormous sum. For that amount I might have said yes to any script.

Twelve thousand francs! When I brought the cheque home and put it down triumphantly on the table, there was a long silence. Then Papa slowly picked it up, regarded it, and put it down again, saying: 'Now we must open a bank account in your name.'

The slightly crazy dream I had one evening in Dieppe, on seeing that poster advertising a photographic competition, had become a reality. I was going to be able to give them comfort and security.

Setback with Boyer

When I was in Dieppe, my conception of glory was very simple: my photograph on the front page of a film magazine. To be filmed, to act, even to play opposite the most handsome of male stars—all that was secondary. I wanted to be the face offered for teenage girls' admiration and for their scissors. To be cut out, pinned up on a wall or preserved in a book, that was success.

Today Maman was waving *Ciné-Miroir* before my eyes. 'Michèle! Michèle! You're on the front page! Look!'

It was me and not me. I don't think I shall ever quite get used to the succession of faces which lie about everywhere—in barbers' shops and kitchens as well as drawing-rooms.

Yes, I was happy, but not in the way I had imagined. Looking at myself, I already had a critical eye. Maman was more ingenuous. I was her daughter, I was in this magazine, and she recognised me, even if not completely. 'It's you all right, but in your expression we can see you're being somebody else.' Seldom should I receive a finer compliment.

Success was like a party—there was the morning after. Despite the photographs, the newspaper and magazine articles, and my name, magnified like that, on a cinema façade, I didn't at all have the feeling that I had 'made it'; I could see all too clearly what was missing. I was to retain this kind of lucidity, and I think it is one of the many little things very useful to an actress with some ambition—at that time I would say 'artiste' and think 'star'. 'Star' was the Hollywood grade, my Polar star which always gave the direction to aim at. I kept my eyes on it so much that after the whirl of *Gribouille's* launching I returned to the school.

Expecting to be welcomed like a pupil who has just won

a scholarship, I met a very different kind of reception. First René Simon's: 'Ah, there you are, you're back with us! Well, you're on, then. Go up and show us what you can do. Who are you going to let us see today?'

It was as if nothing had happened. It took me some time to realise that beneath his cynical and disillusioned exterior he was very proud of his students' successes. You only had to hear him say: 'I taught that young bugger everything, but what an actor! He's done . . .'—and there followed a list of successes for which the said 'young bugger' was responsible. His students' glory was a boomerang which rebounded on him. It maintained his school's reputation, although he was never rich, being very ready in some cases to overlook the fee for attending his school.

I returned to the ranks. Not quite, though: my fellow students and I had a different view of each other. Many of them did not have to spend long envying my luck. Renée Faure made a brilliant Agnès in *L'école des femmes*, at the Comédie-Française; René Simon used her as an example for us. Jacqueline Porel in *Altitude 3200* soon created a character which attracted attention from press and public. As to François Périer, it was in *Les jours heureux* that he showed his capabilities. So we were flying with our own wings, beginning to soar on both stage and screen. I have always thought that as each fledgling left the nest, if I had been René Simon, my pride would have been tinged with melancholy. Perhaps his was.

After the classes we chatted, and of course I was very much the centre of attraction. This was flattering, I may as well admit.

My absence had lasted about six months, and the new students, depending on their characters, tried to mingle in our group or watched us from a distance. There was one of them who at first did not join us but kept gazing at me. One day, however, he did tell me: 'You can't imagine how dazzling I find you.' His name was Gérard Oury, and he was sixteen. Two years later he played the part of Britannicus on the stage of the Théâtre Français, while I was shivering in Lapland for *La loi du nord*.

Was it that day at the school when I noticed he was good-looking, had green eyes and brown hair? I have no idea. He has told me about it so often that his voice has replaced his memory. We were so far from each other then, and remained at a distance for a long time—we who were one day to be so very close.

After *Gribouille*, André Daven received many offers which he told me were unacceptable. Even America, always on the look-out for promising talents, made approaches to which there was no follow-up. 'We'll wait,' Daven told me. But anyone who talks about the United States is thinking in terms of the English language, and mine was schoolgirl English. Berlitz or Linguaphone were good teachers, but England was better. Everybody knew that you only learnt a language properly in the country itself. I may not be a person for quick decisions, but I am good at making resolutions and sticking to them.

'Papa, I have to speak English fluently, it's quite indispensable for me. Do you think our cousins in London would be able to have me for three months?'

These English cousins were part of our family history. Great Uncle Théo Roussel was an artist—perhaps I get my taste for painting from him (there are often side-skips in heredity!). He emigrated to England under the Second Empire, following Victor Hugo's example, I imagine, and possibly for the same reasons, although there was nothing revolutionary about his paintings, either in content or form. The sequel proves it: he became a court painter, married a beautiful lady at court, and founded a family. These cousins were his descendants. They agreed to have me to stay, and it was with their children that I went to see the Crown Jewels in the Tower of London, the Changing of the Guard, Madame Tussaud's— and the works of Théo Roussel, exhibited—supreme honour—at the Tate Gallery.

My stay in London was perfect for its purpose. I duly experienced the dullness of the British Sunday, and adapted very well to the native customs and food, including the famous porridge and roast mutton with mint sauce, not forgetting chicken pies, apple pies, roast beef, etc.—quite a lot of good things in that 'etc.' But then I have always liked tea, an essential taste for anyone living in Britain. I had no boy-friends, and in fact enjoyed very little social life. A typical British schoolmistress, Miss Bacon, gave me private lessons in English. I learnt a great deal of colloquial English, which I found was very different from the language of Shakespeare, and after a studious term returned to France. In April I went back to the school.

Spring stirred up the heart a bit, and made me less reserved. I was intrigued to see a 'veteran' of about thirty at the school. Fancy learning to act at that age! It took someone the age I was then to think things like that. But André was certainly different from the rest of us. Tall and dark, with a small moustache like Fernand Gravey's—who had once been my great hero—this budding actor was a cameraman before, and talked of Françoise Rosay as if she were a close friend.

To listen to him—and how I listened—there was nothing he did not know about the most arcane secrets of the cinema. Without wasting any time, he began courting me—a funny, exuberant, whirlwind kind of courtship, very much in the style of American comedy films. I laughed a lot, and agreed to go for a ride in his car outside Paris. His arrival at Neuilly did not pass unnoticed. He stopped outside my door in a superb convertible. But what was that sitting in the back? A panther. With an explanatory smile he informed me, as if it were the most normal thing in the world, that the panther belonged to a girl-friend; she had lent it him to take out on the excursion.

Was I in love with André? Better say that at that time, trite though it sounds, I was in love with love. I so much wanted to have a man to look after me, and protect me, though I didn't know from what danger. But the feeling of being protected is one I have always enjoyed—I had had enough of being alone, of not receiving 'phone calls, not making dates and keeping them, not playing the exquisite games of love. Quite simply I wanted to be loved, and quite sincerely believed I was *in* love.

66

So it was in full emotional euphoria that a few weeks later I went to an appointment with André Daven.

'This time, Michèle, I have a worthwhile film to offer you. Marc Allégret is going to shoot *Orage* with Charles Boyer.'

'In France?'

'Of course. It's Boyer's return to Paris, a big event.'

The return of such a famous actor was indeed a big event on a national scale.

'For the main part?'

'Yes, Michèle. Would you like it? Do you accept?'

Like it? Accept? I was floating in a dream. In his arms I should be taking the place, still warm, of Greta Garbo. He had just finished making *Marie Walewska* with her.

I think this childish idea and this sense of approaching one of the 'greats' of the American cinema were partly responsible for my semi-paralysis. After Raimu, Charles Boyer. It was a very bad preparation for our first meeting, which took place on the set. Following the best Hollywood tradition, Charles Boyer had his personal chair with his name on the back. His dresser, make-up girl and understudy were constantly in attendance. When I came in, he rose to be introduced, gave me a polite and charming word of welcome, a very eighteenth-century 'Mademoiselle'—and then resumed his seat. It was over already. Surrounded by deferential people, he was the great French actor returned from Hollywood: not at all what was needed to give me confidence.

Lying flat on my tummy in bed, propped up on my elbows, I read the script: adapted from Henry Bernstein's famous play, *Le venin*, by Marcel Achard, *Orage* tells the story of a young student, me, madly in love with a married man, Charles Boyer. I become his mistress, and whereas for him I am only a delightful and flattering diversion, for me he is my great love. When he abandons me to go back to his wife, I commit suicide.

In love with him? Yes, a year or two years ago, when I imagined myself in his arms in the place of all other women. He wasn't flesh and bones for me then. But now?

I tried the Coué method of auto-suggestion. In love with

him, I am in love with him, I am in love with him. I repeated the sentence, but its therapeutic virtues were without effect on me, and I went to sleep hoping that tomorrow at the studio, in the blaze of action, all would go well. After all, he was a great actor, and if I couldn't count on myself, I could perhaps count on him. It may be because that 'perhaps' came into my thoughts that everything between us went so badly: it showed a lack of faith.

In love? Heavens, I was a long way from that next day, faced by his courteous but impersonal attitude. Yet he was around forty, an attractive, nonchalant forty, that would readily charm girls of my age—and others. His well-known 'velvet eye', which I had read enough about in all the magazines, was incomparably soft when the lights lit it; but it went out with *them*. Most disappointing. Not that I wanted him to be interested in me, but I should very much like to have existed and stopped being transparent.

Raimu had made me accustomed to something quite different. So long as he was on the set, he never completely abandoned his character, or anyhow that was the impression he gave me. When I caught his eye, he stayed in the part, there was no break in continuity between him and me. That was a great help to me. I was not yet professional enough to be able to strip off a part, like a garment, as soon as the moment of the sequence has been lived through.

The character I was to portray made demands I found hard to fulfil. There were so many different things to express in quite short scenes. It would have been hard enough for an experienced actress, a fine exercise in her craft; for me it was a piling up of difficulties to be overcome. And I felt no one was helping me.

'Over to you, Michèle. Listen to me carefully.'

When Allégret started in this tone, I had the impression he was addressing a complete beginner, and I could feel myself going to pieces.

'You're coming out of the bathroom. In your dressing-gown pocket your hand finds a tube of gardenal. Your lover is there in front of you. He has lost none of his charm and attraction. You still love him, you love him madly' (if this had been true, how easy things would have been!). 'For him everything is different, you no longer amuse him. He only wants one thing: to go back to his wife. You look at him, you are afraid of reading the truth in his eyes, afraid of learning it; and at the same time you're jealous.'

All that in a look, an intonation. Why on earth did I want to go into films?

'Yes,' I said, and it was true, I had understood what was required; but I didn't feel it. Later I should dare to say that, knowing there was no shame in it; at the time I would have died rather than admit my incapacity. It was repeated once, twice, three or four times, and more. Boyer produced the precise gesture, the right voice, an expression more authentic than nature itself; he didn't change a thing. Nor did I, alas. I was still floundering. If only he would make one little mistake, I should feel less alone. Besides, I was sure I must be infuriating him, only he was to well-bred to show the slightest sign of impatience. His politeness had a terrible eloquence: there are forms of politeness which take your breath away.

'Michèle,' Allégret started again, 'we have to realise that through your despair, in the midst of your anger, your hand which touches the tube brings you the idea of deliverance. We must know that you are deciding to kill yourself. We must see everything on your face, understand everything.'

I felt a desperate void. Everyone was looking at me, no one was getting in a temper. It was so dreadful that I burst out sobbing. Consternation. Marc shrugged his shoulders, the arc lights went out. The ordinary lighting did not give out much light. I sniffed miserably; it was a disaster. Then Charles Boyer handed me a fine white handkerchief, impeccably folded, and I buried my face in its linen. A pleasant scent of lavender refreshed my spirit. It was a kindly gesture of his, anyhow. How complicated it was sometimes to be only seventeen. A few years later, when I was making *Maxime* with him, he was astonished and dismayed when I admitted the fear he had inspired in me.

My greatest support came to me from my 'rival' in the film, Lisette Lanvin. Perhaps she remembered what it was like to be seventeen. All through the shooting she was sympathetic and understanding, making great efforts to boost my flagging morale. In the future she was to do far more for me by introducing me to the woman who was to become my agent and friend, Olga Horstig. Everything is part of a pattern.

Although my mind was weighed down by my difficulties with Charles Boyer, at the end of the shooting one afternoon I did notice a thin young man looking like the black insects with fine wing-sheaths, corseted in lacquer, which sometimes seem to be leaning against the bark of trees in the countryside near Saint-Tropez. Standing with his back against a scenery strut, he was reading a script. His leather jacket was unusual— I had only seen such jackets on the motor-cyclists who carried copies of left-wing papers. Very close to his script I registered a vast brow swept by a brown curl of hair. He had a more intellectual beauty than I generally came into contact with. He intrigued me. Did he guess I was looking at him? He raised his eyes, and looked at me. A sort of big grimace, which pulled his mouth out, seemed to close up his face; then it was transformed into a smile that was at once confident, generous and innocent. With slow, easy steps as in a dance, he crossed the space between us and held out his hand to me. 'My name is Jean-Louis Barrault.'

He was only twenty-seven, and already his career had given him a name which produced strong reactions from everyone. He was an actor with audacity; people used the word 'avant-garde' about him. In the film he was a bit suicidal, a bit of an anarchist, and in love with me; we had several scenes to play together. Charles Boyer and Jean-Louis Barrault: here was the embodiment of two schools of acting. I was too young to appreciate that, but the difference between them made me ask questions about my own acting and nothing could have been more salutary.

Boyer had a classical perfection only to be found in American actors; it is incredible how much I learnt in Hollywood. Everything was wonderfully fixed, and so 'right' from the first rehearsal, that you were amazed they could improve on it; yet they did. Whereas for Boyer professional precision was dominant, for Barrault it was only a springboard which he always hoped would shoot him up into the clouds. He represented a way of acting very different from those I was familiar with. He was already making much use of mime and dance. I remember certain gestures of his hands which enchanted me. They carried the words, tossed them in the air, and caught them again: words as forerunners of bodily expression.

To act with these two men, so different from each other, demanded an agility which was sometimes difficult for me. Here, too, I lacked the experience which would have enabled me to pass easily from one to the other and learn from each what he could have taught me.

Everything was a struggle for me in this film, from beginning to end. Though I shed many tears during the shooting, I shed even more on the evening of the première at the Marignan Cinema. I was in such despair then to find myself so bad (perhaps I wasn't really that bad) that I retired to the cinema's lavatory to sob my heart out. This was my second gala evening, but how different from the first!

Since then I have often thought that such a setback was a very good thing for me. After it I could never again believe everything would go smoothly; that a single film, my first, had opened out a royal road. I had now learnt, a little brutally, that in this profession no triumph is permanent; it can be reversed by each new film.

'We're looking for a girl different from the rest, neither a blushing rose nor a *femme fatale*, but a girl with presence and striking eyes.'

It sounded a bit like a 'situations vacant' advert. The lady who rang me up with this information was Denise Tual, wife of the producer Roland Tual, and a name in film circles in her own right; you met her everywhere. She was small, dark, pretty and dynamic.

We had just had a conversation which left me flabbergasted. It started with an unexpected question: 'Have you seen *Gueule d'amour*?'

'I saw it last night as a matter of fact. Why?'

'What do you think of Jean Gabin?'

'I think he's a marvellous actor.'

She gave a satisfied laugh. 'What would you say to making a film with him?'

I gasped. 'I . . . I'd be thrilled.'

She went on enthusiastically: 'The film will be called *Quai des brumes*—nice title, don't you think? It's taken from Pierre Mac Orlan's novel. You've heard of that?'

I had.

'The director will be Marcel Carné. When I mentioned you to him, he was quite excited. It's a terrific chance for Jean Gabin, and he accepted at once, as you can imagine. The part's made to measure for him, a deserter from the Colonial Army, with dunes, harbour and fog as setting. What do you think of it?'

Among directors, Marcel Carné was the up and coming man. *Jenny* had made him known, and *Drôle de drame*, which had recently come out, was unusual enough to focus the film world's attention upon him. As to Jean Gabin, then thirty-four, he had already made thirteen films, including some peaks like *La bandera*, *La belle équipe*, *Pépé le Moko*, and above all, *La grande illusion*. After Raimu and Charles Boyer, to make a film with Jean Gabin—I should be established indeed!

'As we were looking for a girl with presence and striking eyes, we thought of you.'

I knew the importance of 'presence'. René Simon was always drumming it into us. I was also familiar with the other qualification. I had often looked in the mirror and wondered what was so special about my eyes. I had seen finer, greener and larger ones. Why didn't people praise my nose? No, it was my eyes, my look. This was to become what is called now my 'brand image'. But the brand image without some other solid qualities would not be enough, and even 'with those eyes' many other things were demanded. I am sure it is the other things that have allowed those eyes to appear in films for so long and to continue doing so—but that is another chapter.

'With you in the part of Nelly, at Gabin's side,' Denise Tual went on, 'we'll have a success.'

Was she touching wood? I'm sure I was.

'Did you know that when Gabin came out of seeing *Gribouille*, he phoned Carné and told him: "I've seen a good kid in a film with Raimu"?'

I didn't find anything too exciting in this rather laconic remark; in fact, it was a bit disappointing. But I didn't know Gabin then.

'He and Carné would like to meet you very soon.' Denise concluded.

That I found more concrete and reassuring. An hour later, I followed her into Fouquet's, a privileged and sanctified place for film people where a thousand films are dreamed of for every one that is made.

I had never met Jean Gabin nor even seen him in the flesh. All I knew of him was the personality of his films, which came over in them all: a wit, a bit of a ladykiller, with tenderness in his bright eyes and rages which whitened his lips—one rage per film. There was a satisfying strength about his image, an elegance closer to the suburbs than the Latin Quarter. From seeing him more often as tramp than prince, I had supplied him with a ready-made character, a stereotype from his parts.

What do I remember about that first meeting? The shock of his astonishing fairness; not the bleached paleness of the Scandinavians but a warm fairness like corn in the sun. His blue eyes beneath thick brown lashes. And a most unexpected choice of dress: a smart tweed suit, a tie with club colours, and a cornflower in his buttonhole, his special affectation. Everything about him was immaculate. He was what I might call 'superbly groomed', a man smelling of after-shave and lavender. He wore his clothes with the same ease as those he wore in his films, so that you wondered whether it was the duke or the dustman who was acting a part.

Sitting at my side, he turned his attention to me in a most satisfying and flattering way. I looked at this fine specimen of manhood, swelling out his chest and flaunting his plumage. To make himself attractive must be a matter of habit for him, but I still felt it was a good sign. After all, I was here to please, and to please others besides him. He had taken charge of me with such authority that most of the time I forgot about Marcel Carné, who was talking to Denise but watching us closely. I would have liked to know what he was thinking about us. He was polite, a little dry in his speech, but to my great surprise I did not find him intimidating, though he whetted my curiosity. You could feel he had a quick, exact mind, and a strong aesthetic taste.

Despite this agreeable welcome, my part was not in the bag yet. I was told there would be a test with make-up. Well, that was reasonable enough.

'Look,' said Denise. 'Here's the script, by Jacquer Prévert. It's really very good—you'll see. And a joy for an actress!'

Sitting reading it on my bed that evening, I agreed with her judgment. The style of some of the conversation surprised me, for it did not correspond at all to the idea I had of film dialogue. At first reading, it appeared astonishingly simple: everyday conversation written in everyday language. But as soon as I spoke it, it was transformed and took on a new meaning. Perhaps it was the poetry it contained that somehow made it more realistic than real life! Prévert was certainly a revelation to me.

I was to meet him as well as read him, for he came to le Havre to watch some of the shooting of *Quai des brumes*. I realised then that the source of his poetry was natural, that he spoke as he wrote. He was an alchemist of language, who turned our commonplaces into gold. He did not leave his words in a cage. They flew off like birds or butterflies while he sat on the edge of his chair, dreamily following them with soft eyes. His fingers were yellow with nicotine; at their tips his cigarette, accompanying his gestures, sketched mysterious hieroglyphics in the air. A poet indeed.

But that was for later. At the time I was struck by a most unpleasant idea. No lines were needed for tests with make-up and hair-style. An even more worrying thought was that Gabin had set out to charm me so as to make the demand for a test more acceptable. Tomorrow I should have judgment passed on me again like a beginner. The only difference was that they did it politely.

It was in this state of mind that I arrived at the studio where Jean Gabin was waiting for me; he was always extremely conscientious 'on the job'. Everything was in place, we even had a bit of scenery, the hut of a travelling fair. The clapper-board came down, and the test started: I walked casually towards Gabin as he watched me coming.

When I was quite close to him, I looked up. I was Nelly, lost and vulnerable. 'Protect me!' I cried. The rest of the words followed, so naturally that I could believe they were my own.

Carné, in a suede coat, his hair dark and glossy, was scrutinising us. I forgot he was there, and did not 'come to' again until I heard abruptly a sharp hand-clap and he said: 'Right, thank you.'

Disconcerted, I murmured out loud: 'Wonder if it was all right.'

'What do *you* think?' asked Gabin, a slight teasing smile on his lips.

'I don't know.'

'Can't you feel it?'

'I feel so many things.' I couldn't tell him I had just been living through a dream. He would misunderstand.

He had already misunderstood. Leaning towards me, he said: 'With those eyes you ought to go a long way, and you've made quite a good start.'

I did not answer. You learn quickly that even if silence is not always a golden rule, speech may lead you to places where you don't want to go. I was anxious then not to become involved in any special relationship with him.

Since my arrival at le Havre, where they were shooting the exteriors, I had not had any scenes with Gabin. In fact, I hardly saw him. He was just a pleasant fellow-member of the cast, not at all connected with the gentleman at Fouquet's or the one at the screen test. 'Morning ...' 'Evening ...' 'All well? ...' 'Nice day, eh? ...' 'Drizzling again ...' You couldn't maintain much contact on that level, and there seemed no risk of 'becoming involved'. It was so reassuring— I hadn't yet reached the point of thinking 'disappointing'— that at the time I didn't pay much heed to Micheline's remark: 'M'sieur Gabin has a bit of a roving eye, you know— and I fancy he quite likes you.'

Micheline was a 'character'. She was Gabin's dresser and confidante, and probably knew him better than anyone else. She could talk to him frankly as Molière's Nicole could with *her* master; but she didn't look like Nicole. She was a huge woman with a gauloise perpetually in her mouth, one cigarette lighting another. She was warm-hearted, slow of speech and quick of eye; nothing to do with M'sieur Gabin escaped her. There was an extraordinary telepathy between them: she anticipated his actions, he laughed when she smiled, and both knew why. Jean, who had an unsophisticated taste in nicknames, called her 'Fat Girl' or 'La Miche'

'La Miche' immediately 'took' to me, as she put it. She first summed up my character in one sentence: 'You're the well-bred kind that will never dare stand up for herself', implying: 'If you need it, I'll stand up for you.' Then she gave me the benefit of part of her philosophy: 'Don't waste your time bothering with fools—there are too many of them.'

She was both shrewd and bracing, a good person for me to have around, especially as I was the only female in the film. The average age of the men was about forty-five; Jean Gabin at thirty-three was the youngest. It was worst at table, and the evenings were long, with dinner dragging on interminably. I waited till I could discreetly disappear when the political arguments started. Papa had surfeited me with these for a long time.

Yet they were certainly exciting days. The Popular Front was cracking, the Spanish Civil War had divided Europe—and France. 'They're fighting for freedom down there!' declared both Left and Right. 'Against Fascism!' declared one side, 'Against Communism!' screamed the other. I was inclined to cry: 'A plague on both your houses!' and anyhow I hated all the talk about war. As if it could do anybody any good, whatever the cause people were supposed to be fighting for. It could only be a disaster. I didn't need any arguments to be sure of that. I felt it with every fibre of my being, as women have always done from earliest times and wars.

Back in my room I thought about Nelly. I decided that my third character bore a slight family likeness to Nathalie in *Gribouille*, the resemblance that all ill-used girls have. I am an orphan, given a home by an uncle, tyrannical and jealous, trying to get his own back on the world for his mediocrity and his ugliness. (He was played by Michel Simon, on the surface equally morose and misanthropic, though from the beginning I detected a much more sympathetic person than met the eye.) Anyhow, this lecherous Tartuffe also cherishes a furtive desire for me; how am I to escape from him? With a mean little pimp (Pierre Brasseur) after me as well, I want to run away. At a country fair I meet a real man (Jean Gabin). So love, for me, is a form of escape.

A strange girl, Nelly, always in the borderland between dreams and reality. With her destiny I fancied I would have reacted like her, thought like her; or perhaps I was already giving her my ideas. This wonderful process of osmosis works so fast sometimes, without your knowing it— and it can be quite a painful process at that. Nelly was one of the girls who would become part of my new family, the family of my film parts. One day they would be very numerous, these other 'me's', the children I had created. Some became so alien to me that I have now forgotten them. This often happens in families, there are always the children you don't love, and you convince yourself they don't deserve to be loved.

It was a beautiful February morning. Big dunes, bearing the mark of wind and waves, undulated beneath a blue sky, in which fleecy, round-backed clouds pressed against each other like a flock of frightened sheep.

The ozone was intoxicating. It made you want to take deep breaths and run about. Round me there was a studio-type bustle. It was amazing, in this setting and light, to see all the stuff the technicians were getting out of the trucks. Marcel Carné was dashing around, looking for his angles, jumping from the top of one dune to the hollow of another. When I saw him leaping like a sandfly, I smiled, and could have laughed out loud. I felt like playing truant that morning, I needed to forget Nelly and her torments, to be myself, enjoying the sun and the wind.

'Michèle, you're a bit dowdy this morning, aren't you?' Micheline, who looked after me as well as Jean, tightened the belt of my raincoat, a sort of oil-skin, very shiny.

'There, that's better. You really look quite good in that. It's a find, that get-up.'

There was a story to the 'find', which was born of a *gaffe*. One afternoon after the contract had been signed, Denise Tual came to fetch me. 'I'm taking you to Chanel. We'll see what we can find for you in her collection.'

The fee for *Gribouille* had not yet given me access to the great dress designers, and the name of the famous Mademoiselle left me unimpressed. At Marcel Rochas's I had noticed a dress I liked, and on returning home I had made a rough sketch of it from memory. Knowing very well what I wanted, I put the drawing in my bag. At Chanel's, after we had watched all her collection, Denise asked if Mademoiselle Coco could come and see Michèle Morgan. She was equally unimpressed by my name, but deigned to appear, full of animation and supremely elegant. While Denise was explaining to her in a few words the character I was going to portray, her eyes examined and assessed me. 'You've seen a model which suits you?' she asked.

Completely unconscious of the crime of *lèse-Chanel* I was committing, I calmly handed her my sketch. 'I think I would like something of this kind.'

Did she recognise Marcel Rochas's model? I shall never know, not having dared mention it to her at later meetings.

She took it, pouted in utter disgust, stared at me intently and, addressing Denise Tual (who recently reminded me of the incident), let drop this sentence from the height of her renown: 'What she needs is a raincoat and a beret.'

What a talent Coco Chanel had!

'Here we are,' Carné told me. 'You arrive from here, hurrying along. And suddenly you see him.'

In minute detail he described the scene (which in fact was cut in the editing), showed me the point I was to start from and the exact place where I would stop. Then he had them marked by branches stuck in the sand. 'Now we'll rehearse. It's all yours.'

Obediently I started from one of my marks and stopped at the other.

His eye glued to the camera viewfinder, Carné shouted: 'All right for positioning. We can get started.' A perfectionist, he repeated everything he had already explained to me at length. 'One last suggestion, Michèle. When you stop at your mark, your eyes should be fixed on Schüfftan's left ear.' (Schüfftan was the head cameraman.)

How thrilling: I was to devote all my love to an ear! I went to my starting point, and concentrated: I would forget the ear and look beyond it.

'Camera. We're shooting. Action!' Carné shouted to me.

I looked up, my eyes gazing into the distance, walked to

the end of my 'lap', and stopped. My eyes looked for Schüfftan's ear—and met Gabin's eyes.

'Cut! That's very good,' said Carné.

'With my eyes there,' Jean said to me cheerfully, 'it must
have at least been easier than staring at an ear.'

His eyes were a beautiful blue. They went well with the sea.

Gabin often brought me this kind of help. Playing in a film
with him was a revelation, a third way of acting. Raimu's
was the control of a torrent, Boyer's the triumph of precision,
of imperturbable technique. Gabin's was the unrelieved truth
imposed by the screen. He did not interpret his rôle, he lived
it. His naturalism was infectious; when you play tennis with
your coach, it's easier to return the balls he sends over. In
dialogues with him my responses became real answers. Jean
was the first person to make me realise that in front of a
camera, that merciless magnifying eye, you have to live your
part.

His presence had something reassuring about it which
went beyond the professional context. I was 'pleased' to be
working with him, and 'happy' that he was there: a nice
distinction of language to weave a little romance round. But
I wasn't dreaming of that yet, or if I was, I didn't realise it.

One evening I found hotel life particularly depressing. I
had reached the age of eighteen that morning, and it was my
first birthday away from my family. All the birthdays of my
childhood came back to my memory. Since the previous
night I had received telegrams, and in the morning I got long
letters from Tanine and Suzanne—our trio had re-formed in
Paris (they had both gone there to continue their studies).
I had now just hung up the receiver and still had Maman's
voice in my ear: 'Well, a very happy birthday, my darling
girl!'

'Happy birthday, Michèle!' At the foot of the stairs Jean
Gabin handed me a huge bunch of flowers, and besides the
bouquet there was a special look in his eyes.

Micheline assessed the whole thing in a stage whisper:
'We-ell! When M'sieur Gabin looks at women like that, they
fall like skittles.'

I didn't even wobble; but I cheered up, my depression had vanished. At the end of dinner the traditional cake appeared, with eighteen cheerful little candles making a wreath of light.

'Careful,' said Jean. 'If you want to meet love this year, take a very deep breath—you have to blow them out at one go. Blow—now, kid!'

'Kid' had become his nickname for me. I blew. Four little flames flouted me.

'There you are, you see, you'll marry in four years,' observed Micheline. It was a prediction I should have remembered.

'That still leaves you a little time for living,' said Jean.

A birthday party has to have champagne, and with it went the whole ritual devoted to attracting good luck: I dipped two fingers in the froth poured out, and perfumed the lobe of my ear with it; I was offered the cork of the champagne bottle, which I must keep the whole year. Somebody, I can't remember who, broke a glass to bring me plenty of luck. That gesture closed the party, and I soon found myself alone with Jean, who said: 'You can't finish the evening like that, alone in your room. Come on, I'll take you dancing.'

When did the romance start? The moment I saw Jean—nothing warned me that it was *the* meeting—or when I danced in his arms?

He was very charming that evening. Too much for my peace of mind. I have forgotten what the place was like; I doubt if I really looked at it. It was one of the nightclubs of that period, not to be compared with today's version, noisy enough to give you a headache in the first few minutes. Jean must have chosen the best. It was quiet, intimate, somewhere you could get to know each other; a cheek brushing yours, soft murmurings in your ear which turn into pure poetry.

The instant he took me onto the floor, I realised what a wonderful dancer he was. He spoke little, just as much as was needed, and I kept silent myself. A tango with him was spell-binding, and as for a waltz, it was as intoxicating as in those film sequences where a couple whirls round as if they were air-borne, oblivious of everyone and everything.

We had been dancing for ages, and I was amazed when Jean whispered to me: 'You know, there's no one else on the floor.' (How should I have known? I had closed my eyes!) 'They're only playing for *us*. Look, the waiters are yawning, we'll get thrown out in a minute. Come on, let's go back.'

He handed me my coat, and for the fraction of a second his arms were round me. I shivered: no doubt the draught as the door opened.

It was raining that night in le Havre, a fine rain. The lights of the street-lamps zigzagged onto the gleaming pavements. It was late, very late, or else early—in the morning. For the sky was not so dark, and already there was something rosy mingling with it in the distance.

Jean had his head up, and was greedily breathing in the air, as if he were drunk with it. 'How about a walk?' he suggested, turning towards me.

The fresh air, however, had sobered me up, breaking the charm. I came out of it almost with pain. Should I say 'no', and go back with him in the car? Dangerous. To walk into town might be equally so, sharing a new intimacy. What could I do then? For Jean everything was simple. 'Take my arm.'

We walked arm in arm, not talking. I was fine now. The soft rain refreshed me, things were all right. The hotel was very close, already in view. But the night porter must be asleep, everything was closed. 'Shall we go on walking?' said Jean.

Prudence reasserting itself, I sheltered behind a flat excuse: 'No, I'm on the set tomorrow.'

'Not tomorrow, today.' He leant over towards me, and I thought he was going to kiss me. He didn't. He wasted the moment by murmuring: 'Well?' A very small, ordinary word, to which you can give a yes-or-no answer. To have to make a decision was too much for me.

'See you tomorrow, Jean—I mean today. Tonight's been ...'

'It's been what?' he teased.

'Oh, Jean, I shall never forget it.'

He gently let go of my hand. 'You really are a funny kid!'

'What a silly little girl!' Running my bath four hours later, I began to be tormented by this irritating self-judgment. It would have been so much simpler to let myself go: a fine end to a slightly mad, slightly magical night. And I shouldn't now have to be analysing my feelings.

Was I in love? Yes, I was. But I admitted this with a sigh, not jumping for joy. On the other hand, it wasn't a disaster either. I wished I could freely enjoy the experience which might now be starting. But the word 'freely' reminded me that this was just what made it impossible. Jean wasn't free, and nor was I. Well, in my case the obstacle needn't be so serious; after all, André and I didn't meet or communicate with each other that often. This was because, even without Jean, I was thinking of breaking with him: he was too jealous and full of stupid suspicions. But for Jean things were different. He was married, and there I had my principles. Perhaps it was my upbringing, the idea that you don't break up a home; anyhow my moral code, a particular conception of our obligations to other people, put me against it. Besides, infidelity causes all sorts of unpleasant complications. Having to meet by stealth, watching the clock—I instinctively hated all that. I felt, too, that Jean and I deserved something better than 'illicit love'.

I remember having just reached this point in my mental debate when the ring of the telephone made me jump. Talk of the devil! It was André, to tell me he couldn't endure our long separation and was coming over for the weekend. But he said it not in a way that would melt my heart; he used a proprietorial tone, which exasperated me.

He was not skilful or sensitive enough to change my mood to his advantage; or else scenting danger made him nervous. None of the men I was with found favour in his eyes—obviously to him they were all potential lovers. He even objected to my being friendly with Michel Simon: 'Can't think what you see in him.'

What did I see in Michel? I began to tell André. Michel's

wry, disillusioned philosophy of life was really rather touching. As I have mentioned, from our first meeting I had sensed
the loneliness beneath his cynicism, the humanity hidden in
this man who claimed to prefer animals to human beings.
I might have told André that I liked Michel because he was
understanding and sympathetic towards me. Generally his
language was pretty coarse; he was frank about his love
affairs and visits to prostitutes; but talking to me, he was very
careful not to offend my sensibilities. He was the most pure-
hearted cynic I have ever come across. This was what made
his portrayal of the old man in *Le vieil homme et l'enfant* so
moving.

On the 'phone André began sulking ostentatiously. It was
a way of showing what our relationship ought to be and
wasn't. I didn't care for that at all, and when he arrived that
evening and we went in to dinner, I felt pretty low.

Pierre Brasseur was at the time a bit of a *bête noire* for me.
I was afraid of his teasing, his eccentricities made me uneasy,
and I was much too young to realise that my shyness and
stiffness, which he found rather funny, were liable to excite
him. Unfortunately, when he started drinking he became impossible; and he did so that evening. My being with André
no doubt encouraged him in the exercise of his sarcasm. Having teased me for a while, he turned his attention to 'the
gentleman with you'. André kept his nose in his plate and
pretended not to have heard—whether from prudence or
cowardice, I don't know; or perhaps he really hadn't heard.
All I wanted was to leave that dining-room as soon as possible. I rose and went out, catching on the way a look of fury
in Jean's eyes.

Next day there was a sequel. In the scene we were shooting,
Jean had to give Pierre Brasseur a slap in the face. When I
arrived on the set, he was standing near the camera with his
hands plunged in his pockets, and greeted me with a rather
cold 'Morning, Michèle'. Facing him was a sobered Brasseur,
who seemed embarrassed and looked at me as if expecting
me to speak. But I really had nothing I wanted to say to him.
André had gone back to Paris, and I wasn't in the best of
tempers.

It was an important scene, and Carné, preoccupied and finicky, explained the action to the two men facing each other. Jean's eyes were hard, his face set, his teeth clenched. He did not react or show he accepted what was being said; I felt he was irritated by the slowness of these preliminaries. He had clearly not forgotten the previous evening, but a rehearsal of the dialogue passed off normally.

'Right, let's go,' said Carné. 'Action.'

A short exchange between the two men, then Gabin's hand took off—to land on Brasseur's cheek with terrific force. Brasseur staggered under the shock, went pale, and clenched his fists.

'Cut!' cried Carné. 'Absolutely superb.'

The life of the set was resumed; but for that brief moment reality had taken the place of fiction. This is the true story of the slap in *Quai des brumes* which is still famous. In one cinema anthology you can read: 'No one had ever seen an actor taking a slap like the one given to Pierre Brasseur.'

Poor Pierre, he didn't deserve it. There was a superb bouquet of roses waiting for me in the hotel with a delightful note. Alas, the flowers had arrived too late and the slap was given too early.

A few days later Carné told me: 'Right, Michèle, it's finished for you. You can go home.' I could also stay and give myself two or three days' holiday. This hesitation did not escape Micheline's watchful eye.

It was dangerous to stay, certainly; but danger was tempting. Without enthusiasm I prepared to leave. I told Jean, and he said, 'So you're going, kid?' in a way that gave me a mad desire to stay. Mad but not irresistible. I left the next day. Women are like that.

For two months we were shooting the interiors of *Quai des brumes* in the Saint-Maurice studios. One morning, arriving early, I watched Marcel Carné develop 'his' décor. He scrutinised all the flats and props, seeing they were just as he wanted, barking out orders to have one of them moved or the colours of a poster touched up. Gradually his voice brought about an authentic look, turning it into that unique vision which would make people say: 'That's Carné.'

Then Schüfftan gave lighting instructions, and we heard the familiar shouts: 'Bring up 5, 6, 10 and 12! Strike 30! Tighten 8, widen 20.' I liked the fairground atmosphere; the lights made the scene live in a magical way.

'Right, fetch Mlle Morgan.'

'I'm here.'

'Fetch M. Gabin.'

'No need, I'm here too.'

'Oh, good. Thank you,' said Carné absently, his interest concentrated on the back of a gipsy caravan which he was staring at with a thoughtful frown.

'Know what happens there?' asked Jean.

'Yes.'

'They're shooting our kissing scene in front of that caravan.'

No comment from me.

'Aren't you bothered?' he went on, teasing me. 'You may not have realised that with this Carné kid it's got to be the real thing—no holds barred.'

I smiled. I had received and given plenty of film kisses. The kiss in this scene would be no different.

He turned to Micheline, always within earshot. 'Bet you she doesn't know what a real kiss is like.'

It was in fun, I knew, but it annoyed me. 'Why should you think that?'

'You're too young. You haven't had the chance to try.'

How stupid men were! Not that stupid, though, because I swallowed the bait and made up my mind I'd soon prove him wrong. Also, I thought he was showing off himself, and wouldn't dare give me a 'real' kiss.

'In position,' Carné's voice broke in. 'Here you are, children, you're centred like that, in the 75 mm. Michèle, look out, your hair's nearly out of the frame.'

With points like that to think of, I wasn't likely to go mad with passion. He explained the kiss to me, and my emotions at the time. Little did he know that my chief emotion just then was stage-fright: suppose Jean really dared, in front of everybody . . .

'Lights! Camera! Clapper! We're shooting!'

'You've got beautiful eyes, you know.'

'Kiss me.'

It *was* a kiss 'for real'; he did dare—and I forgot to be embarrassed. There my memory stops. Carné must have said 'Good!' for we didn't have a retake.

7   *Romance amidst Rumours of War*

Our combination at le Havre in *Quai des brumes* was certainly pretty good, ending in that perfect final kiss. It was so perfect that everything after it seemed to be trying to spoil the effect.

The partnership found favour immediately. Journalists spoke of the perfect balance between us, his power and my beauty. Directly the film was released, they unhesitatingly dubbed us 'the ideal couple of the French cinema'. Ideal couples became a fashionable topic in the press, and the widely read *Journal de la femme* hastily organised a competition for them. I have often wondered whether the lucky winners stayed together.

Since we were a 'dream couple' on the screen, we were expected to be that in life as well. Without even needing to discuss it, both Jean and I rejected our rôle, although even today there is an idea among people in the profession that we already had that sort of relationship. Some legends have great stamina.

As with many actors, the cinema, having brought us together, soon separated us again. Jean was off for the shooting of *La bête humaine* while I was to sign several contracts, one after the other—seven of them between 1938 and 1939. When in the innocence of youth I had longed to go into films, I had no conception of the demands of the business. After taking my first steps into that consuming sea, I was unaware how ruthless the system could be.

At the release of my third film, I was in the full flush of amazed euphoria. *Gribouille* had made my name, giving me birth, as it were. With *Quai des brumes* I received the consecration of an official christening: I was no longer one of the hopes of the French cinema, I was a new star. Big producers suggested film after film to me, as if I were someone they had long been waiting for. Even Hollywood showed up this time, contract in hand. I had only to sign to see the gates of my paradise open on a heaven where I should myself be one of the goddesses. It is highly probable that I would have committed the folly of going but for Denise Tual—who had become my manager—and, above all, André Daven. These two told me to sign if I wanted to that badly—an understatement of my wishes—but advised against going to Hollywood at once. 'Your career began in France, consolidate it before you go. You may be very glad on your return to have some firm ground under your feet.'

So I didn't sign. When I think back to that frenzied period, with so many people bustling around wanting to meet me, the journalists eager to exploit my name—I found them terrifying—I marvel that I managed to preserve some sense of proportion. I can't claim that it was my natural modesty or that my head was less easy to turn; and it certainly wasn't any lack of imagination as to the rewards of fame. I think my very useful dual personality stood me in good stead: Simone Roussel was still around, all too ready to give Michèle Morgan a few amused winks, checking any pretensions Michèle might be assuming.

Even so, my existence was never again to be quite the same as other people's. *Quai des brumes* was the point of no return in my life: after this, my films fixed each year's programme. Time from now on was measured by months of shooting, and summer no longer meant summer holidays but the very short period good for exteriors. Sometimes I didn't have any gap, I was positively 'chain-filming'. Free time off the set was at a premium, too, liable to be interrupted by necessary social engagements: 'This weekend, Michèle, you've got a couple of gala performances to attend at Deauville.'

I don't want to sound like the society lady who found all that champagne and caviare rather a bore; on the other hand, I could sometimes feel like the famous 'bird in a gilded cage'. Even my clothes no longer belonged to me. I didn't put on 'my-little-suit-which-is-so-becoming-on-me-and-I-like-so-much', but my russet dress from *Orage*, the beret from *Quai des brumes*.

There were certainly exceptions and compensations. One evening I went home carrying under my arm a box containing a fairy-tale purchase: a fur coat! It was my first, and also the first outlay from my fee of 75,000 francs for *Quai des brumes*. I have never forgotten either the figure or that magnificent beaver. It was, I think, apart from a skunk necklet, the first fur that had ever crossed our threshold so its arrival attracted some comment: 'It's big. It'll give you plenty of wear!'

The fashion was for ample coats with immense pagoda sleeves, and I had chosen one of the most vast.

'It will take alterations,' was the practical assessment of Grandmother Payot, who could already see me ending my days in it.

How refreshing to be brought back to family common sense, which cut everything down to its proper size.

The two contracts I had just signed, for *L'entraîneuse* and *Le recif de corail*, were Franco-German productions, the exteriors shot on the Côte d'Azur, the interiors in the UFA studios in Berlin. This was common practice. The French had certainly never done as much shooting in Germany as during the years just before the war. Dr Goebbels regarded the co-productions as an excellent way of bringing in foreign currency, within the framework of the Franco-German Agreement of 10 July, 1937; they must have made up for the deficiency in exports of German films, which had been progressively declining since the arrival of the Nazi regime.

Germany! Papa, of course, had not let me leave without th facts of the problem. Having been a prisoner, he spoke the language well. He must have told me some very accurate things about this country and the character of its inhabitants. We were within a year of the war, within a month of the Munich Agreement. This was surely obvious in Berlin, which I went through twice a day on my way to and from the studio? To an alert eye perhaps. Certainly to someone who knew German and had plenty of time to brush it up. I didn't.

I found Berlin a fine, slightly grandiose city with its statues and public buildings in neo-classical style. At first I did not notice anything unexpected; I had been prepared for an excess of flags with the swastika and young Siegfrieds in uniform. They weren't all blond and handsome, but they had their flags all right.

I was much more surprised by the Pension Imperiale, a sort of residential hotel where French people working with UFA stayed: an extraordinary ageless place—or preserved from a different age, which is often the same thing. The furniture was antiquated; the dark polished corridors all seemed to lead to an ill-proportioned dining-room where Josef, the head-waiter, an effeminate Viennese who spoke French with a sing-song accent, held sway. He was extremely well in-formed on all aspects of Berlin life, and could give you the latest gossip from studios and fashionable nightclubs; he was never at a loss.

I found François Périer waiting for me. We were acting together in *L'entraîneuse*. After exchanging memories of Simon's school, he gave me his jaundiced view of Berlin: 'I'm fed up to the teeth with this country. You can't do anything. They don't know what liberty means. Everything is *Verboten*, the doors, the streets, the public gardens—even the girls! There's a whistle blown before anyone or anything can move, cars, pedestrians, exits, entrances—it almost goes for us, too. They're giving orders to robots, not men. You'll soon have to pee when the whistle blows. I've had enough of the bloody Fritzes. I can't wait until we can go home and don't have to see them any more.'

The unfortunate inmates of the concentration camps did have to pee at the blow of a whistle. As to his last remark, we had several years to appreciate its irony.

My father had so overdone his forecast of the cataclysm that in reaction I not only refused to see the warning signs but used anything for reassurance: the good humour of Sundays in the woods enjoyed by this beer- and accordion-loving nation. It didn't matter if the songs sometimes received a

martial beat from youngsters in uniform trousers. Youth—
Hitler Youth—was a passing phase. Only it didn't pass, it
grew.

All the same, I found the atmosphere oppressive. There
was a heaviness, a stillness in the air like that presaging a
storm. A few weeks later, in September 1938, I could no
longer cherish any illusions.

For days the tension mounted. Newspaper boys in the
streets shouted the headlines like military commands. At the
hotel everyone gave his own translation of them, and I learnt
with millions of other French people that there was a problem in Czechoslovakia with the Sudeten Germans.

We were in a strange situation. On that date, 15 September, we were at the very heart of the crisis. But we felt
we knew less about what was going on than someone in Paris
or London. Every morning at a set time a car took us to the
studios; and there, isolated from all the excitement, as cut
off from the world as if we were in a bunker, we took part
in the shooting of *L'entraîneuse*, which had no special appeal
for me; in fact I wondered every day how I could have let
myself in for it. Then in the evenings we would be all
together again in the hotel, which remained up to the last
minute a French outpost in Germany.

As we would have done at home, we dashed to the wireless
directly we got in—an enormous set of ornate design which
I felt had something very Germanic about it. It was from
that we learnt of Chamberlain's arrival at the Eagle's Nest,
Berchtesgaden. Then came suspense lasting three days, during which we remained isolated and apprehensive until the
threat of war disappeared with the arrival of Chamberlain
and Daladier to sign the Munich Agreement. On that day,
30 September, I was struck by the atmosphere of victory you
could sense in the streets of Berlin. Showing a lack of awareness which I shared with the majority of the French people,
I breathed an enormous sigh of relief: 'Peace has been saved!'
When I said that to Papa, he answered: 'May God hear
you, my little girl!' The two sentences perfectly reflected
our feelings, and the feelings of the average Frenchman or
woman. I was glad to leave a triumphant Berlin, but went

back there two months later for the interiors of *Récif de Corail*.

After *L'entraîneuse*, this *Récif* was my second mistake. To judge and reject a script you need a maturity and experience I did not have; I think, too, that I let myself be seduced by an attempt to recreate the couple in *Quai des brumes*—who were still pursuing us. It was an unskilful and unsuccessful attempt, which took us to the Mediterranean coast, where the exteriors were to be shot; the co-producers had decided that its beaches would make quite a presentable Pacific atoll. I thought differently, for in October 1938 that sea seemed very remote from Polynesian idylls.

Jean, who was playing the lead, did not join us until he had finished *Le jour se lève*. There is a curious unreality about my recollections of *Récif*. Jean and I spent very little time shooting together, not enough to get to know each other again. I remember fixed images like posed photographs. 'Morning, Jean.' 'Morning, Michèle.' We stared at each other, with the intimacy of two friends pleased to meet again. 'Shall we get going—are you ready?' asks Jean.

Ready for what? To rediscover our relationship? A kind of camaraderie verging on flirtation did begin to grow up, and Micheline even told me: 'M'sieur Gabin's pleased to see you again, you know. I get the feeling he's missed you.' But before the bond had any time to develop, we were face to face again in the departure hall. He was in the same formal navy-blue suit with pale blue shirt and flower in his button-hole; I was wearing the same coat as the day of his arrival. The two memories have become superimposed and confused. The only difference was that instead of 'hullo' we were now saying 'au revoir'.

So there we were. We had met for one film and would now be separated by another. Nor were things much changed by the short time we spent together in UFA's studios. Despite the November wind blowing through the streets and avenues and sweeping under the Brandenburg Gate, which made for clean if very cold air, Berlin was now a place where you could scarcely breathe. It echoed with the noise of boots, of youth in uniform; the wearers of arm-bands marched about as if in a procession, clicking their heels.

At the Pension Imperiale other members of our party were very uneasy, saying things like: 'They're arrogant because they're strong. They're getting ready to attack us.' I refused to listen. I rejected the idea of this coming war which would radically alter the course of so many lives, including my own. Relying on my experience in September, I declared: 'We came through once, we'll do so again.'

But even I could not maintain that optimism for long. On the night of 9–10 November I was awakened by the sirens of firemen and police cars. I opened my window, to hear a noise like a storm rising from the city: shouts, chanting, firing; the red gleams of fires throbbing in the sky. Was this how wars were declared? Or revolutions perhaps—Hitler assassinated? There was no way of knowing. I went back to bed and, with some difficulty, to sleep.

In the morning I passed through a city revolutionised in-deed, and disfigured, by hate: Jewish shops gutted, burnt, pillaged, daubed with great white letters, JUDE. I was shattered by the savagery of this explosion of racism. In my home the word 'Jew' had always referred to the people of the Bible. I didn't know any practising Jews, and had no idea whether there were any Jews among our friends. I learnt afterwards that on that 'Crystal Night'—first in a new series of pogroms against the Jews—men, women and children were killed, besides the destruction of 815 shops, the burning of 171 houses and 119 synagogues—and the arrest of 20,000 Jews.

After that night I felt the same sense of insecurity as many other Europeans; but luckily, as if Fate were doing its best for me before the cataclysm, those last months before the war were very full ones. I was in three films, *La loi du nord*, *Les musiciens du ciel* and *Remorques*; and I also left home, to move into a two-room flat at 33 rue Raynouard.

Poor Maman was disturbed. 'You're still very young to live on your own,' she sighed, already seeing me exposed to all manner of dangers. Without a man like her Papa, how could one be protected? She could understand that I wanted privacy, but in fact that was not the main thing for me. I didn't like being dependent on someone else for my daily needs and, besides the coveted independence, I found it highly enjoyable to be 'setting up house'.

I had very little time to appreciate my new freedom and get used to it before I had to leave for Villard-des-Lans in the Alps to shoot the exteriors of *La loi du nord*. (It was originally called *Le grand nord*, but owing to various difficulties it was not released till France was under the Occupation, and the Germans demanded a change in the title.) As an economy measure, the Alps were to be transformed into the Frozen North. 'Snow is snow everywhere, isn't it?' The producer had reckoned without Jacques Feyder, our director, and it was a lightning visit we paid to the Alps. We left on 28 February, 1939, the eve of my nineteenth birthday. Luckily my family and friends had the good taste not to wait for Leap Years to celebrate my birthdays, and when I left Paris, my arms were loaded with presents, and my sleeper looked like a florist's shop: a real send-off for a star! Charles Vanel, one of the men in the film, gave me a bottle of Guerlain perfume.

Through Papa's climbing holidays, I was used to mountains in the summer, to green prairies. What I discovered now was a revelation. This white universe was a real Christmas card scene. But Jacques Feyder was not at all enchanted. Planting himself in the snow, he hammered at it with his boot, declaring in a fury: 'We're not digging in here. That's not snow. It's grey and flat, nothing like the snow in Canada.'

Assistant producers, cameramen, stage-hands stood waiting respectfully for orders.

'I want all that loaded up again,' Feyder exploded. 'I'm not shooting here!'

Consternation. Nobody moved. They still hoped he would calm down after his outburst. He didn't. 'Who are the cretins that chose this place?' The assistant producers responsible shrank into their skins.

'You can't be frightened here. There's not the space and emptiness. The terror of the white desert—do you feel it, you in there?' (He shook a cameraman by the sleeve.) 'Are *you* terrified? Or you? It's just cotton wool—and those pines, look at them, absurd!' He turned his back on us.

That evening found him perched on a bar stool. With ferocity in his blue eyes he contemplated his whisky. 'I'm waiting for Paris. I'm going to tell them what I think of their economies. I need snow, not boric acid—snow up to here!' His hand went up to his neck. (At that period flakes of boric acid spread on clothes and small surfaces represented snow in the studio.)

He got his snow as he dreamed of it, and so did we—immaculate, inhuman snow. On 10 March we left for Kiruna in Swedish Lapland. A few days later, his fur cap down over his eyes, Feyder, up to his neck in snow and perfectly happy, directed us with authority at a temperature of $-20°$C.

My memories of Lapland are of lively colours, the beaded costumes of the Eskimos sparkling in the sun. On the horizon earth and sky merged, each an extension of the other, a view which suggested infinity or nothingness. There was one colour you never met there, the delicate green of pasture-lands. This green was a sign of spring and new life for me, and I made it my special colour, in contrast to many actresses who think it brings bad luck.

There was a good *camaraderie* out there. We had a solid, united team, full of warmth and mutual affection. As the only woman, I was pampered once more by three men, all very different, each with something special to contribute: Charles Vanel his calm strength; Pierre Richard-Willm, a wonderful musician, his sensitivity; Jacques Terrane his idealism. There was something in him of Don Quixote, not the illusions but the beauty and dignity and integrity. He died in a stupid way, but one that was in keeping with his personality. Having joined the Free French, he was in the battles in Syria; the fighting had been so fierce that a truce was offered to allow the stretcher-bearers to collect the wounded. Jacques, carrying a white flag, had walked towards the enemy lines when a stray bullet killed him. I was very fond of Jacques, and to have to talk in the past of a boy of twenty full of cheerful vitality still revolts and distresses me, even thirty years after-wards. How unfair that such a life should be wiped out!

It was with Feyder that I died in a film for the first time. Since then I have died thirteen times at the latest count. I must be one of the characters scriptwriters kill off, perhaps not knowing how to keep them alive. So much so that my death has often been the last shot in the film.

That first death is a very happy memory! In the film it took place in Arctic cold and thick mist; but it was shot in the studio. Half choked by the artificial smoke spread around lavishly by the props man, my hair swamped with oil so that it stuck to my brow, I expired on a fur bed under a battery of lights. Dripping with perspiration and half dead with heat, I had to shiver convincingly. Leaning over towards me, Feyder, a marvellous actors' director, put me in the right frame of mind; he was like a priest preparing me for death. By the end I really felt I was dying, and lived through the last seconds of my life with an authenticity which apparently was quite impressive. For me those seconds did have an exceptional intensity, and I shall remember them till my real last breath.

In *Les musiciens du ciel*, I had the most important lesson in film-making of my early years when I discovered that I too could forget the technical paraphernalia which till then had greatly inhibited me.

At that time the cinema was an art often dominated by technical considerations. Shooting on real locations was rare because they were difficult to light; so directors preferred to re-create entire streets on which they could stamp their own mark. I think of René Clair's *Quatorze juillet*, the little square swept by the wind the day after the celebrations, blowing away flags and fairy lights; and of Pabst's *Rues sans joie*.

Lighting was not the only concern; we were far from the hand-held camera of a François Reichenbach or a Claude Lelouch. These cameras, heavy and unwieldy to move, required a large and cumbersome collection of rails and trolleys and ropes.

In *Les musiciens du ciel*, a very long 'dolly' (mobile platform) had been provided. I won't swear it was the longest used in a film of that period, but it was certainly one of the longest.

Several dozen yards of rails had been laid and I viewed them with anxiety for I had to walk in the middle of them, step over the sleepers, and avoid the jumble of ropes. It wouldn't have been too difficult for someone able to watch his feet, but as usual I had to be gazing upwards.

The director, Georges Lacombe, gave me his final instructions and I set off. How do you explain a miracle? Suddenly, I had a marvellous sense of liberation—the technical side no longer inhibited me. For the layman this may not seem very important, but I knew that I had just made a breakthrough. When I mentioned it to Michel Simon, who was with me in the film, he said: 'It's professional experience starting to tell.'

For *Remorques*, the next film, I was again to be with Jean Gabin. I had known this for months, and at first hadn't thought much about it. I think I should like to have forgotten about *Récif* and kept *Quai des brumes* as a nice little fairytale without a sequel. But, now we were to meet again, I found to my irritation that I was becoming more and more eager for the meeting, and increasingly anxious about it. Should I find the old Jean of le Havre days, or someone quite indifferent to me?

Between *La loi du nord* and *Les musiciens du ciel* I had met the director of *Remorques*, Jean Grémillon, in the office of the producer, Tolia Eliascheff, who later married Françoise Giroud. Tolia was an astonishing character, with a Slav face and Slav charm. Beside him Grémillon, with his rather bulky figure and florid face, looked very ordinary. He was, I knew, a friend of Jean Gabin, who called him 'the Breton'. This friendship gave him a good start in my eyes, but anyhow we 'clicked' immediately. Grémillon asked me questions in a refreshingly straightforward manner.

'Do you like the sea?' he began. 'The real thing, not a lake for pleasure boats. The Channel with all its moods and tricks?' He spoke of it fondly.

'Yes,' I replied. 'I like it very much.'

'Enough to stay for hours on a tug rolling from one side to the other, pitching and tossing?'

Such a description left me unperturbed. 'I'm not afraid of the sea,' I reassured him.

His eyes rested on me perceptively for a moment, assessing me. 'You don't *look* fragile. In fact, you're certainly tougher than some people might like to imagine.'

He was right there. Because of this, I have often been asked to show a strength of character which I would rather had not been expected of me.

Not much was needed to produce a certain rapport between us; and that sentence did it.

Although I had not finished *Les musiciens*, *Remorques* (adapted from a novel by Vercel) was due to start. The dates for shooting the exteriors at Brest had already been brought forward. When I complained about this to Tanine and Suzanne, they told me, 'Don't complain. It's success.'

That morning in August I felt that success was speeding life up excessively. I sighed mentally: couldn't I have three weeks or a fortnight off, just to give me a breather? I dreamt of this break, but when I told Denise Tual she said: 'Don't count on it. I doubt if you'll have any break between the two films.' I did, however, have a short one!

A few minutes before I left for the studios one day, the 'phone rang. 'Hullo, it's Micheline.' She had no need to tell me. I would have recognised her drawl anywhere.

'I say, have you heard?'

'About what?'

'Jean's getting divorced.'

I remained silent. That must have pleased her. The telephone crackled. 'You know,' she went on, 'he talks to me all the time about you. The other day I asked him: "Like the idea of being in *Remorques*?" And he said: "It's a good script, the Breton's a friend of mine and a fine director ..." He made me wait for the rest, and I was just telling myself it wasn't coming, when he came out with: "Besides, it'll be nice to meet the Kid again."'

She had evidently been given full authority to negotiate and now continued: 'Don't you think it would be rather nice for you to meet before the filming starts?'

I did not answer at once.

99

'Well, can he call you?'

'Yes,' I said.

Five minutes later, I was just opening the door to go out when the 'phone rang again. As I expected, it was Jean. Wasting little time on the preliminaries, he said: 'I'll come and pick you up this evening. O.K.?'

Once again I said yes.

Not long after I got back from the studio and was hastily putting on my 'city face', the doorbell rang and there he was in the doorway, looking splendid, smelling discreetly of aftershave. I had forgotten how amazingly fair he was, and the blueness of his eyes. His smile had already turned into a contented laugh, and the gap of over a year dissolved at once.

It was the kind of moment when anything is possible. Jean opened his arms, and . . . kissed me on both cheeks. Perhaps this charmer needed a Micheline to give him a cue for his advances.

As with the nightclub at le Havre, I didn't take in the name of the restaurant in Paris at which we had dinner. I know it was a good one, with white damask table-cloths and little pink lamps on the tables, not all that common at the time, certainly less so than candles today. We were excited and I think impatient for each other: it was a flirtation blending into real love. Our eyes met constantly, our hands brushed, but no more. There were artificial, awkward laughs, and strained silences. Words changed meaning, remarks spoken in a casual tone became heavy with implications.

'Handsome bloke, your partner in *La loi du nord*.'

'And Simone Simon—she's delightful.'

I pecked absently at something on my plate. I wasn't hungry; nor was he. As he didn't respond to that last remark, I persisted. 'I must say she's very pretty. It must have been nice playing those scenes in *La bête humaine* with her.'

Such trivial observations were trial balloons, of course. Each of us wanted to find out where we stood with the other, and hoped it was a privileged place. It was a moment when every gesture, every silence, was something to be brought up later on with a happy 'You remember?'

We went to the Florence to dance. It was the fashionable nightclub of the time, very much of the Thirties in its décor, with mirrors and wall lamps—terribly old-fashioned today. French band, Anglo-Saxon music. 'Constantinople', 'Tea for Two', slow foxtrots, blues. There must have been a lot of people there, but I don't remember anything about them: for me there were only the two of us.

On the floor, we were in such sublime harmony that Jean murmured to me: 'Dancing is like love, you see, better when it's not the first time.' His strong hand closed on mine, warm and vibrant. 'I'm very fond of you, you know.'

I said nothing. His cheek against mine had become a bit rough. How fast the night was going. The plaintive notes of the solo saxophone—it was the great age of the saxophone—cast their spell. All I wanted was to glide on, not speaking.

'What about you?' Jean asked.

The form of the question offered me a refuge, which I used. 'Me?'

It isn't easy to ask: 'Are you fond of me?' So he side-stepped. 'Yes, you. Do you still see the bloke who came to le Havre?'

It was pleasant to find he hadn't forgotten my boy-friend. 'André? No, that finished ages ago.'

'So—we're free!'

Free. The magic word which opened the door for us, which allowed us to love each other. Jean talked to me openly but discreetly about his new freedom. He brought up his divorce and the reasons for it with an honesty and compassion which I liked; and it brought him closer to me.

We continued to dance. I didn't feel tired, nor now did I notice the night passing.

When we left the Florence, day was dawning, a light, rosy June day. The sounds of morning started up in this empty Paris. The milkman's cart passed, drawn by two sturdy horses; a dust-cart made its door-to-door collections; a workman in a cap whistled.

We drove through the Bois de Boulogne—deserted, not a car in sight. Not even an athlete taking his morning run.

You breathed country air here, the freshness of the morning forest, the foliage full of birds, the city's roar far away.

Our first night together ended in this early summer dawn.

Knowing I attracted Jean made him doubly attractive to me, so that I was an easy 'conquest'. I was impatient to be with him again, frantic to catch up on all that lost time. We didn't know, of course, how little time we had ahead of us; or rather I didn't but Jean guessed.

'Mique'—he hardly ever called me 'Kid' these days—'I've got a surprise for you. At the end of this week we're off for a weekend at Auron, a little village above Nice. In the winter everyone goes skiing there, but there won't be a lot of people at this time of year.'

We no longer needed to keep particular weekends sacro-sanct; so his proposal, pleasant as it was, had something out of the ordinary about it. Still, don't we all dream of going off somewhere with the person we love, for no better reason than to be together?

I woke that Saturday feeling it was going to be a very special time. Jean bustled about, whistling, making all sorts of plans for the day, while I looked at him, thinking that if happiness was like this, it didn't deserve to be quickly for-gotten.

'Penny for your thoughts?' he asked.

'Jean, whatever happens to us, I should like to keep your friendship, your affection.'

'That all?' There was mockery in his voice. A kind mock-ery, but even so it slightly annoyed me: perhaps other women had said the same thing to him. For me, however, it was the first time I had felt this desire and need for a kind of permanence. Perhaps, though, he thought I was drawing away from him.

He came over to the edge of the bed, and sat down. 'Mique—let's only concern ourselves with the immediate future and enjoy the day. Because a bit further ahead'—his hand picked up a paper that was lying about—'the prospects aren't too rosy, you know. They're getting ready to have a go at us again. The next war may not be all that far away.'

I didn't want anyone to talk about war. I refused to believe it was coming. There were a few millions of us in France still putting our heads in the sand. 'The papers are playing it up. For nineteen years I've heard Papa telling us there'll be a war.'

'Perhaps he was nineteen years ahead of his time. All the same, darling, it could be well on its way. The goose-step is making great strides. Who knows how far it will have advanced in a year's time?' He lit a cigarette and, as if it were obvious, concluded: 'I can't forget that I'm in the Naval Reserve, and if the Navy should want me ...'

'What do you mean?' I asked uneasily. 'You'd join up? But you can't—not you.'

'Why not me? Because I act in films? Actors also have their obligations. You won't find me asking for special favours, it's not in my line. The Navy haven't got too many petty officers, and I'm the right age to go to sea again.'

How men can sometimes cast a cloud over one's happiness!

He realised my reaction. 'Don't make a face like that, Mique. We've still plenty of time. Come on ...'

But time passed too quickly. The shooting of *Musiciens* finished in a cheerful atmosphere, with everyone making holiday plans. The whole of France was on holiday, and Jean and I went off for two days to Deauville. Although the rush of cars could by no means be compared with today's, there was a lot of traffic on the roads. Holidays with pay made people carefree; by the end of August it would be time to worry. Besides, wars were only declared in the summer, and in a month work and school and everything else would start again, so ... True, there were some inveterate pessimists who insisted we were dancing on the edge of a volcano. Possibly, but there was no lack of dancers. Others, looking at the summer sky, brought up the old saw: 'When Mars is red, there's war ahead.' But you didn't have to take these quaint country sayings too seriously.

Brest is a town of wet stones and slate. Like le Havre, the sea is its *raison d'être*. But as well as being a commercial port, it is a naval base. That August it was swarming with blue jerseys and red pompons, which made for a cheerful rather than alarming atmosphere. I didn't even find the warships, bristling with turrets and guns, particularly sinister. Jean knew them all by their names, celebrating warrior virtues like *L'Intrépide* and *L'Invincible* or recalling war leaders like *Foch* and *Jean-Bart*. When he looked at them, he became dreamy with nostalgia for ports of call and night watches— that was really life, eh? Like Grémillon, he was a man of the sea; they both spoke of it like lovers. At such times I felt that women were only wives for them—the sea was their mistress.

My love for the sea, though less passionate, was genuine enough, and I stood up perfectly well to the fairly tough conditions of the shooting. We were at sea almost continuously, on board the tug of which Jean Laurent was skipper in the film.

With his cigarette in the corner of his mouth, his eyes bluer than ever, Jean told me cheerfully: 'You know, you're not bad as ship's boy.' He was in his element, and ran along the gangways and climbed the ladders as if he owned the boat; I was sure he would enjoy facing a storm at sea. This pleasure was denied him; it was in the studio that we later weathered simulated storms. Meanwhile, between sessions of shooting on board, we shot some scenes on the beach. I have never forgotten the beautiful scene in which Jean Laurent catches a starfish and gives it to me. Charged with love, it remained the symbol of our passion, and when I went away, leaving him to his wife (Madeleine Renaud), I returned the little dead starfish to him, telling him to give it to her ...

We walked along the wet sand. Jean, with his peaked cap and blue pea jacket, stood out against the sky and the sea. I looked up at him, holding the little starfish between my fingers, and murmured: 'A boat brought me, a boat can take me back.'

'That's perfect, Michèle, really first-class!' cried Grémillon.

Is it easier to interpret love when you are *in* love? On the contrary, though this may be a personal quirk, I find it inhibiting. I have no trouble in freely expressing passionate emotions I do not feel myself; but I am afraid of displaying

Above: Simone Roussel aged two-and-a-half at Cayeux-sur-Mer. *Below:* aged five with Papa and Maman standing behind 'Little Grannie' Roussel and Uncle Teddy.

Above: Aged fourteen at Dieppe. During the holidays Simone always took dance and gymnastic lessons. *Below:* The René Simon Drama School. Fellow students included François Périer (far left) and next to him Gérard Oury. It was here that Simone, in the foreground with René Simon's hand on her shoulder, changed her name to Michèle Morgan.

Above: Michèle, aged fifteen, (standing at the back in a white dress made by her Mother), in her first film, *Mademoiselle Mozart*. *Below:* A radiant Michèle with Jean Gabin at her house-warming party for her first independant home in the rue Raynouard.

Above: Remorques, her second film with Jean Gabin, was Michèle's last film in France until the end of the War. *Below:* On the steps of the Gare Saint-Charles at Marseilles at the start of her journey to Hollywood in 1939. Michèle refused to make films for the Germans.

my own. It embarrasses me that fiction and fact should be mixed up, rather as if I were opening my bedroom door to all and sundry. This is an important enough point in an actor's life for me to return to it, and I shall do so, especially as a very similar situation was to present me the same problem in acute form.

We were working very fast, and the speed increased after 22 August with the announcement of the Soviet–German non-aggression pact. I didn't grasp its full significance and was reluctant to admit even now that war was inevitable. The two Jeans, however, were quite clear about that.

If these were to be the last happy days, I wanted to live them fully and selfishly. Jean and I spent all our free time alone together, our evenings, an occasional free day, walking round Brest, driving in the country, stopping at some quiet inn (you could still find such a thing even in the height of the holiday season), or stretched out on some sandy beach, lazing the hours away as if there were no film and no rumours of war, nothing but the two of us.

September soon came, and with it the war. We were on the deck of our tug, all bent over the newspaper headlines. They took up the whole page: WAR IS DECLARED. Our equipment, no longer of any use, was strewn over the deck, cables mixed with ropes.

About nine months before, I had been in Berlin in the UFA studios. To celebrate the end of the film we were having fare-well drinks in the canteen: actors, cameramen, and the whole production team. For some reason, the party seemed rather heavy going to me, despite the usual jokes, the clinking of glasses, and laughter which sounded a bit contrived. I thought the Germans, mostly men of over forty, seemed ill at ease; there was an uncomfortable atmosphere I couldn't explain. In that atmosphere something strange happened: the first goodbye handshake between a German and a French-man, both grey-haired, seemed to send an electric current through the whole gathering. Like brothers, everyone clasped hands, slapped each other on the back, made vows to meet again, even embraced. But what I most remembered now, the following September, was a superimposed image, the look in the eyes of those Germans, full of messages, with a sort of anguished appeal. What were they trying to make us understand? What did we represent for them? Freedom? I was told later they were men of the left. And now, at this moment, many of them were probably in steel helmets and army boots, and carrying guns.

The sirens, those of the town and those of the ships, blared out in sinister chorus. This first trial alert, with its infinite echoes, was horrifying. We left Brest that evening: everywhere there were posters displayed announcing GENERAL MOBILISATION.

In Paris, Eliascheff decided to go on with the shooting of the film. Every day there were men missing at the studio. 'Specialists, recalled individually,' Jean explained to me. Soon the only males left in the studio were grey-haired or boys. This face of war surprised me. Were they all going to leave? To go where? There was no front. France's frontiers remained unchanged. Whole trains left for those frontiers.

I didn't dare ask Jean: 'When do *you* go?' He had told me about some complicated arrangements for the call-up of reservists, which meant that he didn't have to be among the first.

But everything was now very precarious, and I couldn't enjoy our brief reprieve. Going onto the set I had a new feeling: for the first time the scenery was unconvincing; it no longer corresponded with reality. Around me people were seizing newspapers, discussing the mysterious and reassuring censored communiqués on the radio.

Grémillon was on edge. 'Where's Jean?' he demanded. 'Does he know we're shooting this morning?'

'He should do,' said the assistant, 'it's on the duty sheet.'

'And where's Micheline? She may have some news.'

'I'm here. M'sieur Gabin didn't say anything to me. He'll be here in a moment.'

Grémillon looked round for *me*. My presence reassured him, as if it guaranteed Jean's. 'Ah, good, Michèle, you're here. We'll have the lights. Let's go ...'

When the spots came on, Jean appeared. He was in naval uniform.

'That's wrong, M. Gabin, you're not in your jacket. In this scene, according to the script ... oh, sorry, I didn't see ...'

Jean was in the uniform of a chief petty officer, peaked cap and flat stripe on his sleeve: he had so often been seen in uniform it was natural to think he was dressed up to act in the film.

Our surprise amused him. 'Well, like the other lads—I've come to say goodbye.'

We parted there, on the set, in front of everybody. 'It's better this way,' he whispered to me. 'Smile at me.'

I choked.

'We're stopping. Cut!' cried Grémillon.

The lights went out. He took Jean's arm. 'Come and have a drink.'

With Micheline we watched them disappear.

'You see,' she said, 'it's like that with men when they leave for the wars. They go and have a drink, and as for us'—she shrugged her big shoulders—'we stay behind like stupid idiots.'

How short a romance it was and how sad, if it had to end with the man going off to the wars, perhaps never to return.

As far as the war went, nothing much seemed to be happening. The Maginot Line held; our forces settled down to wait. Maurice Chevalier sang: 'Et tout ça fera d'excellents Français, d'excellent soldats', while the British were promising to 'hang out their washing on the Siegfried Line', and were 'doing the Lambeth Walk'. Paris hadn't changed, even if the city lights at night were a muffled blue. All this might have seemed very soothing, except that the German troops' failure to move was as reassuring as a tiger's stillness before it leaps.

In their hearts the French had no confidence. They were afraid of what would come after the 'phoney war'. Parisians discreetly rented villas and houses on the Loire or the Atlantic coast. If these didn't prove useful in case of disaster, they would come in handy for holidays. On Maman's advice, I bought a little house in the pines at La Baule near the Loire. 'In case we get a drubbing, there'll be somewhere to retire to. That'll be next spring or early summer,' said Papa, whose political pessimism was as prescient as ever. Only for him, the Loire remained the withdrawal line, with everywhere beyond that completely safe.

At the moment we didn't feel safe at all. I seemed to be living from day to day, carrying out minor plans because I couldn't carry out major ones. For instance, Jean loved my wearing tailor-made suits, so I ordered one, in Prince-of-Wales check, from Barclay's: double-breasted coat, flared skirt with pockets.

I moved from the rue Raynouard to the rue Sainte-Dominique. It was a bigger flat, and I decorated it myself with furniture in late-eighteenth-century style, light-coloured, almond green carpets, pink bathroom. I liked all this, though it had an unpleasantly temporary feeling. I came home to it in the evenings as if I were returning to a hotel room. As for Jean, I received laconic letters from him from 'somewhere in France' or 'somewhere at sea'. They did not help much in boosting my morale.

There was little shooting done. The activity of the studios was extremely limited. The taste of the day inclined towards the exemplary French family, guardian of the safe military virtues—they had to be military, of course—allied to an opportunist form of chauvinism. This probably inspired Julien Duvivier's film of cameos, *Untel père et fils*, a sort of fresco, the history of a middle-class family through the three wars, 1870, 1914–18 and 1939.

Shot early in 1940, the film had little luck. The Germans banned it. Entitled *Hearts of France*, it was released in America with a commentary by Charles Boyer. It did not come out in France till 1945, when it appeared old-fashioned and senti-mental with its dated and slightly childish conception of the war as held in 1939.

'I thought of you,' Duvivier told me, 'for a part very dif-ferent from all those you've had before. Nothing dramatic —a light, amusing character. I'm convinced it will be a revelation. You're twenty in 1914 and forty-five now, a real challenge.'

I accepted with enthusiasm. Most dramatic heroes and heroines dream of playing in comedy, tragedians long for a part in farce, comics would like to tackle Ibsen. But having had the chance to see the film again, I am sorry I have been asked so seldom to act light roles, as in *Les grandes manœuvres* and *Benjamin*. Somebody said to me one day: 'Your eyes are so beautiful when they're weeping.' This remark unfortun-ately reflected the viewpoint of producers. So in almost every film I have wept, suffered and, when that was all there was left for me to do, died.

After *Untel père et fils*, I had nothing in view. 'How about going to America?' Denise Tual suggested to me over dinner. 'Don't look so surprised. You've signed with RKO for three films. This may be the moment. This morning they sug-gested a part for you. Would you be ready to go?'

'At once?'

'Yes.'

'The contract allows me a year's delay. That gives me plenty of time, and I'd rather wait a bit. I'm not keen to leave Paris now.'

She smiled. 'I understand.'

I didn't believe this. She was thinking: Jean. It was true. I missed him. If I left, that would probably be the end of our relationship. If I stayed and he came back, perhaps we could go further together. I wanted to try this anyhow, and besides, it wasn't only him. I couldn't desert my family just then.

In this period Providence or chance brought me more closely in touch with Nicole Ferrier again. In fact, she stayed with me for a few days. In the evenings the shutters were sealed, the double curtains drawn. Every ray of light was interpreted as a message for spies and produced whistle-blasts from the air-raid warden. Even if they hadn't brought out the famous 1914 poster, 'Look out. Keep quiet. Enemy ears are listening to you!' the walls of public places, post offices, town halls, stations, etc., were covered with warning slogans of the same kind. So behind our blackout, Nicole and I chatted away.

I talked a little about Jean, and she talked quite a lot about his uncle, that other Jean Gabin. A stickler for certain essential moral principles, he became the *pater familias* and a gentleman farmer on his Norman farm. *My* Jean (if he *was* mine), with his gaiety and tenderness and passionate nature, was a very different person, though admittedly there were sides of him I never met. As with Raimu, I had been warned: 'Look out, patience is not his strong point. He suddenly starts bawling at you quite out of the blue.' He never did with me. Later on I heard him described as gruff and uncommunicative. He may have been at times. In his younger years he could certainly be rude, and it is true that not suffering fools or bores gladly, he was pretty terse and sarcastic in disposing of them. I think journalists irritated him. As to the people who came to the studio 'to have a look', they particularly got his goat. 'I'm here to do my job; if they want to see my face, they can go to the cinema. I wish they'd bloody well leave me alone.' Most of the time, however, he was quite different, and anyhow all of a piece, as wholehearted in his friendships as in his dislikes.

One evening I had asked Nicole to answer the 'phone. After a moment she put the receiver down. 'It's for you.'

It could only be him.

'Mique, I'm on leave. Grémillon asked for it so that I could finish *Remorques*. So here I am for a bit.'

How marvellous! Both the film and our evenings together could start again. I was back with the scenes of *Remorques*, the room at Brest I left never to return, the empty villa where we made love, the pilot's cockpit, behind the windscreen of which I looked at him for the first time—a wonderful shot, with his wet hair and drops of rain like tears. Everything was beginning again without a break. The present could merge with the recent past so as to wipe out in my mind the dismal period waiting for him. In these strange weeks before the *débâcle* we went out all the time, in a frenzy of happiness, as if we were trying to pile it up and put it in store. I have retained in my memory a series of jerky images as from a film being run so fast that you think: 'It can't go on, it must break down.'

In this strange atmosphere of general camaraderie and lightheartedness, Grémillon finished his film. 'There you are, children. It's in the bag.' In fact it was not released till the Occupation, in 1941, after difficulties with the German censorship.

At the end of May 1940, the French Navy had provided us with our only success so far in the war: Narvik. Jean didn't say so, but I knew he would have liked to be there. 'You know where Narvik is, Mique?' He showed me a point very high in Norway, on the map which all French people, including even me, had pinned on their walls. 'It's here, in this fiord, that the British on 10 October and 13 April sank ten destroyers, and now our Anglo–French force have thrown the Fritzies out and taken the town.'

A conversation which started like this wasn't easily diverted to talk of love. I think it was then that I gradually

began to feel there was no future for us as a couple. Our meetings had always taken place under notice of separation, with
absences of several months to follow. How much time had
we had together? About four months, counting up the bits.
I sometimes think if we had been a little more open with
each other, we might have found words to unite us for good.

However, events in the outside world soon stopped all
those private dreams. 'Mique! Heard the news? The bastards
have invaded Belgium!'

Before very long the first Belgian refugees arrived, for-
shadowing the French flight with German tanks in pursuit.

'Listen,' said Jean. 'Why stay here? Go to your villa at La
Baule, and see how things work out. Take the family there.
They'll be safe, and you will be, too.'

He was right. Rather against the grain, I had become head
of the family and it was my duty to bring them to safety.
I felt like saying: 'And you—what are you going to do? Let's
leave together.' But it was for him to suggest this, not me.
So I said nothing; and nor at first did he. Then he tried to
explain: 'I'm not demobilised, you see, so I have to keep
myself at the disposal of the military authorities. That means
I've got to stay here. Besides which, I have some business
to settle.'

He didn't specify what business, but I understood. The
divorce proceedings had not been completed yet, and not
only could he not abandon his wife, he had to make sure *she*
was safe.

There may be cases where war favours love, but ours was
not one. It separated us at the wrong moment: it was the
turning-point most couples know, and we made a mess of
it. We needed a little time and solitude to appreciate what
we meant to each other and transform a passionate affair into
lasting love.

The German armoured divisions were nibbling the north-
ern part of France off the map, and I prepared to leave. Everything was ready. I 'phoned Jean: 'I'm just seeing that they're
safe, then I'll be back.' He gave me a mass of advice for the
journey, and I waited for him to slip in, at the end of a sentence: 'Really I'd better come with you—hang on, I'll be

round.' But perhaps he was waiting for me to ask him. His last words—'Mique, take good care of yourself'—stopped me for the fraction of a second in the act of replacing the receiver. Did those words carry another message? I shall never know, for my hand finished its movement. Once more events beyond our will were separating us. When should I see him again? Should I ever see him again?

There were a lot of things the furnished villa at La Baule didn't have. The first night was miserable; the walls were streaming with damp. Disturbed in their solitude, the mice ran onto Granny Roussel's bed.

Next morning, all the women set to work. There was quite a band of them: my mother, grandmothers and sister. Maman had laid in a good stock of provisions, a reflex from the '14–'18 war, and it was no doubt this that had attracted the little mice.

How long would we be there for? I gave up the idea of going back to Paris. The exodus was developing. My uncles, aunts and cousins arrived, Tanine joined us, and other friends. The house was crammed. You had to step over mattresses.

The stories from the roads to our north were appalling: columns of refugees machine-gunned and bombed. France seemed to be falling, but everyone said: 'Our forces will make a stand on the Loire. The front will be re-formed. We'll stop them there.' Panic spread like an oil-stain. It caught me, too, and like others I lost my head. We *must* cross the Loire— but we needed a car to take ten people, and anyhow there was no petrol. Something must be found. And I thought of something. I would buy five of those little pedal cars you hired on the beach in the summer to ride over the wet sand.

I told my mother about the idea, and she laughed a little hysterically. 'My poor darling, your grandmothers will never be able to pedal.' The humour of the situation now struck me, too: five little pedal cars fleeing at full speed before the German tanks—a real black-comedy scene.

I bought them all the same, and we set off. We crossed the Loire, and disembarked at Saint-Brévin with bundles, blankets, cases and umbrellas—just in time to hear the sirens pierce the air. The Messerschmitts with their sinister black crosses flew very low, hedge-hopping. Flat on their faces in the dust, the whole Roussel family waited for them to pass.

A small abandoned cottage offered us some meagre shelter. We collapsed into it in a stupor of weariness.

In the morning, the sun rose in all its glory. There had never been such a beautiful summer. I opened the window. The little street was quiet. A hand pulled a shutter, making it clatter. As if responding to a call, other hands appeared and clattered shutters. Everything was so calm and peaceful.

'Hey, you up there!' cried a man's voice, 'close your shutters. Can't you see *they're* coming!'

I obeyed hastily, but remained on the look-out behind the shutters. Through the slits I could watch a piece of deserted road, white in the sun. The silence was broken by the noise of a motor-cycle; all I could glimpse of the man riding it was his round helmet, surmounting a vast shapeless waterproof outfit in a dull green. I had been expecting to see a ferocious blond giant.

Other motor-cycles passed and a curious little square car, then all was quiet again for the moment. I felt a strange new sensation, that of humiliation, shared with millions of other French people.

On that day, in silent groups round the radio, we heard the croaking voice of Marshal Pétain, announcing the Armistice to us. The most sinister and inappropriate *Marseillaise* in our history was followed by a silence which choked us.

Papa rose, and in a solemn voice delivered his verdict. 'When a man is the victor of Verdun, he hasn't the right ...' He repeated: 'Hasn't the right', then broke down. Tears flowed over his face to get lost in his moustache.

It was all over. The next day we returned to La Baule.

'Why don't you go to Hollywood, Michèle?' Denise Tual asked me one fine autumn morning. It was much the same as asking a cripple: 'Why don't you go for a walk?' In lucid moments my mind had been playing with the idea; but despite the magic of the word Hollywood, it had found too many difficulties in leaving: France was cut in two, and my parents were on the other side, at La Baule in the occupied zone, while I was here at Cannes. Marc Allégret had sent a telegram asking me to come in connection with a film project, and I had been here three weeks. To cross into the unoccupied zone had been easy enough; to cross the Atlantic was a rather alarming prospect.

I looked up at Denise, who was regarding me thoughtfully, and gave her the result of my reflections: 'It's not the right moment.'

'I think you're wrong. There will never be a better moment. The Americans have asked me if you were prepared to honour your contract. At present you can leave, but quite soon everything may be different. The Germans have reopened the studios in Paris. *They* will be the new producers. They'll try to collect as many actors and directors as they can. Don't forget you worked for UFA before the war. They'll certainly try to get you back.'

As far as *they* were concerned, I could give an immediate answer. 'Things are different now. I shan't make films for an occupying power.'

'Fine, but think a bit. To refuse their offers will put you in a very tricky position. And you may be without work, perhaps for a long time.'

'I'll find work in the free zone. Marc has an excellent project, and if he succeeds in setting it up ...'

Denise shook her head vigorously. 'There won't be many films made on this side. Paris will be the centre more than ever. Labs, studios, equipment—everything's there. You're going to have to make a choice.'

From the terrace of the Grand Hotel where we were sitting, the sun-bathed Riviera seemed unreal, a backdrop on a film set behind which we were sheltering—with our heads in the sand like ostriches. For these three weeks I had been living here on the fringe of the national disaster. We formed a small band of young men and girls of my age: Michel Auclair, Louis Jourdan, Danielle Darrieux, Micheline Presle. October had provided an Indian summer, and we had become carefree, enjoying the pleasures of an extra holiday: bathes, tennis, cycle rides; while in the evenings we played pranks in the hotel corridors like schoolchildren in the playground, laughing, shouting, singing, improvising operatic arias with the stories of our lives. It was a way of wiping out of our minds the disgrace of defeat and the mess our elders had made. The present helped us to forget our fear of being without a future; and it was just this future Denise was making me remember, reminding me that I had a decision to make.

Micheline Presle's voice made me start. 'We're going for a bathe, Michèle. Coming with us?'

'I'll be with you in five minutes.'

During those five minutes I made my decision. 'Right, I'll go. But how?'

'I'll inform RKO. They'll organise your journey.'

'What about my passport and my visa?'

'You'll get them in Nice at the Prefecture and the American Consulate.'

'Good, but I shan't leave without seeing my parents and asking them what they think about it.'

'Write to them.'

'On an inter-zone card? With little crosses for the answers? The authorities didn't include provisions for journeys to America. I'd rather go up there.'

'Suppose you can't get back across the line? It would be better to send a letter by someone. That's quite easily done.'

It still was at that time. So I wrote to my father, and very soon, with the help of the same courier, had my parents' answer: they both completely approved of my going, sent me all their love, and were already wishing me *bon voyage*. I could imagine them round the table trying to picture the America I was about to visit. I wonder whether I should have gone if Denise had not done the necessary.

Although *Quai des brumes*, specially released in America as *Port of Shadows*, had been very favourably received by both critics and public, I told myself the Americans were not waiting enthusiastically for my coming. They had within reach the most dazzling creatures in the world, incomparable talents—I imagined them in even greater numbers than they were. The failures were equally impressive. The only French stars you could quote as successes were Claudette Colbert, Charles Boyer and Maurice Chevalier. Several times my fellow actors and actresses had warned me in a friendly way (or perhaps it was not so friendly): 'You must realise, directly American film companies see a talented young actor or actress appear in Europe who may be a rival to their own stars, they pounce on him or her with contract in hand. What does it cost them? A few dollars. Once there they are competing with American stars, who are well known and loved by their public. It's an unequal struggle. When the contract is terminated, it's not renewed. They depart in triumph, but their welcome back to Europe is less brilliant. The star is now half forgotten, and has to start all over again. I wouldn't go to America, not if they built a bridge of gold for me.'

I soon realised, certainly, that the Americans did modify European actresses to their taste, so as to turn them into stars 'made in U.S.A.'; but the other part of this reasoning was false. American companies didn't put them under contract in order to remove them from the international market; the companies were just as keen to achieve successes with new stars, whatever their nationality.

Disquieting as these warnings might be, they did not slow down my preparations for departure. Having only come to Cannes for a week or two, I had left my belongings at La Baule and in Paris. So I ordered a travelling coat and two suits, one in turquoise and one in almond green.

The nearer my departure date came, the more I realised how alone I was, leaving France for who knew how long, and without my nearest and dearest to say *au revoir*. I wrote letters to friends, especially Tanine and Suzanne, who would know how much I missed them at this time particularly. I could imagine their questions and advice, their laughter and emotion, all that warm-hearted excitement I so much needed—if they had been here to join in preparations for the trip.

I wrote also to Micheline Bonnet. Today I must be honest with myself. Having no news from Jean and not wanting to write to him, I chose, without admitting it to myself, the intermediary he had used himself, and persuaded myself that the little sentence had come from my pen in all innocence: 'I've no news of Jean—if you see him, say *au revoir* to him from me.'

I believe I had hoped up to the last minute that something would happen to stop me going. To leave France was practically impossible, even departures for North Africa were under surveillance, so . . .? But Denise Tual's tenacity and the efficiency of the American film company surmounted all the difficulties—my itinerary was fixed: 'You'll cross the Spanish frontier at Port-Vendres. At Barcelona the head of RKO in Europe will join you—he's going back to the United States. You'll then cross part of Spain and embark in Portugal . . . New York, then Hollywood . . .' The details that followed were calculated to encourage me to the full.

My boats were almost burnt! In melancholy mood I was putting my new suits in tissue paper—how pretty they would have been in the Riviera sunshine!—and getting ready to close my first case, when the 'phone rang: 'Michèle, it's Jean.' Three words, but what a lot they meant: 'If you need me, I'm here.'

'The Fat Girl told me you were leaving for Olivode' (a

joke stage-French pronunciation of ours). 'You must be pleased. You'll see the great Greta.'

His tone was bantering. I laughed, slightly put out.

'Don't worry,' he went on. 'I think you're right to go.'

'You really do?'

'But of course. The Fritzes are going to want us to act for *them*. They tried to contact me in Paris. So I may soon be doing the same as you.'

His approval of me was so important that I wished I could have kissed him.

'Listen, it just happens I have to come down to the Riviera.' The 'it just happens' was very warm and loving.

'In three days ...'

'Yes, I almost missed you. You were running away without giving any warning.'

Oh, I had given warning all right, and he knew it.

The next day he was at Cannes. We had two days to go, both too short a time and too long. Then I was with him on the platform at the Saint-Charles station, sinister with its blue glass roof, crowded, noisy and dirty. Without him there, in the midst of that bustle and noise, I should have felt lost. But he projected a serene, reassuring strength. Nothing could happen to me when he was there.

Leaving for Hollywood ought to have made me joyful, but I didn't manage to be. I couldn't stop myself finding this departure a sort of exile. It was easy for me to imagine what it would have been like in normal times; family, friends, press, photographers, flowers, hands waving—a typical picture, like a wedding photograph. But there we were, just the two of us, alone. He had given me papers, sweets, placed my cases in the luggage-rack. Now he was on the platform, head raised, and I was at the window leaning towards him, looking at him, smiling. A scene from a film, but the dialogue was ours and we were playing it sad in heart. No one would know we had tears in our eyes.

Jean on that railway platform remained for a long time my last image of France—and of him.

We were to meet again, but it would never be the same. Something had finished that day. I never 'broke' with Jean, we just parted. That's why I have put in here what I wrote in my diary on 15 September, 1976:

'Monday morning. Wake up with this message: "Madame Morgan, *France-Soir* on the line. I'm afraid I have some bad news for you. Jean Gabin is dead."'

It came so much out of the blue that I remained speechless. The pain, I knew, would only come later. At the same time I knew the journalist was waiting for some reaction from me, preferably dramatic. He waited in vain. What could one say in such a case that was not platitudinous or banal? He had gone too soon, much too soon. He didn't have time to wipe out that slight sense of unfulfilment, that permanent melancholy that was always in him: the feeling that he hadn't lived life to the full. Yet he had everything. He adored his wife, his children, his home, his films; he had several close friendships, and youthful affairs of the heart to look back on. But did he ever know real happiness?

'I can still see his fine hands, his fair, silky lashes, that way of smiling he had, and that way of acting a part without acting ...'

'Tuesday evening. In homage to Jean Gabin they're showing *Quai des brumes* on TV. What memories it brings back! I see him again with my more mature outlook. I didn't know much about my craft then, but Jean—such an impressive note of authenticity, his natural gestures, his striking voice. I look at him and think that in a few hours there will be nothing left of him, or so very little.

'A few days have passed, I am in bed with 'flu. I have just watched the ceremony at sea on the small screen. I've seen the boat move away. Did he love the sea to the point of sinking in it? A sailor will scatter the ashes. Goodbye, Jean.'

Crossing the Spanish frontier, I had the unpleasant sense of not only leaving my country for a long time, but of leaving it like a deserter; perhaps I shouldn't have listened to the song of the American sirens? I was met by a friendly young man who drove me to Barcelona. On this red soil, which in some places had gaping holes like wounds, the signs of war were very much in evidence. I was shattered by the piles of ruins and such widespread destruction. I had been going to Simon's drama school, learning to become an actress, while here there was a foretaste of the conflict now destroying *us*. I had ignored the Spanish Civil War, and reproached myself for having been blind to so many horrific things.

At Barcelona, I was met by RKO's Mr Nicolson, who was to be my companion on the Atlantic crossing. He too was a warm, friendly man, but his flowers and smiles did little to cheer my spirits.

Lisbon, with its buildings intact, its lights blazing at night, its peacetime life, astonished and almost shocked me. The boat we were travelling on was called the *Exhocorda*, which means 'Exodus', and it was an apt name, for it was full of people with no belongings except their past, and they were running away from that. I was a long way from presenting the stereotyped picture of a star on a sea trip.

With eyes smarting, we watched the coast disappear. I felt a bond with that mass of people. I was like them, even though it was not quite the same for me. Though my situation was less dramatic, I still felt myself a refugee. When would I cross the sea the other way? When would I come back?

I shared a narrow cabin with a French woman and two German Jews. After a period of silence, conversation developed naturally. To talk of yourself and your past is a way of holding onto something and not feeling uprooted. One of them summed up their line of thought: 'To save one's skin is all very well. But afterwards, you have to live.'

The dining-room was as cheerful as a monks' refectory. There, or on deck, I often found myself in Mr Nicolson's company—Harry's, I should say, for he told me to call him that at the first handshake. He was typical of one sort of American, smile whiter than white, clear complexion, clean-shaven, on the plump side, with a permanent good humour and good conscience. My air of being far away, verging on melancholy, surprised him. Despite his stay in France, where he was stationed, he couldn't understand why I was not deliriously happy from morning to night. He was so far removed from my cares that when I spoke of Occupied Paris, he patted me on the hand and said: 'Too bad.'

It was a long crossing. To avoid mines and submarines, we didn't follow the usual route and had a lot of manœuvring to do. So when it was announced to us ten days later that New York was in view, everyone rushed to the upper deck. The excitement of the landing changed the ship's gloomy mood. There was laughter and tears, the Statue of Liberty was greeted with shouts of excitement and nothing could have seemed to us more symbolic.

Though New York was not Hollywood, my first experience of American publicity started here. First, of course, I had to answer the punctilious and somewhat absurd Immigration Office questionnaire, declaring with all due solemnity that I, the young blonde lady in a turquoise suit, had not come to this country with the intention of assassinating the President of the United States. After that I went straight to my hotel suite; and before I had time to realise what was happening, the strong hands of a ginger-haired photographer had perched me on top of my trunk, just opened while a good fifteen journalists, informed by RKO's press office of the arrival of Michèle Morgan, star of *Port of Shadows*, bombarded me with questions I only partially understood. The English of our London cousins had little in common with the nasal American of these journalists.

'What about your romance with Jean Gabin?' The question was asked point blank. They're well up on my affairs, I thought, but before I had time to answer, the photographer, his eye in the viewfinder, ordered: 'Cross your legs!' With an imperious hand he pushed my skirt up onto my thighs, in my estimation almost beyond the limits of decency, then approved the pose: 'O.K. ... Now say cheese!'

What had cheese got to do with it?

If New York is a vertical town—this is not my phrase but Jean Cocteau's—Hollywood is a horizontal one, lying on the edge of the sea. In fact it isn't a town, it's a district, only a vast one stretching from Los Angeles to Santa Monica. The air there smells of ozone and orange groves. I breathed it right from the airport, where I made my arrival in accordance with the tradition of the newsreels: I came down the steps of the plane with a big 'cheese' smile, waving my hand in the air. Surprise! Julien Duvivier was there. I was quite touched, for I knew him as a difficult, rather than welcoming character. He and Mr Brown, RKO's public relations chief, protected me from the journalists, pressing them back with the statement: 'Miss Morgan will give a press conference at 5 p.m.' The thought of this ordeal terrified me.

The limousine went quite slowly from Hollywood Boulevard to Sunset Boulevard, so that Miss Morgan could see everything. I found it all enchanting, the splendour of these white villas in the middle of their well-kept gardens, full of flowers. It was a dream, I was being driven through my dream. Then Julien Duvivier damped my enthusiasm by remarking: 'It makes a big impression when you arrive, but after a few months you feel you're living in a cemetery.'

Later on, I found his warning well founded.

I came down into the hall of the Hotel Roosevelt. Mr Brown was briefing me for the press conference at five o'clock: 'Very important for you, Miss Morgan.' No doubt it was, but I felt fairly demoralised at the idea of 'showing my legs' again like Mistinguett, facing a running fire of questions, and showering the journalists with 'cheese' smiles. My face showed my anxiety.

Chewing his cigar—I guessed he must have slept with it— Mr Brown reassured me in his fashion. I heard with stupefaction that RKO were the best in the world at launchings. Their publicity office, directed by Boris, a Russian who spoke French—a European, see?—had studied me in depth. He had a complete file on me, my tastes, and my typically French family. Oh dear, they must picture my father with a Basque beret screwed onto his head and a long loaf of bread under his arm. As to my life, Boris knew about it down to the smallest details. A pleasing prospect! I was choking so much I couldn't even explode with indignation.

Mr Brown assured me that they knew what was good for me, and that my guardian angel on the road to success would be Boris's assistant, Miss Adele Palmer, a very remarkable person who had 'thought up' my personality and knew how to present it to the American public. Again I was stupefied. He seemed to be saying: 'Be beautiful. We'll do the thinking *for* you.'

I wanted to shout at him: 'I don't need anyone to exploit my life or think up my personality. I refuse to become a manufactured product. I want to remain myself. They can like me as I am or I'll clear off.' But where? This very short question calmed me down. Still, I was not in a very co-operative spirit as I prepared to meet my Pygmalion, Miss Adele Palmer. Three hours later, I was ready to cling to her like a drowning man to a buoy.

Adele Palmer had very white, very short hair, a young face, a smile to cheer you in a black mood (as I was to experience later on), tip-tilted nose, and the energy of a particularly dynamic bee. Directly she arrived, while welcoming me on quite intimate terms, which was heartening, she fixed my air-conditioning, checked that my iced-water dispenser worked all right, made sure my hotel Bible was there in the drawer of my bedside table, arranged the flowers, and finally handed me a mysterious little pot. 'I've brought you a beauty mask to rest your face. If it suits you, I'll tell you where you can buy it, I know all the right addresses in Hollywood.'

Impossible to tell her that I didn't use any product, only the most natural light cream possible to protect me from bad weather, plus a little powder, and *never* any tinted foundation cream; that my most important ritual, which I carried out religiously twice a day in all circumstances, was to carefully clean my skin.

With the authority of a nurse, she drew the double curtains of my windows and telephoned the desk with the most stern instructions: 'Miss Morgan is not to be disturbed for an hour on any pretext.' Then she turned an innocent eye in my direction. 'There we are, you must stretch out in the dark, drink a glass of water, make your mind a blank, and relax, Michèle. Take it easy! Everything will be all right!'

It would be all right, would it?

Yes, perhaps it would. When I got up again, I decided that Adele Palmer's methods were quite effective.

In the car, a veritable mobile *salon* which took us to RKO, she explained my personality to me. 'For us Americans you are "the typical French girl", emotional and amorous, shy but not prim. You like scent, intelligent men, Burgundy, cheese . . .'

'Cheese again!'

'You do like it, don't you? It's very French.' She looked down and set her mind at rest. 'It's in your file anyway.'

Her eyes travelled over me professionally, assessing me. I could see her reviewing the image I was presenting to her, and finding it satisfactory: hair sensibly done, well-cut dress, all 'so simple and unpretentious'. I must correspond to the machine portrait of a French girl.

If I could also talk the way they wanted, perhaps everything *would* be all right. 'Adele, what will they ask me?'

'Don't be scared. You look so respectable they won't dare to be indiscreet.'

'Suppose they do dare?'

'Answer everything by talking to them about California. We really do like people to like us.'

The ordeal began curiously by contradicting Adele. 'You don't look like a Frenchwoman.' They debated it seriously. 'More the Swedish or Norwegian type,' declared some. 'No,' insisted the others, 'her Germanic ancestry is obvious.' Was I quite sure my grand-parents . . . ? My cousins from London did not satisfy them, and a Walloon grandmother left them indifferent. Anyhow I didn't live up to their strictly defined rules for a Parisian woman: small turned-up nose, dark, plump and excitable.

'What are your likes, Miss Morgan?'

Scent, intelligent men, cheese, and the wine of . . . California.

Victory! Discreet applause and approving laughter at this important declaration.

I was no longer Miss Morgan, I was Michèle. And Adele was ecstatic: the good old tricks, well applied, always succeeded.

Now it was clearly established that I was French—my

accent certainly was—they looked at me mischievously with winning smiles, as if to say: you can make advances to *her*. I have always disliked this reputation of Frenchwomen in the United States, and it exasperated me throughout my stay.

'Michèle!...Michèle!...' The questions came from all sides. What the journalists expected of me was some gossip about my private life—the main theme, of course, being Jean Gabin. But I kept to the very different scheme I had worked out for this conference: to talk about my country, and Paris under occupation. They would have to listen to me.

In Hollywood, and generally on the West Coast, the war in Europe seemed very far off. Papa always said: 'You'll see, my darling—when the Americans get into it ...' Yes, but for that they must hear the echoes of it, and for them it was still light years away.

At my first party I plunged straight into the Hollywood of
its thirty most prestigious years. Seventy-two hours earlier
I had been on the high seas in a boat full of refugees that was
manœuvring hazardously between the mines. Now I was getting out of an RKO car to make my 'entry into society', the
high society thronging into Ginger Rogers' villa on the fabulous Beverly Hills. Quite a contrast!

I thought I was walking on a set for a Hollywood super-
production. It was all there, the neo-Mexican style villa, the
blue velvet, starry night, and in a corner of the park raked
with floodlights, the silver crescent of the moon glittering
into the swimming-pool. The cars, with their tyres swishing
over the gravel—the lights transforming a cluster of trees into
an enchanted forest—completed, in the words of a song of
the time, 'a night more lovely than the day'.

Ginger Rogers had slipped her siren's body into a lamé fur
to receive her guests at the front door. The array was complete: Olivia de Havilland, Orson Welles, Ronald Colman,
Mickey Rooney, Ava Gardner, Humphrey Bogart, Clark
Gable, Gary Cooper, Tyrone Power—and many others to
be discovered in the drawing-rooms. I would have been content just to look at them, and then tiptoe away, postponing
till tomorrow my entry into the real world of my dream.

A voice greeted me. 'Hullo! My name is Cary Grant!' Did
he think we didn't go to the cinema in France? With my
most charming smile I said: 'Michèle Morgan!' A good point
for *him*, he avoided the 'You're French!' which punctuated
every introduction, as if to say 'How can one be anything
but Anglo-Saxon?' He extended his hand and led me
through a crowd chattering in American the same remarks

you heard in France in the same kind of gathering: 'My film's being edited' 'We've just opened in New York, Dallas and Chicago, excellent press' 'He had the nerve to offer me a small part, I said "What?"' I was quite sorry I understood English.

'Come with me, Michèle.' Ginger took me away from Cary Grant. 'I want you to meet my mother.'

She led me off to the basement, one of the curiosities of her house. Surprise: Ginger's mother looked like Ginger's sister, a not much older sister at that. She was standing in front of a huge nickel-plated organ-like apparatus dispensing ice-cream. From this Mrs Rogers adroitly extracted litres of ices, chestnut, vanilla, banana, apricot, chocolate—and Chantilly. With her finger on the keyboard, she said amiably: 'So you've come to film in America, Miss Morgan. Can I give you a milk-shake?'

How could I refuse? I was presented with a Himalaya of chocolate and apricot ice crowned with a Mont Blanc of Chantilly, and nibbled away at it under the equally blue pairs of eyes of the Rogers ladies.

After the bar, the second marvel was the bathroom in pink marble, almost a swimming-pool. The room served as a setting for an impressive collection of French perfumes, a little like a chapel built round the high altar. Incredible! I went from a gigantic bottle of Lanvin's *Arpège* to a tiny Chanel No. 5, not forgetting *Vol de Nuit* and *Soir de Paris*, from magnum to sample bottle. The whole gamut of amber liquids from the deepest to the lightest glittered in the softness of the indirect lighting. These rare essences were bought, apparently, at Tijuana on the Mexican border.

Bathrooms played a big part in such parties, replacing the boudoirs of duchesses. The women did their hair there, adjusted their make-up together. Seeing them re-powder, I followed suit. Behind me in the mirror, I suddenly noticed a very beautiful woman—Joan Crawford, wearing a long-pleated dress in white crêpe-de-chine worthy of the finest French *couturiers*. Her hair, her long black lashes, her dark blue eyes, and above all, her mouth—the outline of which I had imitated at the age of ten, a little prematurely—in a red made darker by the whiteness of the face: all this presented a mythical apparition. There was no point in turning round, she would never be as fabulous as her reflection in that mirror.

Anyhow, that evening it was the reflection of these stars that I enjoyed. I didn't want them to have daily preoccupations and cares, to be the same as me and everyone else. Like Alice I was visiting Wonderland—let no one wake me up! But I didn't need to go behind the looking-glass to enter another realm of fairy-land; the glass doors opened for me.

There I saw hundreds of blouses, shirts, dresses, coats, shoes and bags, dozens of fur coats, nightdresses and bedroom slippers. You couldn't wear out such a mass of garments in a lifetime, and when I remembered that such a wardrobe went out of fashion from one year to the next, my mind boggled. Was it really necessary to indulge in such extravagance? They corresponded to a particular image of a film star which I found rather disgusting.

I visited this house rather as if on a sight-seeing tour, and would have looked at it with different eyes had I known the part it was to play in my life. I already, it seemed, had something of my own to contribute for Ginger Rogers, who had seen *Port of Shadows*, wanted to hear more about Jean Gabin.

'What's he really like?'

'He's really like himself.'

This answer made her laugh, but she pressed the point. 'Has he as much charm as on the screen?'

'Oh, far more, you know.' I began a eulogy of our French star which may have sounded a bit over-patriotic. But it was quite true that not a single male that evening, however 'gorgeous', had the charm of Jean. Perhaps because they didn't know how to lean their bodies towards a woman as a Frenchman does!

I didn't say this to Ginger (that would have been going too far), but I told her of Jean's admiring curiosity about her. He had even irritated me with remarks like: 'Ah, Ginger! She's a great girl! I'd love to meet her.'

I said goodbye to my hostess well before the party ended. When I returned to France, I was often asked with a wink: 'I say, you must have seen all sorts of extraordinary things at those parties over there.' I had to say I couldn't produce any spicy stories, perhaps because I always left them fairly early, before much drink had been taken.

There was one last sight to see in the world of my childhood dreams: a gala evening at Grauman's Chinese Theatre, when all the stars in their finest clothes paraded along the red-carpeted sidewalk of Sunset Boulevard. Squeezed between a teenager and a granny with blue hair haloed by a spangled veil, jostled by a crowd predominantly of youngsters, I watched the procession of celebrities moving forward through the double line of smiling, curious, admiring faces—celebrities I had always been certain I would one day see in the flesh, only it was good to have such a 'certainty' translated into fact. Sometime I should be one of them myself, but before that, as it turned out, I had a year ahead of me that often made such prospects look very doubtful.

Boris, the public relations chief, took me to the RKO studios, which affected me in a strange way. Of course, I was staggered by their vastness and perfection: even when you have heard about something like this, actually seeing it makes a big impact. A French film actress, used to having to gallop between Billancourt and Épinay, could not fail to be impressed by these factory towns: the vast sets, the viewing theatres and cutting rooms and projection boxes and labs, and above all the backlots with their permanent 'scenes', New York streets or villages for Westerns, Mexican quarter or Roman forum. After America had come into the war, I often saw French villages which, if not very true to life, were still recognisable, a sort of synthesis of European folklore.

I had been expecting all this. Nor was I surprised that there were cafeterias and restaurants for different grades—which did not stop the executives taking their meals with the technicians or the cameramen—and that you needed a car to travel through the studio 'streets'. But it was the human relations which upset me. Even though in this truly democratic country, a studio sweeper might greet the producer or director with a jovial 'Hello, Harry!' or 'Morning, John', some distinctions remained insurmountable. As for myself, the repeated 'Hello, Miss Morgan' and 'How are you?' seemed a little mechanical. This universe might be perfectly conceived for maximum efficiency, to produce 'the best films in the world'. but I found it decidedly chilling. I felt I was transparent for all these people I was meeting. Everyone had his own daily problem, his preoccupation of the moment. In the confines of the studio they hadn't time to be human; they were paid to be units of efficiency. If I held their interest for a few seconds, it could only be on a strictly professional basis. Yet they were quite friendly, and would stop chewing their gum to give me wide grins.

In this gigantic factory, I was just a tiny cog which had not yet found its place: Michèle Morgan, a young French actress, known on the European market, of less interest since the war had started as she could only be displayed for the American market. It was the first time I experienced the reality of my wise forebodings—that I was not the girl everyone was eagerly waiting for.

At the end of my visit, Boris kissed my hand—after all, he was a Russian—and abandoned me in the lair of a gentleman as busy as he was important. Giving an audience behind his magnificent desk of precious wood and chrome, on which stood batteries of telephones, this personage, who might have come out of one of his films, told me in paternal and authoritarian tones: 'We're going to look after you. A good script and a good director, that's what you need.' The originality and accuracy of his observation filled him with satisfaction: at first throw he had hit a bull's eye with me.

Paralysed, sitting on the edge of my chair, I felt like a patient in the consulting-room of a great physician, awaiting a verdict from which there could be no appeal.

Jovial and dynamic, he informed me: 'You can have confidence in us.' (How could I do otherwise?) 'We shall find a way to use your looks and your accent. We need a very French story-line for you.'

It was the language of an efficient machine, benevolent within its limits, but completely alien to anything I could be or think.

I ventured to ask: 'Do you think you'll have me in a film soon?'

'Certainly. But first it's essential to make the American public eager to see you on the screen. We need a big publicity campaign for that. We must also improve your English.'

The Parthian shot had been left to the end. Although contradicting what he had said a moment or two ago, he explained that the main thing troubling him was my French accent. Amusing, charming, even seductive in a society gathering, in intimate surroundings it would turn even the most dramatic rôle into a comedy one. Did I understand? Yes, I understood very well. A Russian comedian might play *Tovarich* but not Racine; and for them my accent was something like that.

My enthusiasm was somewhat damped. To improve my English before being in a film meant how many lessons and how many months? Two very different evenings: last night I was in dreamland outside the Chinese Theatre, and tonight I realised it would be some time before I would be walking beneath the glorious platform, leaving my hand- and footprints in the cement of Sunset Boulevard.

In my memory, that first year in America has largely merged into those that followed. Hollywood became my new home, a major aspect of my life. If I isolate that year, 1940, from its context, it was fairly painful and can be summed up in two words: work and loneliness—despite an environment of sunshine and palm-trees and swimming-pools, a world of picture postcards in Technicolor, into which now and then I plunged and drifted. These times of idleness and oblivion were a drug more dangerous than might be thought: there were many in my sort of situation who became 'hooked'. Luckily, and here again I think my middle-class upbringing helped, I had my feet too firmly on the ground to let myself go in this way.

From that first interview at the studios it became clear that RKO were not going to put me in a film until I had lost my accent. So my life was organised round overcoming this obstacle. In theory, it sounded simple enough. The invaluable Adele Palmer had obtained an apartment for me (I had to learn not to say 'flat'), and there my specialist tutor, Dr Michneck, appeared one morning to start a course of lessons as demanding in its way as anything I had met at René Simon's.

This Dr Michneck was short in stature but long in knowledge. Russian in origin and a real polyglot, he had taught at Columbia University, where he had acquired his title of doctor. He owed his renown in the film world to his speciality: removing the accents of foreign actors who came to him from all over the world.

My morale went up a notch or two when he told me he had received instructions to take me on as priority and declared: 'With me you'll speak English like an English lady living in America.'

That very morning he revealed to me my main enemy, the syllable stress; and it was indeed a revelation. Without knowing exactly which part of a word had to be stressed, you couldn't possibly be understood in Arkansas or Minnesota. To put the accent on one syllable rather than another was something so far from obvious that it soon became like a Chinese puzzle for me. I had to say *pine*apple, not pine*apple*, ban*a*nas, not bana*nas*, for no other reason than usage. When since infancy your ear has not been initiated to these mysteries, how can you find your bearings in their midst?

To relax me, Dr Michneck made me read aloud from Shakespeare and become familiar with the best American authors. In a few months I became quite an expert on contemporary literature. The polish you acquire through familiarity with good authors is one of the positive aspects of our profession.

Day followed day, lesson followed lesson, and I remained pretty sanguine as to my progress—until the Hitchcock episode.

One morning in November I was summoned to the studio by Mr Hempstead, one of the RKO producers who was apparently interested in me. I found his interest extremely flattering, for he had just had Ginger Rogers in his widely discussed production *Kitty Foyle*.

'Miss Morgan, some very good news for you: a screen-test with Alfred Hitchcock.'

This time fortune was knocking at my door. As I had done

in France, I was going to make my début with one of the élite.

'He's planning a film called *Suspicion*,' Mr Hempstead continued, 'with Cary Grant as the hero. We'd very much like to give you the female lead.'

And would I like to be given it! The future began to shine in very bright colours—which were quickly wiped out.

'There is, however, one small difficulty. Hitchcock wants a British actress for the part. Even so, you'll be given a test. Dr Michneck assures us he will make you talk with the most perfect of English accents. Here's the script. You have a week to work on it.'

A week of suspense, alternating between hope—my teacher encouraging me with, 'Perfect, we're there!'—and disappointment—'That's still not quite it, let's try again.' So I would try again, and became increasingly nervous.

To start off in a big film seemed of prime importance to me. Besides the fact that I should be well directed and in a good cast, it would be widely promoted. I should be launched at one flight into that firmament where, as I already knew, there was not much free space. So I just had to succeed.

I was pretty tense when I arrived for the screen-test. Hitchcock, short and plump, with incredibly piercing eyes, had a charming yet ironical way of receiving you and giving you his instructions. This in itself was enough to put you into the atmosphere of suspense which he had already made his special realm.

'Action!' The camera whirred, we were off. From the first words, I felt ill at ease. There were two Michèles, the one acting and the one listening. If my own ear was not satisfied and my accent upset me—not quite French any more, already American, but not at all 'English'—what was Hitchcock going to think of it?

'Cut!' he ordered. 'Cut,' the cameraman echoed. 'Thank you, Miss Morgan,' said Hitchcock. It was polite and enigmatic—but not for long. The next day the verdict was delivered: 'English inadequate.' Joan Fontaine played the English girl's part which had been rather prematurely suggested for me.

My debut in America, contrary to what I had for a moment hoped, was not going to be at all like what it had been in France. This setback heralded a long series of mis-adventures.

It was time for me to remember Saint-Exupéry's saying: 'The strong are strengthened by defeats.'

The next day there was a stern post-mortem with Dr Mich-neck, who shook his head: 'The less you speak French, the quicker you'll speak English.' It was a diplomatic way of advising me to cut off all ties with the French colony. 'Live,' he told me, 'eat, learn, read the papers, listen to the radio, enjoy yourself, in American, with Americans.'

That very evening I had my first lesson in telling my French friends: 'Sorry, but I'm not free.' Never again should I have so many headaches, important dates, professional obliga-tions. Nor should I ever again be so lonely.

Dr Michneck didn't dare say this to me in so many words, but he was plainly suggesting it: among the diversions which would be excellent for my accent, a boy friend occupied a privileged place. Flirtation sharpened the wits.

My relationships with American men were a bit hesitant. I found them handsome and quite attractive, yet nothing much passed between us. Was it they or I who lacked the vocabulary? Our conversations were short-lived.

One morning somebody called me to ask: 'Would you enjoy meeting Robert Taylor?' The ideal male, the inacces-sible hero of my mid-teenage years, the Armand Duval of *Camille*, whose photographs I pinned over my bed—and it was suggested I have dinner with him this very evening!

In the living-room, with a glass of California champagne in my hand, I awaited his 'entry', quite prepared for the fit of shivers which I did have when he appeared in the doorway. I was introduced to him, and his smile made my heart beat faster; I think I went so far as to blush. He was even better than on the screen: wonderful, tender, with understanding eyes, a perfect nose, a mouth to dream of, magnificent shoulders, what a figure—altogether perfection!

We exchanged a few polite commonplaces, and his voice

did not disappoint me. I sat down at his side. As long as his conversation was up to his image, I was ready to swoon in adoration.

In a thrilling silence we swallowed our oyster cocktail. The meat course gave him the chance to ask me if I liked beef. I stammered a 'yes', which had the profundity of a religious confession. Delighted, he outlined the family tree of my steak, for, as he explained to me, he was very well up on anything that concerned cattle and his ranch was famous throughout America. 'Do you know anything about stock?' he asked, looking at me seductively.

I cursed this gap in my education, and improvised something as best I could. 'In Normandy we have cattle which weigh about 1500 kilos ...'

He burst into scornful laughter. 'For us that's the weight of a calf.'

I was slightly put off by this expression of national pride, but, hoping to please, began to discourse on the comparative merits of rib of beef, chops, rump-steaks and *entrecôtes*—a fine effort of vocabulary. He seemed to find me fascinating. I opened out, thinking that we should surely be changing the subject soon. At the end of each sentence I hoped to hear some remark from him about his tastes or mine, about his profession, which was after all not that of a cowman but the same as mine; a question about my films, why not? That, too, could be a topic of conversation. Not for him. At the coconut cake he had still not exhausted his subject: cattle. It was clearly inexhaustible, for with the coffee he was telling me with deep feeling about the calving of one of his cows. This was too much, it brought tears to my eyes—and I just managed to stifle my hysterical laughter.

Gosh, he was handsome, Robert Taylor!

Peter was less handsome, not famous at all; he was a young technician with Metro-Goldwyn-Mayer. But his conversational appeal was greater: he asked me questions about myself, even about France, my remote and so unusual country. I met him at one of the parties of which Miss Palmer said: 'O.K. It's good for you.' We had been chatting for a bit when he said, 'I'd be very happy if you'd give me a date.'

'A date?' I enquired in some surprise.

'Yes, to have dinner with you.'

Why not? Engagements in my diary were all too scarce.

We had a nice dinner and a pleasant evening. Peter didn't dance at all badly, and it was quite late when he took me home. On the steps outside the house door, he was clearly finding it hard to leave me. He certainly couldn't be expecting me to invite him in and have 'one for the road'; nothing in my attitude could have given him such a hope. I had been warned enough that this 'one for the road' always meant you would spend the night together; to send a man away after asking him in for a drink would be to break an unwritten law. My shoes were hurting, I was sure the end of my nose was shiny, I was longing for a good hot bath, and as I didn't see what he could be waiting for, I held out my hand to him. 'Good-night, Peter. It's been a very nice evening.'

Surprise: he came towards me, and asked me boyishly for a good-night kiss. My rather sharp 'no' must have displeased him, for he grunted a good-night, got straight into his car, and slammed the door with some violence. There was something I couldn't quite grasp, but I was too sleepy to bother.

Next day it was forgotten, and a week later, with the same innocence, I granted a date to a certain Will. He was in public relations, and hawked all the Hollywood gossip with some humour. I thought it might make an enjoyable evening. It did; I enjoyed it a lot, and continued laughing in his convertible as it glided poetically into the blue night. The end of the evening was again: 'Kiss me.' Again I refused the kiss, and William in his turn slammed the car door furiously.

'When you go out with a man in the United States, do you have to finish the night in his arms?' I asked Adele, who with much amusement explained to me the rules of the game. 'To accept a date means, even if you don't want to go any further than that, being ready to let him give you a good-night kiss at the end.' It was evidently a way of thanking him and needn't be taken too seriously.

Too bad. I still wasn't going to kiss either out of politeness or on command. I suppose it would have been too much to expect these boys to understand that when I went out with them, without even realising it myself, I was primarily looking for someone I could communicate with, who was interested in what might happen to me for good or ill, who made me feel that, in this country too, somebody recognised my existence as a person.

In Hollywood I went through the longest and most testing period of loneliness in my life. Not to be able to speak your mother tongue with anyone means cutting off your roots. It's hard to appreciate how much you can miss the intimacy of shared stories and songs from childhood and adolescence. It is a terrific bond to have in common your history, your countryside, your great men, your style of cooking and meals, and other features of everyday life.

How far away my country was! The war occupied little space in the newspaper columns here, and the news they did offer me was disheartening in the extreme: Germany victorious, London bombed, Rommel master of the desert, the Balkans occupied, then Greece—everywhere the Nazi jackboots were crushing freedom. The right to live was left only to those who gave in, or rather, 'collaborated'—this positive word had already taken on its malign connotation. Such news was all the more depressing because it was quite impossible for me to assess its importance. There was no one to explain that perhaps it wasn't quite so bad as it looked because of such-and-such.

How could my parents live through this war? I only received their news through the Swedish Red Cross or Consulate, and when a letter reached me, written months before, it said nothing of their miseries and privations. Everything was going as well as possible, Denise Tual was a real friend who had helped them a lot. But was I happy? Had I already been in a film? How glad they were to imagine me not having to go without anything. It was enough to make one weep, and I wept. And almost every day I went to the little Catholic chapel I had discovered, to light candles for them, for me, for the end of this war, for our seeing each other again soon, very soon.

I posted them parcels, which I stuffed with all sorts of things, and sent through the Swedish Red Cross, without knowing if they would ever open them. It was terrible not being able to do anything for them, and on my worse days I reproached myself for having left them. Who could I confide that to? Could you confide it to anyone?

My refuge was work, and Adele Palmer, who had very quickly become indispensable to me, and Nina Moise, my tutor in dramatic art, were the ones who offered the most attentive ears and the most open hearts. Without them I don't know how I could have borne those first years of exile. How precious you can find others' curiosity, how much it encourages you when you are over 10,000 kilometres from home!

Nina Moise was a highly intelligent and cultivated woman with a passionate interest in her job. Our first contact gave me an unpleasant surprise: I performed for her, as I would have done for René Simon, one of my 'party pieces', feeling relaxed and self-confident. I waited for her reaction, and heard a reproving, 'Tssk, tssk, that's not it. Miss Morgan, your voice isn't steady.'

Not steady, after nine films and René Simon!

'Sit down by me, darling, and listen. You have the thin voice of a little girl going to her first party. It doesn't tally at all with your looks.'

She was right, and I owe her far more than that. It was she who taught me to act in the rhythm of the American acting style, a lesson which has often been useful to me.

New Year's Eve, 1940. It was a fine day. Paris would be grey—there might be snow, perhaps it was very cold. I thought of our little flat in Neuilly, from which we could see the top of the Eiffel Tower, used at night as a site for Citroën advertisements. My brothers and I—my sister wasn't born then—used to fight over which of us should have the chair to climb on and 'see the lights'.

It was a day to avoid thinking too much, when it was best to thrust memories aside, to enjoy the pleasant little things of the present and attach yourself to them, for the future was as dangerous as the past.

In Hollywood, you aren't left alone for Christmas or New Year's Eve. There are plenty of parties, and I received many invitations. Ralph Blum, my impresario, and his wife Carmel, who were now good friends of mine, asked me to go with them to a party at Jack Benny's.

'You know him, Michèle?'

'Of course, he's a radio star and has just made the film *Buck Benny Rides Again*.' (Jack Benny's first big film success was with Carole Lombard in 1942, that masterpiece of the comic cinema, *To Be or Not To Be*.)

'He gives magnificent parties, you'll see.'

'But I thought he was supposed to be stingy.'

Ralph laughed. 'Don't worry, you'll have a bit more than a hamburger. I suspect he uses his stinginess as a publicity gag, and even invented it himself.'

However that might be, the party showed no signs of money stinted; it was a millionaire's party, with all Hollywood society there. We drank and danced. Robert Taylor smiled at me, and I did not melt. Cary Grant handed me a glass, and I felt depressed. Why should I be suddenly so miserable? I must have looked it, for Carmel was kind enough while dancing to give me a smile to cheer me up. It didn't help, I was a prey to a strange sensation: a great weariness in my limbs, a general malaise, the painful sense that something was happening elsewhere, something I ought to know; as if I were being sent a message I wasn't managing to grasp. What sort of message? My distress became unendurable. I abruptly said, 'Excuse me', tore myself from my partner's arms, and fled to the bathroom, where I began to sob my heart out.

It might be thought that I was the worse for drink, but I hadn't drunk anything. I didn't care what people thought, I was completely in the grip of this ... this sorrow which had come upon me from another place and was making me cry.

Just under an hour later, a disappointed but sympathetic Carmel took me home. I cried all night. In the morning the storm had passed; the sun was there the same as ever.

Three months later a letter from Maman arrived: 'I'm

afraid there is some bad news to tell you, darling. Granny Roussel is dead. It happened on New Year's Eve between three and four in the morning.'

Between three and four in the morning! Taking account of the time difference, it would have been about 10 p.m. in California.

Being unmarried, and French as well, was a very uncomfortable position. Women dreaded your charms; and thanks to the reputation of Parisian ladies, men would set you traps which were sometimes more subtle and intriguing than my unprofitable evenings with the good-night-kiss-seekers.

My splendid isolation from my compatriots was not so complete as I have made out. I did, for instance, see Madeleine Lebeau quite often. With *her*, apart from being an old friend, I had an excuse; she was in process of getting divorced from her husband. One afternoon she rang me up to say: 'One of my bachelor friends has asked me to go to a party with him. Would you like to join us?'

'Where are we going to?'

'I don't know. I forgot to ask him. I expect it'll be a pretty big affair as usual.'

But we could see immediately it wasn't one of the usual parties. There were no other cars arriving, and we had the whole parking area to ourselves. A ceremonious footman in livery showed us into an empty drawing-room. Perhaps we had come much too early. I looked at Madeleine, and her expression of amusement made me think she had taken in the situation already: soft music, mysterious lighting, voluptuous cushions deep as divans—it was all there. For us French girls!

It was a situation I had never had to face before. Should we pretend to be innocent and then refuse to 'play ball', or should we leave immediately? While I was pondering these alternatives, our host made his appearance, suave, friendly and welcoming. He offered me a cocktail, and plied me with salted almonds. I thanked him coldly, but did not quite have the courage to add that I had not expected to be coming to a party on this intimate level. Whereas Madeleine seemed to have accepted the situation, I was fuming inside. It just showed what sort of reputation French girls had, and how much they respected us! Anger had given me courage, and I was about to say what I thought of the cheek of this invitation, when the door opened on a small man of about fifty. His brown hair had turned silvery, but his smile took twenty years off him. It was Charlie Chaplin.

Unexpected—but to be invited in his honour was not reassuring, either. *His* reputation was going through a bad patch, his affairs of the heart received daily attention in the press, and that morning again, in the *Los Angeles Times*, his photograph was displayed over several columns. With him was a young actress, hitherto unknown, who accused him of having fathered her child and was suing him for acknowledgment of paternity.

This was not at all the kind of press notice I aspired to, and I doubted whether Adele Palmer would have described the present evening as being 'good for me'. I prepared to be as dignified and reserved as Chaplin was nonchalant—but it was difficult. For all his genius in silent movies, his charm as a man lay in words. He was dazzling at dinner, fantastic after dinner. You forgot the well-cut dinner jacket, the silk socks and polished shoes; he had transformed himself into the little man with the stick the world knew. We were treated to a Chaplin festival, from the dance of the loaves to the flea-trainer. Only the seducer, who was later to appear before audiences in *Monsieur Verdoux*, was missing. A last look, a final gesture, then silence, which turned into slight embarrassment. Here we are, I thought. The men were furtively looking at each other, as if to say: chance missed. Were they going to grin and bear it, or try their luck even now? I kept my reserve: this French girl was not going to let herself be caught by a charming Don Juan, however much of a genius he might be.

With a shade of irony in his blue eyes, Chaplin resumed his improvised act. The evening had definitely changed direction. He told us his story, which has since become famous, of the five-pound note.

London, on a foggy night; Big Ben has just struck midnight. Some rich gentlemen come out of the club. They have had plenty to drink and are in high good humour. One of them sends off his Rolls to his friends' astonishment: 'But you live miles away!'

'I'm going to walk for a bit. The fresh air will do me good. Then I'll take a taxi.' Automatically he feels in his pockets. 'How stupid, I haven't any money on me.'

One of his friends hands him a five-pound note. 'This any good?'

'Thanks, old man.' Cigar in his mouth, fur-lined coat buttoned up, he walks towards Waterloo. A fine night, a bit frosty. On the bridge, right in the middle, he sees the figure of a woman, about to climb over the rail. He dashes up, catches her by the arm, and restrains her. 'You're mad!'

'Let me die, sir. I don't want to go on living.'

'At your age? But why? Have you been jilted?'

She shrugs her shoulders. He notices her shawl is in shreds. 'Oh no, but I've no work. I'm starving, sir.'

He is deeply affected. The poor girl, he will look after her. 'Listen, I'll give you work. I'll take care of you.'

Is he making fun of her? The poor girl looks at him like a dog that doesn't dare believe it has found its master.

Quite overcome, he reassures her. 'Oh yes, everything will be all right. Here's my address'—he hands her his card. 'Be at my office at nine o'clock tomorrow. Till then you must eat and sleep. Take these five pounds, it's all I have on me. Trust the future. Till tomorrow ...'

She kisses his hands; he gently releases himself, and goes off with a light heart. What a good thing he decided to walk back!

Next day when he opens his paper, he reads: 'A girl threw herself off Westminster Bridge last night. When her body was retrieved from the Thames, she was dead.'

Horrifying, incomprehensible. Why didn't she have confidence in him? Why didn't she keep the appointment?

A few weeks elapse before he meets again the friend who lent him the five pounds. He wants to pay him back. The friend refuses, and asks maliciously: 'Have any trouble with your taxi that night?'

'No, why?'

'Because of the note. It was a forgery. It was a fake note.'

A good example of Charlie's black humour. So the evening with the two innocents, which might have led to our downfall, ended pleasantly enough.

Not long afterwards Chaplin met a delightful young brunette, Oona, who was to become his wife and the mother of nine children. And I thought at the time of their wedding: how unlucky to be always falling in love with young actresses under half your age.

'Miss Morgan, we are producers. May we come and see you?'

This is the gist of what Robert Hakim said to me on the 'phone. No doubt his brother Raymond was on an extension, because they seemed inseparable. They entered my living-room together. 'We are two young independent producers, and we thought of you for an important rôle.'

It was a long time since I had heard such a splendid opening statement.

'We're going to make a film of *Johnny Belinda*, and we think you could play the principal part.'

I beamed. The Hakim brothers were speaking in French, a charming sing-song French. They wouldn't find it hard to convince me.

'It's a very unusual and exciting part because the girl is a deaf-mute,' said Robert.

'You realise,' said Raymond triumphantly, 'as she can't speak, you won't have any difficulties with the language.'

Nearly a year's hard work, a dearly won victory in syllable stresses, and then to hear that!

'Besides,' said Robert, 'you can express anything with those eyes!'

My eyes again! I was almost mute with rage. Before I could explode, they went on pressing me; they would leave me the script, could I let them know in two days' time? Oh well—I grudgingly agreed.

With Hitchcock, it had been the English that counted. With them, now that my English was all right, I was to be silent. If only the offers had been the other way round! What bad luck.

It was even worse luck to have been stupid enough to turn down *Johnny Belinda*. The film was a masterpiece. Jane Wyman had the good sense to accept the part, and was awarded an Oscar for it as the best actress of the year.

I know to err is human, but you make some mistakes for which it is hard to forgive yourself.

Jean was in Hollywood, and we celebrated our reunion by having a meal *chez Oscar*, a French restaurant, with little napkins in little squares, bifteck-frites, and real French Beaujolais. Sitting opposite each other at table, we let the time pass; and each minute drew us closer. These reunions in a foreign country are really good. I laughed as I hadn't laughed for ages. Soon I was shooting a barrage of questions at him and then he conjured up images which brought me nearer to tears than laughter.

'What's Paris like, Jean? Tell me all about it. And the occupied zone, the rations, the films? Who's in what?'

'Well, I'm mainly in the unoccupied zone. I don't like what's going on in Paris. The collaborators; the disgusting racial laws; the queues for bread, for a pound of leeks, for everything. And the black market: we pay for our clothes with butter and our cigarettes with a pair of boots. You can imagine the way it is.'

I didn't find it that easy to imagine. Especially as all sorts of new catchphrases and slang had grown up, and even the inevitable German words, like *Ausweis*—apparently you were continually being asked to show your pass or identity card.

'And the last straw: at noon every day, the Fritzes have a band goose-stepping down the Champs-Elysées right to the Unknown Soldier. Enough to make him turn in his grave.'

Other images came up. So that was what Paris had become? Sad at heart, I felt like saying: 'Enough,' but said: 'Go on.' This disfigured France he was telling me about was my country, and it showed me how much I loved it.

'Now it's your turn. Tell me about your life here.'

I wished I had something to tell him. An admission that I wasn't doing anything would have been over too quickly.

So I evaded the issue a bit, talking Hollywood shop, giving him some of the gossip.

Jean was not deceived. He dropped back in his chair, lit a cigarette, and observed: 'I see. In fact you came to Hollywood to wait.'

It was so true that, like a prisoner in the dock pronounced guilty, I lowered my head. Realising this, he reached a soothing, philosophic conclusion: 'Even so, you're better off here than you would be over there.'

A short pause, and I returned the ball to his court. 'And you?'

'I've come to wait, too. Like you, I had a contract to honour. From here I shall see how events turn out. Who knows, perhaps a day will come when I can have a bash at the bloody Fritzes.' (The day did come: he later joined the Free French forces.) 'But apparently,' he went on, 'you don't see the French over here any more. You've given them the brush-off.'

I explained to him my method for Americanising my habits and language, my forays with syllable stresses. 'Adele tells me every time I speak French, I take two steps back.'

'Hey, at that rate, after our lunch you're going to land up at Timbuktu.'

We both laughed.

'I don't know if yours is a good system. Personally I pick up the accent by ear. I listen, and when I've caught it, I work out a set-piece to mimic it. I'll give you a sample.'

It was amazing. He had an incredibly accurate ear, and he was very soon coping quite adequately with the English— or rather the American—language.

We talked and talked, the eager chat of two good friends meeting after a long separation. We were no longer any more than good friends; or we were that again.

'You know everyone now in your Olivode,' he remarked with a slightly overdone casualness, 'and there's someone I'd rather like to meet.'

As hypocritical as Jean, I said: 'Oh yes, and who's that?'

'Ginger. Are you friendly with her?'

'We know each other.' Very gently, I reassured him, 'I can

even tell you that you impress her a lot. She thinks you're very good.'

He was impressed by that. His blue eyes sparkled. Dear Jean, who liked to know there was going to be firm ground under his feet before he started exploring any new terrain!

A few days later we were together again round the table in my apartment with a few friends and Ginger. That day I don't think his 'ear' was much use to Jean, his English was still hesitant; but he managed very well talking to Ginger, and I was amused to see how quickly his charm worked.

His idyll with Ginger Rogers occupied him for several months, and we saw very little of each other. Having arrived in February 1941, Jean too had to wait a good year before being in *Moontide*. Then, on a visit to New York, he met Marlene Dietrich. The collision of these two great charmers was explosive, a thunderbolt in the Hollywood Olympus; and what lightning it produced! In counterpoint to this often stormy passion, Marlene prepared some admirable spaghetti dishes for Jean, and cooked him her masterpiece, pot-au-feu Marlene.

Hollywood tongues wagged, and I didn't see Jean again for several years.

I had waited a long time for my first film in Hollywood, and had indulged in many fantasies about it. When it came, the disconcerting thing was that for the first time I seemed to have the right qualifications, and yet they were still wrong.

Everything started very nicely. Mr Hempstead gave me a script, saying: 'Read this, it's a fine vehicle for you, by a French author, Jacques Théry—know him? We're sure you'll like *Joan of Paris* a whole lot. It's the story of a girl who goes into the Underground, I think you call it the Resistance. It's a great story, very patriotic. And we're giving you Robert Stevenson for director.' Bob Stevenson had just had a huge success with *Back Street*, and any actress would jump at the prospect of working with him.

There was less prestige to the name of the man I was to play opposite; in fact, it was unknown at the time. A young Austrian, the son of a Baron, Paul Henreid had come to Hollywood as a refugee from the *Anschluss*. I found it rather quaint to have him cast as a Resistance man fighting for a France that was under the heel of the Nazi jackboot; but Mr Hempstead could not see anything funny about it, and solemnly explained to me that in this rôle Paul's Viennese accent would provide added realism. I had a moment's panic: perhaps for this production I should be asked to reassume my former accent.

My euphoria went down sharply anyhow, after reading the script. This modern version of Joan of Arc didn't strike me as at all convincing. True, Jacques Théry had told me over a cocktail: 'I'm working for you. I'm planning a part that will just suit you.' Either he hadn't the right measurements for me, or not much was left of his script after its retouching by the specialised production teams. To my way of thinking the part was highly implausible, though admittedly we had little idea then what the word Resistance meant, let alone what it really was. Still, I rather doubted whether Théry, who had arrived in Hollywood in 1941, knew any more than I did. Apart from a few reasonable scenes, my character's psychological level was about that of the heroine in a schoolgirls' magazine; as to my heroic exploits, they were so foolhardy as to be more crazy than patriotic. Naturally, by risking my life I found love and shed many passionate tears.

Were there the elements of a good 'vehicle' here? It seemed unlikely. But rather innocently I thought that such a film, the first to speak of France's struggle for freedom, would be shown in all the American cinemas. This idea encouraged me to accept; anyhow, I didn't see how I could very well refuse. Besides, there was Bob Stevenson. I imagined him possessing a sort of fairy wand: he would transform this trumped-up stuff into a masterpiece.

I did not know that at that time a good many directors attached to the major film companies were quite ready to be business executives rather than creative artists. Like barristers given a brief in court without being asked whether it had any interest for them, they were handed a script perfectly worked out to the smallest details, with casting decided by the studio, which they had to put into celluloid form. They did this with more or less satisfaction and enthusiasm. In Bob Stevenson's case, it was clearly less.

Our relations might have been compared to two planets pursuing their courses in the firmament without any hope of ever meeting. He was about forty, pleasant enough, good-humoured and calm, and, as I have suggested, a little distant. There weren't many worthwhile scenes, but I had hoped that those few would have been better exploited. I wanted to give everything I could, and he asked very little of me. For my first film in English, I was expecting firmer direction from him. This was worrying, but who could I ask for advice? Not Mr Hempstead; he seemed to be solely concerned with the modifications to be made in my figure. Yet when handing me over to make-up men, dress designers and other stylists, he had given instructions: 'No transformation needed. She must remain as she is: typically French.'

After the first shots, he surveyed me from all sides and frowned: my figure did not correspond to his idea of the French girl, Parisian, and in the Resistance at that. I was not sexy enough; I didn't have big enough breasts. In vain, I protested that heroism could not be measured by the size of the chest. He laughed heartily and summoned the dresser, who immediately corrected the defect with a padded bra, explaining to me in charitable tones that I mustn't get worked up about it—they did this in all productions, expanding the girls' breasts; even big ones couldn't be big enough.

The following evening, viewing the first rushes, Hempstead knitted his ginger eyebrows. Before I had time to worry about this, he announced what was wrong: 'Miss Morgan's breasts aren't big enough.' A new and more generous padding was required. That evening he made a new survey. 'Still not enough.'

This criticism was repeated several times. Consequently, having started the film with slightly rounded breasts, I ended up with Jane Russell's. There was nothing to be done but laugh about it. So I laughed when I saw my figure with its varying dimensions on the evening when *Joan of Paris* was presented at the RKO Pantages Theatre. The film struck me as pretty mediocre, and I could not understand the success it achieved. As to the notices, they too were miraculously good.

More fortunate than I, French cinemagoers never had to see this *Jeanne de Paris*.

In August 1969, I was listening with half an ear to the radio when the sudden dramatic tone in the announcer's voice captured my attention: 'Last night the actress Sharon Tate, married to the film producer Roman Polanski, was brutally murdered with several of her friends in her Beverly Hills villa ...' The details of the crime were appalling, guests hanging from the main ceiling, Sharon on the divan with her throat cut. I remained paralysed with horror, and for a moment my mind flashed back to September 1941.

It was 2 a.m. Sitting up in my bed, I peered into the darkness. Somebody had been walking beneath the veranda in front of the house. No, the sound must be coming from the living-room. Was it really steps? Worse, it was the sound of things being brushed against; there was definitely someone there. Furious with myself, I lit my bedside light, and for a moment was reassured by the delightful reality of the pink and white room which I had decorated and furnished with such pleasure and care. I picked up a book, read a few lines, then listened. This time I was sure of it, there *was* someone. I should have to get up and go round the house. I did so, and saw there was nobody, nothing. The idea of an invisible presence chilled me still more. The house was alive with a strange disturbing force. I remembered table-turning sessions I had attended as a girl, a game like any other. Tonight it was not a game. I told myself this was a new house, only just built, so it couldn't be haunted. No good; I was still terribly frightened.

This wild ridge above Beverly Hills was fairly isolated, of course, but it couldn't be called a desert. It was rather splendid to be living opposite the former estate of Rudolph Valentino; after Benedict Canyon, at the bend in the road, there was Ray Milland's villa; closer still, Harold Lloyd's. Even so, I could have screamed for an hour and died twenty times before anyone heard me. Sure, there was always the 'phone; or was there? I went to the movies often enough to know that wires were cut, that no doors were impregnable, especially mine. I had chosen the 'Early American' style for my villa, a whole front of bay windows and glass doors, looking very attractive but open to all the winds. I was mad to have had such a house built when there were well-protected apartments.

It was all the fault of Ralph Blum, my agent. 'Michèle,' he said after *Joan of Paris*, 'you've just made quite a bit of money from your film. There'll be other films soon. You ought to put your dollars into something solid.'

What could be more solid than American stone on American land? Land and house became mine for $20,000—a wonderful investment if I had kept it.

That night, unable to get to sleep before daybreak, I resolved to put the villa on the market the same day.

Having made my breakfast in a model kitchen, I ate it in the vast and comfortable living-room with its country furniture in light eighteenth- or nineteenth-century wood, dominated by its great ceiling, and the little ladder which led up to the first floor. This environment reassured me. It seemed so welcoming and peaceful that I was ashamed of my terrors of the night. Only I quite realised I should be a prey to them again in the evening, so I decided to call up an appointment bureau and ask them to send along a couple; I did so, ending: 'I need them at once.'

'You're in luck, madam. I just happen to have a husband and wife, both free. They're Irish and have very good references. I'll send them to you.'

Maureen and Patrick made an excellent impression. *He* was a tall burly redhead. They both looked about forty, had florid complexions and innocent blue eyes. I gave them their instructions: 'I shan't be alone this evening. I'd like you to prepare a dinner.'

'Will it be a big party, madam? Fifty or sixty people?' asked Patrick, with a strong Irish accent, in the competent tones of a professional ready for any task.

'No, there will only be two of us.'

At seven o'clock Madeleine Lebeau arrived. At eight Patrick had not yet appeared, and I heard no sounds from the dining-room. At nine I had still not been told dinner was ready, but then people dined late in the United States. We went on chatting.

At half-past nine I opened the dining-room door: the table was not laid. I went to the kitchen. Patrick and Maureen, their feet under the table, were evidently enjoying a very good dinner. They both stared at me, making me feel I was out of place here. I ventured a diffident question: 'When do you think you'll have our meal ready?'

'Needsh toime to cook,' replied Maureen in a slurred

voice, slouched over the table. Between them, speaking
volumes, stood a bottle of Bourbon. I returned to Madeleine
wondering whether I had really found what I needed.

At ten, the echoes of joyous Irish songs reached us, interspersed with shouts and insults concerning 'the bloody
Frenchwoman'.

Indignantly, I went back to the kitchen. Maureen hadn't
the strength to get up, but red-haired Patrick, six foot and
about fourteen stone, advanced towards me belching, stink-
ing of alcohol. I tried to reason with him, but this only added
to his fury; Madeleine, coming to lend me moral support,
arrived in time to see him smashing crockery and threatening
that if I tried to stop him he'd be after smashin' me up
too.

We returned to the living-room and called the law. The
typical sequences of crime films followed in a few minutes:
sirens, squealing of tyres, car doors slamming; two enormous
cops, as Irish as the offenders, burst in and removed Patrick
and Maureen with great vigour. End of scene, pan on to
devastated kitchen, ending in middle ground with Madeleine
and me eating at a corner of the table amidst the debris of
my new china.

The second night was as sleepless as the first.

Next morning I was in no mood to appreciate Ralph
Blum's facetiousness. He told me a guard-dog was what I
needed, adding: 'But I'll find you one that's on the wagon.'

My Great Dane stared at me, some eight stone of muscles,
bone and jaw, a fine mouse-grey in colour. I had no idea how
to talk to him, and he did not seem disposed to encourage
any dialogue. I had taken the leash handed me by Ralph, and
was then dragged off by the dog at full speed, going just
where he wanted for as long as he pleased. As with Patrick,
our relationship was inverted immediately: he was the
master.

In doubt about the future, but hoping at least for a peaceful,
recuperative night, I let my guardian off the lead at sunset.
Like an arrow he made for my bedroom and installed himself
with a great sigh of contentment on my pink bedspread.

'Get down! Will you get down?'

'No!' he barked in answer, teeth bared. I went out; he made no protest. I gently reopened the door, and was greeted by furious barks. We played this game for a bit, then I tired of it: too bad, he could sleep in my room, I'd stay in the living-room.

Stretched out on the divan, not daring to look at the night's blackness swarming with indefinable things pressing against the windows, I spent my third wakeful night.

For a time Madeleine came to stay with me. She confessed afterwards that she was frightened.

So what was the matter with this house?

It was at the end of a small road that was called 'the road to Heaven', on which I once, astonishingly, met Greta Garbo out for a walk. Had I been asked on reaching the States who I would most like to meet, I should have answered Garbo— and now here she was, like me, in sloppy jersey, slacks and big shoes, as taken aback as I was by the encounter. I looked at her, and she turned her head, presenting me with the famous profile and her short, pale blonde hair. Then she strode away and disappeared, as if terrified I might address her. I never saw her there again, nor anyone else out walking on that road. The house *was* isolated, as I have said.

It was not the situation, however, which aroused these obscure fears in me; it was the building itself. Yet how could a house without a past, a house I myself had built, have been haunted by its future?

I never got used to living there, and after I had left, it passed over the years from hand to hand. The last owner of the house on 'the road to Heaven' was Roman Polanski, who went on a journey in the summer of 1969, leaving his wife Sharon there; and on the night of 9–10 August—as I heard over the radio—she was murdered in the living-room, in that house where I had so often been afraid.

Time in the United States could be divided into Before and After Pearl Harbor. Within a few hours this pre-emptive attack, while a Japanese delegation was still engaged in negotiations with the United States government, brought the American man-in-the-street a new awareness of the

European drama and an involvement in the war. A whole country's indignation was very spectacular and it lasted a long time. For years the slogan 'Remember Pearl Harbor' covered the walls in American cities.

I, too, remember 7 December, 1941, very vividly. I was in my kitchen, getting myself an orange-juice. The radio was putting out music, a pleasant background noise, which suddenly broke off, to be replaced by a very serious announcer's voice informing the country of the Japanese attack on the Pacific Fleet with heavy losses for the American Navy in ships and men.

I dashed to the 'phone and called Léonide Moguy. After hearing this news, I had to contact my compatriots. My first question was: 'So what does this mean for us?'

'The United States will come into the war.'

I heard my father's voice, always prophetic, assuring us: 'The day the Yanks come into this war, we'll be well on the road to victory.'

'Come over to me,' said Léonide. 'We'll all be there. We can talk things over.'

What I wanted to know was simple—no doubt, too simple. If the Americans declared war on Germany (in fact, they did so four days later), would it speed up the end of the war as my father had predicted? I conceived this question, I am afraid, very much on a personal level: it really meant, shall I soon be returning home?

I found myself in the middle of a very French argument. After ten minutes I was completely bewildered. Politics and strategy became hopelessly confused, grandiose ideas jostled each other, and I felt very stupid with my simple little questions. Perhaps it was because they were so simple that no one could answer them. In rapid contradiction I learnt that Papa's victor of Verdun was a traitor, an old dotard, and that he was a noble figure who had saved us from a *Gauleiter*; that General de Gaulle was a fanatic who got everybody's back up, and that it was thanks to him France would recover her liberty and her greatness.

Among the French in America, the General at that time was far from receiving unanimous approval. Anyhow we didn't know much about him. Even so, a good many of these same Frenchmen later joined up in the Free French forces.

As usual with French arguments, everyone remained fixed in his position, nobody convincing anybody of anything. Taking advantage of a moment of silence while they were refilling their glasses and rallying their forces, I asked: 'But how is the war going to end?'

A happy impulse. Most of them could already see themselves entering Paris, taking their old places again, chasing out the usurpers. It was a long time before Yalta, but they were all sharing out the world, which also led to quarrels. 'Nothing for the Russians,' said one side. 'The Eastern front will be fatal for Hitler,' said the other. 'We'll have to reckon with the Russians.' The latter were quite far-sighted for it was only the end of 1941, and at that time the Germans were marching victoriously on Moscow.

The historic event of Pearl Harbor had very fortunate private repercussions for me: *Joan of Paris*, with a Parisian actress in the title role, became *the* film on the French Resistance. It shot to the top of the charts, its fame rocketed. The programme Adele Palmer proposed for me was impressive. 'You will present your film in San Francisco at a great gala evening in the presence of your consul. Then Washington: lunch at the White House, you'll meet President Roosevelt.'

'On my own?'

'Not quite that, I'm afraid, but still ... Washington is the starting point for a propaganda tour intended to raise the troops' morale. You will be visiting New Orleans, Dallas, Houston, etc. Mickey Rooney, Ava Gardner, Betty Grable and Rosalind Russell. There! Wonderful, isn't it!'

I didn't contradict her, though I found it scaring as well as wonderful for she told me that, in connection with my film, I should have to make some emotional and patriotic pronouncements about the Resistance.

The audience at San Francisco was very enthusiastic, the consul most understanding, with the diplomatic politeness not to show astonishment at the Paris presented to him by our film. He was also kind enough to laugh when I forgot my French in my excitement and spoke to him in English. What a pity Hitchcock couldn't hear me now! I must at least remember not to speak French to Roosevelt.

Everything went very well. It was Mrs Eleanor Roosevelt who received us, in a black dress with a pearl necklace: charming, very much the American hostess, benevolent and attentive. When the double doors of the drawing-room opened and the usher announced, 'The President of the United States', I had a shock as a wheel-chair entered, pushed by a secretary. To see this great personality seated in an invalid chair was a moving sight. What a smile he had! It was there all through the meal, directly he addressed any of us. I had a small personal success, too: in view of my lack of accent, he expressed astonishment that I was not American. I beamed joyfully, for the RKO representatives were within earshot.

The gathering ended unexpectedly for me. Going to powder my nose after the meal, I met Mrs Roosevelt who said: 'You haven't visited the White House? Then follow me.' It was a unique experience to have the wife of the President of the United States showing you into Abraham Lincoln's austere room and accompanying her on 'a tour of the house'.

The Washington reception had given us a fine send-off. Now our propaganda tour got under way. Trains, planes, towns, military camps: an unusual way of seeing the United States. The countryside and the towns might be diverse, but the welcome given us was the same everywhere: overwhelmingly warm and enthusiastic. A bit too much so for my taste: invariably, after the showing of the film, we had a reception offered us, during which the female stars had to 'make' the G.I.s dance. Never before on a dance-floor had I been so shaken up as I was between the robust hands of these future warriors. The animation of their jitterbugging was dangerous for the straps of my bra, and I felt nostalgic for even the most whirling waltz...

My early relationship with Bill Marshall, from our first meeting to our wedding, had some of the elements of a typical American film comedy.

Opening scene: I am in a hurry, and dash across the road from the studio to make a 'phone call. Damn, the booth is occupied—by a tall fair guy, who proceeds to turn his back on me. I stamp about outside for a bit, then he comes out without seeing me, bumps into me, says, 'Sorry', and walks off. I take his place. On the ledge there is a huge, heavy Colt-type revolver. 'Excuse me,' I shout, 'you've forgotten something.'

He returns with long strides. He's very handsome, with broad shoulders, slim waist, a cowboy belt around his narrow hips, and high-heeled boots. 'Thank you, it's my revolver.'

'So I see.'

We laugh. He has a fleshy mouth; his teeth shine, his eyes are blue. He introduces himself. 'William Marshall, my friends call me Bill.' Then he departs again.

I don't remember feeling any special euphoria over this encounter. Watching him go, noticing his swinging gait, I probably thought: 'An actor, I suppose, or with that get-up he could be a stunt-man in a western.' Anyhow he made no great impact, and I might have forgotten him, if—but then one always tells oneself that.

I'm sure I was quite fancy-free the day Bill greeted me in the studio with a warm 'Hello! Remember the guy with the revolver?' It was funny, though: for months before that we had never met, and now we were crossing each other's path all the time. I didn't feel that I was becoming involved either that day or the next time, or the time he invited me to sit by him at lunch. I found him amusing, not like the rest; and that 'not like the rest' should have served as a red light. But I was so far from seeing it as such that when Bill, grown suddenly shy, asked me for a date, I shook my head at once. I had no wish to start the sessions of 'Kiss me good-night' all over again, nor to get annoyed with such a pleasant person.

He looked so put out, almost unhappy that when he pressed me, I gave in and granted him a date, but a good way ahead, as if to leave the door open for all sorts of contingencies, like my having a cold or some work on or changing my mind, or his meeting another girl.

None of these things happened.

Second scene, therefore: at the appointed time, a smiling Bill is framed in my doorway, superbly shaved, carrying a square box adorned with a magnificent ribbon in violet satin, which he hands to me. I protest and open it. On a bed of tissue paper rests what is called a 'corsage'. He has done things in a big way. It is a spray of six mauve orchids adorned with a cascade of violet ribbons. My dress is green; I can't possibly wear them. Yet politeness demands that I pin this Niagara of flowers on my bosom. Impossible. It will disappear beneath them.

Bill, with the modest attitude of someone expecting a compliment, looks at me, confident and smiling. I must do something. 'Oh, Bill, it's superb, but they're too beautiful to be sacrificed. I'd never forgive myself. I'll go and put them in a vase.'

As I might have expected, he took me to the coast, to one of the countless Hawaiian restaurants scattered along it, the smartest of them all: girls in grass-skirts, with necklaces of shells clinking on their bras, served us to the sound of ukuleles and a background of slightly lewd dances.

I felt myself plunging into boredom. An evening like all the others, with a programme lacking in surprise: the man thinking of only one thing, how to get through your bedroom door.

How could I escape? I had no skill in feigning an opportune

headache. So I must last out to midnight or one o'clock. Oh dear!

It was past three when Bill took me home, after my best evening for ages. He had begun to talk at exactly the right moment. He was very entertaining, and with a slightly zany humour told me all sorts of Hollywood stories. He seemed to know everybody, and to be on intimate terms with all the great names. He was so animated and convincing that I didn't feel any surprise at his having such extensive and privileged relations in the movie world although he had only been in one film for Michael Curtiz in 1940, *Santa Fe Trail*. I had not yet discovered that he had the imagination of a novelist. When he left me, there was not a gesture, only his eyes were tender; he didn't commit the folly of claiming a good-night kiss.

The next day he called me to see how I was, and he called me again in the evening so that I should feel less alone. The habit was quickly picked up, and soon, without admitting it to myself, I was waiting for the ring of the 'phone, then the noise on the road of his car slowing down to announce his imminent arrival.

We went out together more and more frequently, and now Bill talked to me about himself. 'I'm only twenty-five but very ambitious. It's not the cinema which interests me, though. I want to become a singer, not an actor.'

He had made his début in Fred Warring's band. Crooners were the fashion, and he put his vocal timbre between Bing Crosby, then all the rage, and Frank Sinatra, a young man of Italian origins who was becoming talked about. If he was right about that, I thought his voice must be extremely attractive. I found later that it was, and always regretted that he did not follow this, his real path. He didn't need it to charm me, however; and when he asked me, 'Like to see California with me? I'll take you to an extraordinary place, Carmel del Monte', I answered 'Yes' without thinking, though not without registering that this was slippery ground where I might easily trip up.

He stopped his car outside the house, and we stayed sitting there together, talking on and on. All lovers have known this unwillingness to move, as if by moving you might break the spell. He told me about his family, talking about them in just the right way to appeal to me.

His father was dead, and Bill had greatly admired him, a man of tremendous integrity, rather austere as befitted a zealous Methodist, which I soon learnt was a strict Protestant sect. That night I rather liked the sound of it. It was a sort of guarantee of their being good, honourable people, with the same Christian ethic as I had been brought up in—it brought them closer to my own family. When he talked of them, Bill's voice took on a special affectionate note which I found very touching. He described his brother, whom he adored, and his sister, who seemed to be more or less perfect in his eyes. I could imagine my brothers talking about me with the same tenderness, and this was very reassuring. As to his mother, he made me very keen to meet her, and I told him so. He said he wasn't surprised. Then there was a great warm silence, perfumed by that night in the early Californian summer, which drew us still closer.

I wanted that good-night kiss as much as he did.

We had a rather short engagement, a month and a half.

The weekend at Carmel del Monte was unforgettable—and decisive. The petrified forest of San Francisco is certainly a unique, almost nightmarish place: miles of fossilised trees, twisted, clawed like witches' arms and hands, branches that have become stalactites, in all shades of grey, mauve, blue and ochre; a wild desolate landscape like the end of the world—but sublimely beautiful.

Bill had a real artist's sense of setting! We were leaning against a huge tree-trunk, a mauve haze had come down over the horizon, making the forest seem even more eerie and insubstantial.

'Will you marry me?'

'Yes,' I heard myself answer.

'Only, my love, promise me one thing.'

'What's that?'

'If ever we feel we may be falling out of love, wherever we are, very close or very far away, we'll tell each other.'

'I promise.'

With slow steps we returned to the car. Behind us the forest sank into the twilight mist, and disappeared.

In the car, leaning my head against the seat, I closed my eyes, but not to sleep. I was wondering why I had said yes. I wasn't indulging in any deep analysis of what had happened; it's always afterwards that you do that, when you have sufficent perspective. But I had enough judgment to be astonished at my 'yes', seeing that I wasn't really a person to take quick decisions.

In fact my 'yes' seemed incredible. It was obvious that I was in love, but not to the point of marrying him. Then why? He was good-looking, but that was not enough. I felt good with him, but how was I to know it would last? I hardly knew him ... I half opened an eye: it was with that profile I was going to spend my life! Amazing. Not for a moment did I think: if it doesn't work, I'll get a divorce. My models for married couples were parents, grandparents, uncles and aunts, all happy unions.

When we got back, Bill said to me ceremoniously: 'Would you like to come and have tea with us?'

My introduction to the family was as perfect as the rest had been. I had against me being French and Catholic, but it was greatly in my favour that Bill loved me. I very quickly realised that for his mother everything her elder son did was well done; without hesitation she approved his judgments, and that approval was essential if I was to be accepted by them. I felt I was accepted.

She was a slightly formidable lady, with green eyes behind her glasses, and grey hair, naturally waved, which gave added softness to a face that was benevolent despite the severe expression proper to Methodists. His sister was a lovely girl, spontaneous and exuberant; his brother as tall as he, less handsome, but very pleasant. In contact with them I found that family warmth I had been missing for so long.

I had three cups of tea and two slices of home-made chocolate cake. Bill's mother was a marvellous cook. They were so perfect it was like a coloured photograph in a magazine representing the average American middle-class family.

Why did I marry Bill? I have often wondered.

I have an idea that when an event is *meant* to happen, everything will contribute to it, a series of minor factors will link up together, even the weather will play its part. Either it's raining so that you are offered a lift in his car, or it's a beautiful day and you decide independently at the same time that it would be nice to go for a walk and you choose the same place. You see the friends you need to see just then, and they unwittingly say the things which will lead you uniquely towards the end of which you are still unaware. When you read a book, see a play or film, you find an analogy with your own situation, and everything seems to occur for a particular reason. Like my going to dinner with Jean-Pierre Aumont and Maria Montez, who were such a marvellous couple— I don't think I ever told Jean-Pierre how much his example influenced me. You tell yourself that's happiness, and realise that a tall fair stranger, as the fortune-tellers say, has now entered your life ... it all happens as if decided by some external force. When you at last recognise the existence of these signs, it will be too late. You will have lost all powers of judgment.

I don't think one can attribute everything to destiny, unless it is part of destiny that a meeting like ours should occur at the right psychological moment. It couldn't have been more right than that spring of 1942. Everything pushed me towards Bill: my loneliness and my realisation that it was going to be a long war, that because of it my future would for a long time be here, would depend on this country where I was a foreigner.

My morale was very low, and was further reduced by small experiences like a walk in the Hollywood cemetery. Seeing those neat lawns without any tombstones, I was overcome by a terrible depression—I didn't want to die and be buried *here*.

The idea of such foreign earth over me was suddenly unbearable. I came back from the walk in tears. I felt as if I had only just grasped the full meaning of the words 'my native land'.

I was also what actors call 'resting'. Since *Joan of Paris* no parts had been offered to me. RKO had changed hands; the studio bosses were new or not yet appointed, and no one knew what to do with this little French actress.

If you add my age to these reasons—I was twenty-two—and a very natural need to love and be loved, you will appreciate that Bill arrived at a crucial moment.

On the announcement of my engagement the climate around me changed. No one had made the slightest criticism of my having a flirtation with Bill, but as soon as they heard we were going to get married, opinion among both professional friends and in the French colony proved almost unanimously against the match. Adele Palmer, Ralph Blum, Charlie Feldman, Léonide Moguy and Madeleine Lebeau—all with different arguments tried to dissuade me, and duly achieved the opposite effect. I demanded my right to love and happiness; as to my friends' revelations about Bill, I treated them as slanderous gossip.

Bill hadn't seen any of my films, not even *Quai des brumes*, though he did know about the existence of Jean Gabin! I rather liked this touch of jealousy. As far as work went, I wanted to make him understand that compared to my career in Europe, to have been in only one film in two years was very demoralising.

He agreed: 'I can see it must be depressing, Mike'—he had Americanised my name in this way—'but personally I'm not surprised, I think you've been badly advised.' His tone became grave and warm, that of someone who knows and will sort things out. 'You see I don't think you've had the right people around you.' But what followed was some 'good advice' I didn't appreciate.

'I'm sure you'll agree about our house, darling. You'll understand that a man can't live under his wife's roof, a roof she's paid for—so I suggest you sell it.'

This idea hadn't occurred to me, and I pooh-poohed his scruples.

His face darkened. 'No, I can't think that way. Really, it's something that just isn't done. We can rent or buy another house, I've visited one on location at Brentwood which looks pretty good. How about we go and see it?'

Compared to mine, it had nothing; but you don't start a marriage by saying no. Shouldn't I be happy anywhere if it was with Bill?

So I sold my house, and with the money we bought another, which as it turned out was to remain his.

The weather was superb. The church was overflowing with flowers, the minister solemn but friendly. Bill slid the ring on my finger. I had just pronounced the sacramental 'yes', and sincerely believed I had committed myself for life. As we left the church, great handfuls of rice were thrown over us. Then, following the custom, Bill carried me over the threshold of the house we had rented.

The reception in the afternoon, for family only, took place at his mother's. On a central table stood a majestic wedding-cake. I pulled out the little figure of a married couple on top, and amidst applause carved into the edifice. Then I made a discreet sign to a servant, who opened the first bottle of champagne—which was to be the only one! The noise of the cork popping created as much furore as a train hold-up in a western.

That morning when I asked Bill not to forget the champagne, I received a scandalised response: 'You mustn't think of it, Mike. No drop of alcohol has ever entered my mother's house.'

'But, Bill, a wedding without champagne is a wedding without happiness. It's a very important French custom.'

This assertion carried the day; and his mother had dutifully pretended not to notice the entry of the prohibited bottle.

But when it was time for the toast, no arguments could persuade her, or Bill, or any other member of the family, to accept any of the wine in their glasses. So with the light sparkling cheerfulness of my golden wine I clinked glasses against the dark colour of their coca-colas. Again I felt almost as if I were acting a scene in an American comedy film.

But that was the end of the sequence. After that we were back in real life.

Mr and Mrs Marshall and Baby

It was not only Bill I had married, it was his family, and beyond that, America. My life became that of a young American woman. A good wife, I made the coffee while Bill fried his eggs and bacon. On Sundays, we had breakfast at the drug-store or the nearest cafeteria before going to church with the family. I found the service rather boring. The Methodist God, without incense, purple and gold, or the warm radiance of candles, the body of Christ distributed for communion in the form of small pieces of bread, was alien to me. I didn't dare ask anything of *Him*.

After the service we went back to my mother-in-law's. I can still recall the taste of her dishes, and feel nostalgia for them even now—I appease it by asking Mike, my son, to cook me one of his grandmother's dishes. Like all mothers she confided to me the tastes of her son. 'Billy adores fried chicken and turkey with cranberry jelly. Yes, I've made a meat loaf today. I'll give you the recipe.' All that was delicious, though it would have been even more so had there been a glass of wine to go with it rather than iced milk.

That first year of marriage went by very quickly. I was happy for the most part, and as happiness leaves no scars, I remember only the smooth, calm surface of a pool warmed by the sun; if a small cloud sometimes passed, it was soft and fluffy.

Professionally, my career was no longer at a dead end. I was in two films in quick succession. One was for Universal, another Resistance story, *Two Tickets to London*, directed by Edwin L. Marin; the other for RKO, *Higher and Higher*. I remember little about the former, and have bad memories of the latter. After a few preliminary conversations, I had met my future director, Tim Whelan, in the RKO producer's office. He didn't make much impression on me at the first meeting. About fifty, he had been a gagman for Mack Sennett and Harold Lloyd, and had then worked with Frank Capra for the comic Harry Langdon. These references for guaranteed mirth were the only thing I was to find amusing.

The two wise men, Whelan and the producer, informed me that they wanted to launch on the screen a young singer called Frank Sinatra—the man Bill spoke so highly of as a crooner—and that they had thought of me as his partner in a film called *Higher and Higher*.

For a moment, I was speechless. Then I protested: 'But I can't sing or dance.'

The producer was slightly irritated. With casual assurance he said: 'You'll learn. An actress should be able to do anything.'

I supposed he was right, Many actresses here did have such versatility. With a gesture he swept aside anything I might have to say. 'For you it's not the musical scenes that are important, they're very short anyhow: it's the rôle and that's magnificent. We're counting on your looks and your personality.'

I could be gently obstinate on occasions. 'Are you quite sure it's my line?' I insisted.

His voice became sharp and authoritative. He knew better than I did what would suit me. 'Miss Morgan,' he told me firmly, 'each to his job. Yours is to act. Ours is to know what you should act in. Look at these.' With the end of his cigar he pointed to the photographs of the studio's great stars who lined the walls of his office. 'Do you imagine they were asked their opinion? They all trusted us.'

I didn't answer, and reserved my decision till the next day. This time I was not on my own. Ralph Blum was against it, too: 'I think you should expect to be offered a part closer to your natural gifts.' But Bill saw things differently: a film musical, his dream, could not help attracting him. Flattered to be having a sort of casting vote, he was highly optimistic: 'You need to be a complete actress, and you can do anything if you try. I can give you some coaching and keep you at it.'

Why not try? So my lessons started again: singing, dancing, tap-dancing. From my first lesson in singing, I was quite
sure I had no future there.

A week before shooting began, I was summoned for ex-
amination by the producer and director, who studied me intently, moving round me like horse-dealers with a filly who
was not all they had hoped. 'Michèle, your face isn't quite
right for the part.'

'Then why did you engage me?'

'Because it's very near. With only a little done to it it'll
be perfect. Don't worry. If we just accentuate two or three
small details and suppress three or four others, we'll make
you exactly the woman for the role.'

I was taken off to Tommy, RKO's chief make-up artist,
who examined me rather as if I were a freak of nature. Under
his professional eye, Marlene herself would have had doubts
about her face; and his verdict, delivered from the corner
of his mouth, was too dismaying for me to even find it funny:
'The blonde hair's rather dull with those blue eyes. The
eyes—yes, they must be enlarged with false lashes. Then the
eyebrows, mmm, they must be accentuated, re-drawn. The
mouth is too thin, not sensual. I'll reshape it for you with
this coloured lipstick or perhaps that one.' Then Tommy
bluntly dismissed producer and director. 'Leave me to work
on her. My inspiration fails when I have witnesses.'

I became Tommy's property, a sort of wax doll. He sat
me down in his chair, which reminded me of a dentist's, and
began his creative task. At the end of the session, I was dizzy
from all the different mouths and eyebrows and hair-styles
I had seen displayed in the mirror. My skin, made up and
then un-made up, was taut and smarting. I no longer dared
to open my eyes. At the last attempt Tommy, after vigorously wiping his hands, contemplated his work with delight
and telephoned that all was ready.

In the mirror, an unknown woman regarded me, very
pretty, with a look in her heavily made-up eyes which was
slightly disconcerting; the deeply bowed mouth surprised
me too, and even more startling was the crow's-wing hair-
style taken up into a bun on the crown of my head. But I

Above: On her arrival in Hollywood, Michèle was welcomed by Ginger Rogers and Ginger's mother. *Below:* Michèle Morgan's remark: 'Hollywood for me was a series of mistakes' is partly proved by this uncomfortable R.K.O. 'pin-up', publicity photograph.

Above: Michèle Morgan with her first husband Bill Marshall. *Below:* their son Mike.

Above: Michèle's portrait of the blind girl in *La symphonie pastorale* won for her the award for best actress at the Cannes Festival of 1945. *Below:* Michèle with her brother Paul and Olga Horstig her agent, close friend, confidante and counsellor.

Above: Michèle and Henri Vidal (left), with Edith Piaf, celebrating their marriage. *Below: La Belle que voilà* was Michèle's first film with Gérard Oury who became the third man in her life.

found the whole effect rather amusing. Like most people in show business I had a strong feeling for disguise, and was attracted by the production of a new character. Why indeed not act with this face? For Tommy, his creation was a triumph. When superlatives failed him, he contemplated me with an expression of wonder and gratitude, though I really hadn't done anything myself. In fact, I was beginning to be rather against it. Something inside me rebelled, the vague anxiety at having become an artificial product. This beauty from the make-up box, if it *was* beauty, had made me into an American girl like so many others. I quickly stifled that reaction in the form of the voice of reason; after all, these people had created the likes of Marlene Dietrich and Ginger Rogers and Joan Crawford. I accepted their confidence; they knew better than me. Even so, I felt unnatural throughout the shooting; was it really me dancing, me singing? Could it be called singing and dancing anyhow? Even when acting, I had the sense of being somehow off course in relation to myself, and to everyone else. How could I be at ease singing with Sinatra? I was not likely to gain confidence from awareness of his brilliance or the seductiveness of his voice. Every time we were together, I wondered whether the film was not a producer's folly.

To catch a glimpse even for a moment of this slim, dark, vivacious young man with his sweeping lashes and velvety eyes, girls in their early teens pressed against the doors of the studios; for whole days they besieged him, shouting and screaming and swooning. For me the extent of their delirium was unexpected. At the time I left France, the idols of song had not yet come into being. Admittedly, it was said that women would throw their coats onto the ground where Tino Rossi was walking. But apart from him the arrivals and departures of singers—or actors for that matter—had not required any special public control.

My relations with Frank Sinatra were very friendly when we met; but that seldom happened. He would arrive on the set surrounded by his entourage of secretary, impresario, prompter, band, etc., which didn't make personal conversation easy. I was not really anxious for it anyhow since, as the weeks passed, I became increasingly sure that I had made a terrible mistake. On the evening of the première there were the usual compliments, but I never gave them much credit; I set even less store by them today. Despite such compliments I was shattered to watch that sophisticated woman, who had lost all charm and naturalness, moving and acting so clumsily. For me, the film made horrific viewing.

Poor Bill spent a miserable night, kept awake till the early hours, his ears buzzing with my regrets and complaints, dramatising the situation more and more as the night wore on. He patiently assured me that I didn't know my public well enough, that this Americanised version of Michèle Morgan would be very popular, that actresses always had to change faces according to their roles, etc. etc. I contradicted everything he told me, and found only one small consolation in the thought that the French public would never see me in this ghastly performance.

A false hope. The film was shown in France directly after the Liberation, and achieved what kindly critics called a moderate success.

We had not had any honeymoon; the shooting schedule for *Two Tickets to London* had made it impossible. Bill consoled me half jokingly by remarking that we had the privilege of being in the very place where other Americans took their honeymoons, and this should be adequate compensation.

Our honeymoon was at home, therefore, and was very happy too. It would no doubt have lasted longer if Bill had not been called up, an event which he announced to me with shining eyes, as if life had just granted him an unexpected promotion. Women have a different way of receiving this sort of news. The idea of being deprived of him, on my own again, was painful to me, and I told him so. To reassure me, he explained that he was nowhere near leaving for the front, and would be doing his training with the Air Force Cadets at Santa Anna in southern California. 'It's really quite near, you know. You can come and see me every Sunday.' He decided we should have a lovers' celebration.

Restaurant on the coast, dancing, the pattern of our first

date. But alas, it contained a different and unexpected moment—a jealous scene from Bill, unexpected and all the more unjustified for being retrospective. Well before we got married, I had confided to him any secrets there might have been in my private life, which amounted to very little. I did so because I have always thought lying was no guarantee of tranquillity, that the marriage of a couple who couldn't bear the truth about each other must be extremely fragile.

I don't remember how the discussion started, but it very soon degenerated into a quarrel. Bill's insistence that a girl should keep herself for her husband struck me as almost funny. I told him that there were moments when his principles were becoming irritating. At one point he informed me that he was willing to accept everything (a very meagre 'everything', I thought)—except Jean Gabin. I was amazed. Could it really be Jean's presence in Hollywood which was upsetting him? What had he to fear there? As everyone knew, Jean had been going through his 'American period'— with Ginger and then Marlene. We were no longer in touch; he didn't care about me any more except in a friendly way, nor I about him. Whereas till then Bill had always been rather discreet, he now showed an unpleasant insistence on hearing more, even pressing me for details. It was horrible, but after all he was my husband and perhaps believed he had a right to them. So I gave in, and told him all that had passed between Jean and me. Naturally I didn't make too much of my actual feelings, and in fact understated them. By then he wasn't listening properly to anything I said, except to turn it against me, and in disgust at his undeserved reproaches I lost my temper.

We went on with the futile argument until I was overcome by an immense weariness, and we went home. Although the memory of the spoiled evening remained with me for a long time, I didn't realise its importance till much later. I had intuitively picked up a revelation of his real character.

Neither of us said anything about it next morning or in the days that followed. We never openly 'made it up', but he seemed as friendly and affectionate as before the scene, and I responded accordingly, greatly relieved. He suggested rather firmly that it would be a good idea if his mother came to live with us, as he was soon going away, and I readily agreed. I, who later was to appreciate solitude so much, did not enjoy the prospect of living alone. So it seemed quite a natural arrangement; despite our quarrel, the idea that his mother would keep watch over me never entered my head. Yet in retrospect I dare say that was one of the motives behind the suggestion.

Mrs Marshall was gentle, vigilant, a little authoritarian— inclined to say, 'Bill prefers ... Bill likes ... Bill doesn't like ... When he was small, Bill did this, Bill did that ...' She was there in the house, and acquired a position that was never to be taken away from her. She was generally friendly, but even with her there the evenings were long, and my mind invariably slid towards images which became obsessional. I saw again the advertisements on the walls of the Métro tunnels, 'Dubo ... Dubon ... Dubonnet', the lamps in the Neuilly streets, my parents sitting round the table in the evening ... So I sat about brooding, my thoughts far away.

When I read in the papers that Paris had been bombed, my fears rose like a fever, and for days I was on the look-out for a letter. The ringing of the 'phone made me jump. When I found some indication of a district in an article, I reasoned with myself, 'it's not theirs', then became anxious for they might have moved. Or perhaps they had gone for a walk near the Auteuil race-course the day it had that air-raid. Eventually, enough time passed to reassure me. I should have been informed if anything had happened.

Imperceptibly, I slipped into the mould of the American woman. I went to see my husband every Sunday at the training camp. I didn't know any of these young women I met; we exchanged a smile, a 'hullo'. They were all very young, some accompanied by a child—which made Bill start hoping for an heir; and he gently coaxed me towards the same dream. An accident helped to transform this still vague thought into a real desire. Bill had a fall during exercises, he hit his head and was taken to hospital. Anxiety often serves as a gauge of love, and mine grew still more when my husband was taken to a New York neurological hospital. He had a 'cranial traumatism' I was told. I left at once to be near him.

I found him pleased to see me, apparently recovered from his fall, and impatient to leave the hospital. 'They've no reason to keep me. I feel fine. I'm ready to return to camp.'

But active service was over for him. The medical officer, who asked to see me, gave me explicit advice: 'In future, Mrs Marshall, you should make every effort never to oppose your husband. Avoid any grounds for causing him anger, which would be very bad for him.' In consequence I adopted the habit for a long time of answering Bill passively, 'Yes, darling', 'No, darling'.

The dreams of glory in the skies were finished for him. Did this sadden him? He didn't talk much about it to me. It was in New York, on leaving hospital, that he was given his new occupation: he was transferred to the Forces Theatre. Rehearsals were beginning almost at once for a show called *Winged Victory*, glorifying the United States Air Force. It ran for over six months on Broadway, and during that time I lived in New York.

A second honeymoon! I rediscovered the Bill of our engagement days. So had I really lost him before? Not really; and yet for a keen observer there was still a definite change.

The shooting of my two films, and then the Air Force, had inevitably drawn us away from each other; nor had we been enough alone together. His mother and family had a big place in his life, which wasn't a thing I could reproach him about. All the same, whenever we were on our own, our little differences had always been more easily resolved. Now we were closer and sure of our marriage, we decided to have a child.

I recognised the importance of this decision. Like many women, I felt my life would not be completely fulfilled, that I should always be missing something without that. I had a deep sense that not to have a child was not to have fulfilled one's function as a woman.

The new arrival was bound to have an influence on my professional life, and although I couldn't immediately weigh up all the effects, I wasn't running away from them. To realise myself completely as a woman was as important to me as to succeed in my career.

I thought about it a lot. The only factor that escaped me was the effect the baby might have on our married life. It seemed obvious to me that it could not help reinforcing the bond.

Three months passed, extremely happy ones. I liked New York life very much; it was less narrow than Hollywood's. So when I was offered a part in a film to be directed by Michael Curtiz, *Passage to Marseilles*, playing opposite Humphrey Bogart, I hesitated. Again we were going to be separated by my career, and I knew now that this was bad for us. Besides, my last experience had been unnerving, I had no wish to find myself once more with a new face, playing something completely wrong for me. But Bill insisted it would be a mistake to refuse. 'Don't funk this. A film with Bogart is sure-fire. Don't forget you missed *Casablanca* and were sorry afterwards.'

It was true. Ralph Blum, taking into account my contract with RKO, had asked too high a fee. As the film was very successful, it was the third time I had missed out on a big American hit.

I also had to consider that, except for his Air Force pay, Bill hadn't been earning anything for a year. And then it did seem that a baby was on the way. A little sad to leave Bill, I returned to Hollywood. The very day I signed my contract, my doctor confirmed to me that I was pregnant.

That evening Bill and I talked on the 'phone for over an hour. I shall never forget the tone of voice when instead of 'au revoir' he said: 'Darling, think of me, of us. Take good care of yourself and of my son!'

His son! Throughout my pregnancy he talked of the baby always as 'him'. How could I be so clumsy as to have a girl?

We called each other every evening. I found it half touching, half irritating, when he said: 'Ask my mother for advice. She knows, she's had two sons.'

'Darling, do you really think that in my condition the precautions to be taken are so different for a girl or a boy?'

174

We laughed. Every remark, however trite, delighted us. It was quite obvious no married couple had ever had a baby before us.

'Are you sure you can act in ·your condition? You could pay the breach of contract money and send them packing.'

'But, Bill, I'm only three months pregnant!'

'Three months already! These are the most important weeks,' he declared authoritatively. 'It's at this stage everything is decided.'

I was swamped by a flood of advice. He must have bought a handbook for mums-to-be.

I had an untroubled pregnancy without special incident, only the incomparable pleasure of a life developing inside me. I knew it was too early yet for him to be moving, but that didn't stop me from putting my hands on my stomach and imagining them penetrated with a warmth that was not mine, that came from him. These moments belong only to us women.

During the shooting of *Passage to Marseilles* I was busy setting up the baby's room, decorating it with a delightful pinky-mauve wallpaper, furnishing the cot. From the pleasure I experienced sewing it with that white satin-stitch, I discovered the serenity of mothers preparing the nest.

It was lucky I had that. For professionally, nothing was easy: I lived in fear that Michael Curtiz would notice I was pregnant; an alert eye could guess from a certain heaviness at the waist and the subtle rounding of the figure. He would be furious that I had concealed my condition.

In a few hours, he had shown himself to be the most disagreeable director I had ever had. This Hungarian with the looks of a Tartar quite terrified me, and without knowing why or how, I had become his *bête noire*. He watched out sadistically for each of my failings, provoked them in fact; and, of course, they multiplied as I felt his hostility increasing. With an insulting malice, at the end of each take and the beginning of every new one, he would find some cutting word to reduce my morale, already low. I slept badly at nights, thinking of meeting my tormentor again the next morning.

As to Humphrey Bogart, 'Bogey' to his friends, I was not going to get support from him: he retreated into sullen neutrality, he had his own problems. With cigarette hanging from his disillusioned lip, he stayed in his corner, brooding over his marital troubles. He had not yet met the charming Lauren Bacall. From the first day, Bogart kept his distance with Michael Curtiz, and gave him short shrift.

When *Passage to Marseilles* was at last in the can, I could expand freely—and literally. No point now in tightening my belt. I had the right to expose to view my approaching maternity.

Bill was still in New York. I should have liked to join him but felt a bit lazy, with a desire to enjoy life; and in his absence our little French circle revived me. Charles Boyer, whom I hadn't seen since *Orage*, invited me to dinner. In his house with its exquisite décor I was warmly received by him and his wife, the British actress Pat Patterson; their marriage was a model for Hollywood society, a life's partnership. Like Jean-Pierre Aumont and Maria Montez, they gave me an idea of how wonderful such a partnership can be.

By a happy chance I was placed next to Kisling, the artist. This even led to him saying: 'I'd like to paint your portrait, would you sit for me?' Much flattered, I accepted, and the next day entered into the magic world of painting. To have Kisling as initiator into its mysteries was a great piece of luck for me. In fascination and excitement I watched a woman's face grow with every stroke of the brush. I don't know if it was my face, since re-created by him, I became a 'Kisling woman'. But what loving care there was in the use of pine-marten brush which, immersed in an oily paste, produced a work of art! I believe that when an artist has attained a certain degree of technique and talent, the model is only a pretext for a particular composition.

But in this pretext there is still something of you, the model. Why didn't I ask Kisling if I could buy it? I hadn't the heart to deprive him of it. I have realised since then that there comes a time when an artist can part easily with his work: he is fairly fickle, more attached as a rule to tomorrow's canvas than yesterday's. Who was I sold to? I've no idea. I have sometimes wondered whether I was put up for auction. Am I hanging somewhere on a wall I shall never see? She was a strange creature, that Michèle Morgan who was not quite me and had a destiny outside my own.

When the sitting was finished, I asked Kisling if he would let me watch him paint. Seeing him at work, I felt tremors of envy, so I dared to say: 'If I were to ask you to give me lessons, would you be willing to?'

He gave me a long look, his eyes searching me as they had done a little while before when he was painting me. 'Yes,' he said finally, 'but on one condition, that you promise me you'll keep on with it.'

It is a promise which with some difficulty I have kept.

At last Bill rejoined me. He was staggered by my size. 'Mike, you're going to have twins.'

The confidence of his pronouncement disturbed me, and we began seriously wondering whether it would not be best to buy another cot and double the baby-clothes.

Waiting for the baby was perhaps responsible for a certain indifference on my part to anything except him; at any rate I did not react to Bill's switches of moods. He was nervy, rather irritable, often withdrawn: A change seemed to have occurred in him; I noticed it without becoming too worried. It was especially my friendship with the French which made him grouchy. The important thing was that the good moments between us should be more numerous than the bad, and they were. There was only one thing outside my condition that greatly concerned me: to have our marriage blessed by a Catholic priest before our child's birth. Bill was not too keen: 'We were married in church—that's good enough.' 'No, Bill, not for me, I want our marriage to be recognised by my Church. It's very important to me.'

This faith of mine might sound childish, but I was born with it. Throughout my childhood and youth I had basked in that atmosphere of kindness, tolerance and simplicity of soul, closely linked with the idea of Jesus Christ, the Holy

Virgin Mary and the Saints. I still retain a wonderful memory of it even today, for it is indeed a miracle to grow up amidst these feelings of purity and hope.

6 June, 1944. Radios and papers proclaimed the news: 'Allied troops have landed on the coast of Normandy, Operation Overlord has been successful.'

I was shattered, imagining my country aflame and deep in blood. When I was not reading the papers, I was listening to the radio or dashing to the consulate, trying to get news of my family. The newsreels choked me. That coast which it was so hard to make out in the smoke and explosions of battle, that piece of beach and countryside was Normandy; this section of wall was a French farm. Between the tanks and guns, the steel helmets and the shoulders in battle-dress, I could see a fragment of my own country—and that brought tears to my eyes.

I did not find the advance of the victorious troops reassuring until the war correspondents replaced the accounts and pictures of ruins with cheerful descriptions and views of delirious crowds acclaiming the victors.

Of course, we French were not the only people in America to be feverishly following events and, feeling solidarity with all the women whose menfolk were fighting to liberate my country piece by piece, I stopped feeling a foreigner in America.

This did not stop me having a violent nostalgia one morning when I heard Charles Trenet singing on the radio: 'Revoir Paris ... Un petit séjour d'un mois ... Revoir Paris, et me retrouver chez moi ...'

To see Paris again, and be at home once more—it was out of the question; and even had it been possible, I was only three months from my confinement. It was the American custom to give a big party called 'a shower', tea or a meal, or cocktails. My mother-in-law chose a tea party to announce the approaching birth. It was the occasion for female friends to bring a 'shower' of presents for the baby, little silver objects, mugs, rattles, pram. I was given so many things I didn't know where to put them all.

The party was a success. Bill was happy, so was his mother, and I was happy with them. I was becoming used to them, and to my mother-in-law being ruler of the household. I told myself: she's doing it from kindness, why think otherwise? After all, they *are* my new family, the family I've chosen.

I had just stopped my car outside our *pâtisserie*-cum-baker's. The radio was broadcasting some very good jazz when the music was broken off abruptly for a news-flash: 'Paris is liberated!'

The tears spurted from my eyes and flowed down my face without my being aware of it. I was trembling. A war correspondent described the 2nd Armoured Division's entry into the capital in words that overwhelmed me. I heard a hubbub of French voices and French words mingling with the American commentary. Behind the roar of the tanks, I could hear the clamour of a crowd *en fête*: it was a unique moment. The announcer spoke of tricolour flags decking the houses, of women and girls kissing their liberators—and I was here in America, in a car parked along a sidewalk. It was very hot, I was wearing a pink and black dress with a big floral pattern, I had a huge stomach, and I sobbed loudly with my head close to the radio set. It was on so loud that I didn't know whether it was my apparent distress or the reporter's voice which made passers-by stop. When I became aware of them, I gave them a big smile and assured them I was perfectly all right—and very happy.

On 12 September, 1944, at midnight I entered the Cedars of Lebanon, a Los Angeles hospital. The pains which made me leave the house in haste were the only ones I was to feel. Tenderly escorted by my mother-in-law, calm with experience, and a frenzied husband, I was taken in charge by the nurses, given an anaesthetic by injection in the spinal column, which was high fashion at the time, and—at 8.27 on the morning of 13 September my baby was born. The first thing I asked the nurse was: 'Is it a boy?' 'Yes, Mrs Marshall.'

God be praised, I had not failed! All through my pregnancy Bill and his family had talked about this boy almost every day. In the end I had been terribly scared of giving birth to a girl.

So Bill had a male heir! Here he was, in the crook of my arm. I couldn't have my fill of contemplating him. He was wonderful, with a little silky hair, eyes drawn towards the temples, turned-up nose. What a fantastic feeling! I kept repeating to myself: There it is, I have a child. I've produced a human being, a baby of 9 lbs, perfect, unique, mine.

Bill leaned towards me crazy with joy, and we looked at each other. An exceptional moment, a peak of happiness. 'Well, Mike 1,' he said, 'Mike 2 is born!'

I painted my future in the rosiest of colours. Soon I should be seeing my family again, showing them my child. I would give my son the chance to get to know my country. How happy all three of us were going to be!

How good life was! We were the typical happy family of the American illustrated magazines, a young couple rejoicing in their first offspring, and with no fear of enforced separation. For Bill would not be going off to the wars; he was demobilised, and had just signed a contract with Fox. I had a charming mother-in-law and an adorable baby. When I went shopping with Mike, even the assistants in the supermarket thought him beautiful. Everything was just as I had desired. As I kept telling myself, I had every possible reason to be happy.

I have often thought back to the period in Hollywood at the end of the war—placid, a little uneventful but underneath so important a time for me, for us. Those months carried within them all the ferments of the fifteen years that were to follow, during which I had to adjust my life as a woman to my life as an actress.

How can the two be reconciled? This is a question which often comes up in interviews, and of course there is no simple formula to answer it. This problem, however, which was soon going to crop up for me in a serious form, was not important at that time. My career as an actress seemed to have come to a full stop, and was not likely to threaten our marriage; it was threatened, alas, for other reasons. With hindsight I can say that there was nothing to be done. I can even conclude that the marriage was a mistake, though because of my son I shall never regret it. But at the time I wanted to believe that things would sort themselves out. I clung to happy memories which were so recent, and thought they could be the guarantee of my future, transforming everything. I dreamed of our happiness as a trio, living partly in

America, partly in France. That dream was very distant, as I realised from one small scene, which has remained in my mind vividly.

I was alone in my room, writing a letter to my parents. Communications had been re-established, we were in regular correspondence. I heard Mike cry, and after a few seconds during which I finished my sentence, I crossed the passage. When I opened the nursery door, Bill and his mother were already there at the cot. She had the baby in her arms, and he had stopped crying. When I went in, they both turned their heads towards me. Both pairs of bluey-green eyes registered clearly the same scandalised astonishment: What had *she* come here for? I wondered myself. *They* knew what a Marshall needed. I looked at them, and felt dispossessed. I was to feel on many other occasions this sense of having produced a child for *them*; but I remember that occasion with most precision, perhaps because it was the first on which I was really aware of their 'taking possession'.

I did not return to my unfinished letter. I felt frustration not only for myself as a mother but for my child. All mothers know the importance of physical contact with their baby. To give Mike his bath, powder him, put on his nappy, feed him—these were actions I didn't have to learn, they came to me from generations of mothers. Yet Mrs Marshall disparaged them by giving instructions in front of her son. With her expertise she was always impatiently relegating me to the position of a young novice daughter-in-law. What could I do? It was no good talking to Bill. He would answer something like: 'What's bugging you? Mother's looking after Mike very well, he's happy, and you can go out without worrying.'

Innumerable young couples have known this situation, and I fear that a vast proportion of them have come out of it very badly. I suffered so much from the presence, however benevolent, of this gentle but inflexible woman, who was imperceptibly separating me from my son—that, when I became a mother-in-law myself, I took great care never to interfere in the household's life and to avoid giving advice, even in the form of helpful remarks!

Nineteen forty-five was dragging out painfully, but it was very good to have renewed the bond with my family and friends in France. As my parents were going short in many things, I sent them food parcels twice a week, with rice, cocoa, coffee and tins of all sorts, and even—to the amazement of the Beverly Hills post office—7 lb sacks of coal. In return I received newspapers and magazines; France and Paris were spread out on my knees. Against a background of the Eiffel Tower and the Seine banks, young women showed me the new fashions. There were some relics of the Occupation fashions to be found there, platform shoes, small hair-slides on the crown of the head, bouffant hair-styles, wasp waists—the wasp-waisted corset was born—and short skirts with slits, which made me feel old-fashioned. In America we were still at the stage of normal heels and flat hair-styles *à la* Veronica Lake.

If I could only go back home, even for a very short time! Tanine and Olga were pressing me. 'Come quickly, we're dying to meet your husband and your baby.' Olga Horstig had become very important to me. We had first met through *Gribouille*. She was a Yugoslav journalist who in interviewing me had shown so much understanding and kindness that a real bond had grown up between us. Our correspondence after that transformed the bond into a deep friendship, especially during the war years, which she spent in London, her diplomat husband having a post there. In her letters she talked a lot about the film circles which she frequented professionally—she was ready to become my agent. Denise Tual also told me that I should be well received.

I should have loved to respond to these appeals coming from France; but the thought stayed within me like an unsatisfied desire. It wouldn't have been a good time to talk to Bill about them. He already frowned on any connections with the French colony in Hollywood. All attempts to bring him into our little group were in vain. Admittedly—and I *can* admit it today—they didn't really like Bill; not being involved, they perhaps had a better and clearer judgment than I did. His suspicious and rather withdrawn attitude didn't help matters. He didn't speak French, and like most foreigners had a defence reaction, imagining that we were making remarks about him and above all were laughing at him. As I did not want him to feel rejected, I didn't insist on his coming with me, and I spaced out my own meetings. Anyhow the little colony was gradually losing its members, as one by one these French people returned to their own country and mine.

Mike was a little over a year when a new source of discord came up between Bill and me.

'Open up!' he shouted through the bathroom door. 'Right, just a second, I'm coming.' I finished tying the lace of Mike's little white shoe. My voice had broken off when I heard Bill's steps in the passage; but not soon enough.

'You're talking to him in French again!'

I managed to stop myself shouting: 'Yes, I was committing that crime! I had the audacity to sing to my son, *Sur le pont ... d'Avignon*, to speak words of tenderness to him in my mother tongue which is also his. If you don't like that, you shouldn't have married a Frenchwoman!' But I said nothing. I had no wish to worsen an atmosphere which was too often unpleasant anyhow.

'If you talk French to him,' Bill went on vehemently, 'he'll have an accent when he goes to school, and the other boys will laugh at him.'

'That's ridiculous, Bill. A child easily becomes bilingual, and doesn't have an accent in either language!'

His rejection was indiscriminate. 'No, the effort will hold him back. My son is American.' (I didn't yet appreciate the full gravity and importance of those four words.) 'I've told you a hundred times, French won't be any use to him. He can learn it afterwards if he wants to. But not now, not now. I forbid you to do it.'

'You have no right to forbid me to do anything which concerns my son ...' Farewell my resolutions, the discussion had become a quarrel.

He went out, slamming the door. Furious, I took myself off for a walk. I knew that directly I had left the house, he would go to his mother, who would find him in the right.

More than ever I felt I was the foreigner, the Frenchwoman. I didn't blame her for that, I still respected her and understood her feelings. She had dreamed of a young American wife for her son, and with such a daughter-in-law she would probably have had a different attitude, she might have been less inclined to monopolise her grandson. But I was an intruder, coming from another country, from a city the very name of which suggested sin to her: Paris.

But it was no help to understand my mother-in-law and find good excuses for Bill's unreasonableness. I resigned myself to the obvious truth that while any marriage has its complications, coming from different countries adds to them considerably. My dreams of 'commuting' between our two countries now seemed very remote. We had last discussed it not very long before.

I had been thinking about it while doing the housework and all day. In the evening Bill was affectionate, and it seemed a propitious moment. 'I'd very much like to go and see my parents. It'll soon be five years we've been parted.'

This was something he could appreciate very well.

'Yes, darling, I hope you'll be able to do that soon. Well, fairly soon. Shipping's still difficult, and one can't make quick trips there and back.'

'Wouldn't you like to see Paris and meet my parents?'

He became evasive, but was still conciliatory. 'Yes, perhaps one day.'

I pressed him, explaining that I was as attached to my country as he was to his. I knew already that I oughtn't to go farther than that. But I was so fed up with the force of inertia opposing me, his refusal generally to make any effort to understand me, that I went on: 'In France we'd have a different life. I'm a star, my friends tell me that everyone's waiting for me, that I'll be offered a film directly I arrive.'

He reacted with a deliberate misunderstanding. 'Do you think I'm incapable of looking after you and the baby? I don't need a wife who works, and I'm not going to live in France. Ever!'

'But it's nothing to do with looking after me, Bill. Of course you can do that very well. Only could we perhaps think of a few months here, a few months over there? American actors are appreciated in Paris. They'd be happy to have you. You'd get work.'

He rose, and stubbed out his cigarette. 'No. It's no use, and I don't want to hear any more about it. You married an American. You're my wife, and here's where you'll live.'

At that time there were many mixed marriages, and many wives experienced this sort of difficulty. Back in France I received a lot of letters from G.I. brides of 1945–47, which generally began with 'My case is a little like yours, so I think you will understand me ...'

They almost all told me the same story: 'I met Jim (or Harry), looking very smart in his uniform, cheerful and optimistic, quite sure of our future together. He took me to his own state, and now I'm in the back of beyond in Kansas (or Minnesota, or the Middle West). I can't adapt to it. I don't understand anything about this country, and he doesn't understand me. I feel as if I were living on a different planet.' In many cases the situation was aggravated by the presence of a child, which all too often, when they wanted to return to their home country, became the cause of strains and quarrels. Very few of these G.I. brides adapted successfully.

What answer could I give the ones who asked me for advice? My case was not really like theirs, for I had continued to make progress in my career and they had not. Often they had married a ranch-hand, having thought they were marrying a gentleman farmer. Girls with an easy-going life-style landed up in puritan families. Brought up with a good European education, they found themselves tied to a small Bronx radio repairer addicted to baseball. They were completely thrown by the shock of their disillusionment. I sympathised with them, but although I was familiar with some elements in their situation, I couldn't think of any comfort or advice to give them.

In spite of everything, Bill and I still loved each other for much of the time. He may well have sensed the point of exasperation which I had reached, and felt a need himself to return to our old good times. He set up his mother in a little house in the San Fernando Valley—but perhaps regretted this gesture once he had made it, for after that his moods seemed to get worse again. I could not help asking myself what there was left of the boy I had married, apart from his looks. I had once been so disarmed by his amusing talk, his way of telling stories, his imagination; now he was proving gloomy, pessimistic, touchy, complicating the simplest things to suit his purpose. If he had been like this when we first met, I should never have got married, and this made me think that his accident may have had something to do with the change in his character.

I found it increasingly difficult to put up with his jealousy. At the beginning it seemed flattering, but it's always a mistake to confuse jealousy with evidence of love. It now irritated me by its extravagance and stupidity: if a man looked at me in a club or a restaurant or at a party, Bill was on edge. If I averted my eyes or plunged my nose in my plate, that showed I felt guilty. If I pretended to laugh, it was to annoy him. Whatever I did the evening was now spoilt.

The 'phone rang. Bill answered, then handed it to me: 'It's for you—a Frenchman.'

'From Paris?' I blushed stupidly as if I had been caught in some misdeed.

'No, it's from over here—a Mr Bercholz.'

When I spoke to this Frenchman, he had a Russian accent and sounded very nice. He would like to fix a very quick appointment with me, as he was leaving in three days.

My financial situation, our situation indeed, was far from satisfactory. Since coming to the States I had been in four films, but had paid 80 per cent in war taxes, and had no new contracts in view. As to Bill, being with Fox only ensured him irregular fees, and not very large ones at that. In these circumstances the prospect of being engaged for a film seemed like the result of a divine intervention.

It was in this state of mind that I arrived next day at the 'Players', a French restaurant on Sunset Boulevard owned by the director Preston Sturges.

A man alone at his table, about forty, with greying hair, rose to welcome me, a smile on his face, his voice friendly. 'What can I get you to drink?'

'A glass of milk?'

Bercholz looked astonished. 'They told me you were Americanised, but that's taking it too far!'

This remark irritated me, and I deliberately 'over-acted' by choosing a typical American menu: hamburger and apple-pie.

'And to drink?'

I would shock him to the limit. 'Some milk, please.'

Nevertheless, he chose a bottle of excellent imported Bordeaux, and without fuss poured me out a glass. Out of politeness I moistened my lips—and thereafter abandoned my milk.

'Now then. We have acquired the rights in an André Gide novella, *La symphonie pastorale*. The rôle I'm offering you is that of a young blind girl, very beautiful, very pure-hearted—and she becomes involved in a love affair with cruel results. I've brought you the book. The film adaptation will be made by Jean Aurenche and Pierre Bost, and the direction is being given to Jean Delannoy...'

At last I heard names mentioned which linked me to the people I had made films with in France. I had heard a lot about Jean Delannoy's brilliance. His film, *L'éternel retour*, the biggest success of 1943, had brought him immense prestige.

A blind girl? I had missed *Johnny Belinda*'s deaf-mute, so I was not going to pass up André Gide's blind girl. I said yes to Joseph Bercholz without even thinking about it. I just could not refuse.

I heard Bercholz as if in a dream. He was talking to me about Pierre Blanchar, who was to play opposite me as the Pastor, and describing my character, that of Gertrude, in touching terms. I think he must have talked at some length, before a last sentence brought me back to reality: 'You'll have to be in Paris by the end of October at the latest, to try out costumes.'

So in this way my return had just been decided. How was Bill going to take it?

Not badly at all. I opened by making a lot of the name André Gide. 'You know him, don't you?'

A slight hesitation was followed by a cautious: 'I've heard of him, of course.'

'Do you think I can refuse a film written by Gide?'

He was not going to compromise himself by a direct answer. 'How long will you be away?'

'A few weeks. They're offering me a fee of a million, with journey paid and all expenses while I'm there. Come with me, and we'll take Mike. His grandfather and grandmother will be so pleased to see him.'

There was something like astonishment in his eyes. His son had another grandmother besides his mother? He frowned and shook his head, declaring that the journey would be too long and uncomfortable. He had a point there, too, for I had no idea of the conditions in which I—or we—should have to travel. 'For such a short time,' he said, 'is it worth upsetting the rhythm of a child's life at such an early age, and changing his habits? He'll be well looked after here by my mother.'

Oh yes, I knew I could have confidence in *her*; but a part of my dream had collapsed. So I resigned myself to leaving alone, torn between joy at this return so much longed for and the pain of leaving my little son.

With some difficulty I obtained a passage on a Liberty Ship through the French Consul in New York. This ship, designed mainly for troop transports, had no cabins, only dormitories; there were forty of us women crowded in together. But what did the length of the voyage matter, or its discomfort? I was returning to my country. I had left as an *émigrée*, but now I was returning.

At Cherbourg journalists invaded the deck and dashed towards me. On the quay I was surrounded by men and women whose French, in their rustic accents, was like music in my ears. They asked me for autographs, they talked to me about my films, the pre-war ones. I was staggered that they remembered them, amazed they had not forgotten me. For them I still existed as I had been then, as I was now.

I wanted to register everything down to the smallest detail, to capture all these images so that they stayed in my mind. But somehow my sight was blurred—I found I was crying.

Cherbourg on that rainy night smelt of the sea. It was the smell of *Quai des brumes* and *Remorques*, welcoming me, and taking me back several years in time.

'Michèle, it's me!' Olga hugged me. 'I'd like to introduce a journalist friend, Jean Vietti, and Serge Lido, a photographer.'

When I compared this return with my arrival in New York—the French was certainly on a more intimate level!

'You're going to come with us by car, we're driving you to Paris.'

For me these simple words were still unreal, magical. I had lived through this moment too often in my imagination to believe in the present reality: the soil of France. I discovered that the love I had for my country was passionate: I loved France, as one can love one's mother or one's child. I had a mad urge to kiss that soil of my native land.

It had taken my exile to make me feel so deeply the charm of its villages, its countryside, its people, to whom I felt bound; they had belonged to this soil from time immemorial and formed the great chain of my ancestry.

The scenic effects on this night journey were extraordinary. First darkness would mask the scars of the Allied landings; then the headlights, conjuring them up out of the night, would make them even more tragic, picking out the ruins of these villages like a stage back-cloth.

I was astonished by the dimensions of things. I had forgotten how small the houses were. After the huge tower blocks and skyscrapers, everything seemed so tiny—and so charming.

About ten in the evening an authentic country inn agreed to serve us with a bacon omelette and some bottled cider. Here were tastes I had forgotten; they blended with the smell of the old beams and the wood fire smouldering beneath the ashes.

At midnight, Olga and Jean Vietti put me down at my parents' house in the rue Pergolese. They were all waiting for me. Maman wept tears of happiness. She had aged, and so had my father. They had been ill and suffered from all sorts of privations. And my sister? I had left a little girl of eight, and now found an adolescent who was rather shy with me. My brothers had beards—they were men.

'You're sleeping at the hotel?' Maman asked hesitantly.

'Oh no, I'm staying here.'

'Ah, I thought you would. The room is ready.'

'And there's Uncle Teddy and Aunt Yvonne...and Grandfather and Grandmother... and ... and ...' We had marvellous reunions, in a night-long party. At dawn our excitement subsided, and during the morning, half asleep, I imagined I was back in my bed at Beverly Hills.

I didn't return to reality till Maman, half opening the door, suggested, like someone offering a treasure: 'Would you like some Nescafé? We have a little through friends with a cousin working for the P.X.'

The French had just discovered powdered coffee, milk and eggs, and were thrilled by them, while for years I had been able to enjoy them every day; and now Maman was offering me jam as a great luxury. I had lived in abundance without being aware of it. Their poverty, the whole country's poverty, was shattering to me.

It was still quite early when I ran to the post to send a wire to Bill. I was amazed to see so little traffic; outside the main arteries the streets were empty. I walked and walked in the joy of rediscovering my city, delighting in the greyness and asphalt of the capital, the zigzag reflections of the lamp-posts on the wet streets; all the charm of Paris! These October mists—how much I relished them! I, who had lost touch with anything but sun, breathed them in ecstatically.

I crossed the road carelessly and nearly got run over. 'Hey there, you silly bitch!' the driver bawled at me. 'Look where you're bloody going, can't you?'

There was no doubt about it: I had come home.

La symphonie pastorale will remain one of the most important films of my career. To return to the French cinema in a work like this was a real renewal of my good luck.

The Claridge Bar, which had housed the staff of the Panzer divisions, had been restored to civilian owners. It was here I met Jean Delannoy for the first time. In this rather run-down, old-fashioned setting I found him the picture of robust health, blue-eyed and pink-faced; not at all like the film people who call you 'darling' straight off and confuse familiarity with human warmth. The contact between us might even have seemed distant, but that was only an appearance: we knew we could understand each other, that we were on the same wavelength. We have given proof of that understanding with six films together, and I hope there will be more to come.

Jean Delannoy is precise. He takes his time; he talks as he directs, with care. You feel he has the necessary detachment to look at things in depth. It is not the outer view they offer that interests him most, it is the glimpse they give of hidden and buried passions. Not that I worked all that out at the time—I was much too captivated by his film but I sensed it.

I began to steep myself in this woman, Gertrude, whom he was to conjure up in the film, by reading André Gide's novella. She became astonishingly close to me. When I told Jean this, he smiled and said: 'You see when Gide talks to you about her, you'll understand her even better.'

I was to meet André Gide. The mere thought was awe-inspiring.

These meetings of author and actor are one of the joys of our profession. They are almost indispensable for the actor.

It is through them that you can really study and get hold of a character. It is so exciting to ask an author questions, to talk to him of his creation as if the character created were alive; to ask him what her tastes and quirks are; to assess with him whether she would like this or that, whether such and such a thing would annoy her; to calmly assert: 'No, she would not act like that—she couldn't do it.' You have to know everything about this woman you are going to lend not only your face to but sometimes much else of yourself, and who at the same time, by a curious phenomenon of osmosis, is going to make *you* become *her*.

I have rarely been frustrated in this excitement, but it has never given me such joy as it did with Gertrude in *La symphonie pastorale*. Your name, when you have one, can sometimes spoil things a bit: it may happen that you are chosen not because your looks and personality tally with the heroine in the minds of the author and the director, but because they represent a certain commercial value. Too often this detracts from authenticity—but then why accept characters with whom you don't feel in perfect harmony? That is a situation I know very well from bitter experience, and I shall be 'justifying myself' later on. At the same time I was still far from all that, and the only thing that concerned me was this Gertrude was created by Gide, to be brought to the screen by Delannoy, after an adaptation by Aurenche and Bost so perfect that Gide himself said they had been extremely faithful. Gide's prestige at that time was at its peak. I remembered boys at the Simon School who identified themselves with Nathanael, quoting passages from *Les nourritures terrestres*, who, after reading *Les faux monnayeurs*, proclaimed the beauty of unreasoned action. It was with these ideas that the whole of my generation had gone through the war. Their successors of 1945 would soon be calling on Jean-Paul Sartre to be their guru, but for the moment Gide remained a sort of Pope of literature; and it was him I was going to meet. No wonder I had something like stage-fright.

The first shock I received when Jean Delannoy and I met André Gide was a matter of clothing. His smart outfit was audacious for that period, though today it would be the height of fashion. He wore a wide loden cape, and a cap of the same tweed covered a superb Roman senator's head. The face was white and clean-shaven, the eyes quick and perceptive. The very curious impression he gave me was of being with us and yet not with us. He spoke to me of my role, Gertrude, and of *La symphonie pastorale*, and listened to what I said in reply; but I somehow felt he was pursuing a chain of thought to edify a different company from us. I was fascinated by that intellect, his rather slow speech, searching for the right word, with every word counting, and even these spoken sentences 'punctuated' to perfection. Hearing him talk was an experience in itself.

The three of us had quite a long conversation. It was remarkable to watch a close sympathy and understanding growing up between these two men, so dissimilar. They listened to each other with great attention. While the film was being shot, Gide came to the set several times to watch us at work. I have never seen an author more admiring, more pleased with the transference of his work into visual images. Seeing technical possibilities unknown to him, he was full of youthful enthusiasm. As with Cocteau at the end of *his* life, one did not feel that Gide had aged at all in spirit.

Sometimes when the name Gertrude was spoken, he would give me a quick glance, as if making a confrontation between his model and her double. Indeed this young blind girl was already beginning to have a definite existence inside me. The period of incubation a character needs is different each time. With her I recognised at once that I should identify very quickly; so much so that when I went for a walk, though I had not yet reached the point of describing the scenery to Gertrude, I sometimes felt she was with me and I was looking at things *for* her.

After that, I must make it clear that I don't 'think' my character. I am not an intellectual actress, more an instinctive one: the creation which comes out of me is not the fruit of research. I don't deduce: 'Gertrude, having such and such motives, would do this.' I think directly: 'Gertrude will do this.' I 'receive' first, then check by reasoning. My professional training and my experience allow me to 'place' my character and consolidate it; I use these endowments only to save me from the technical traps you often meet during shooting, or on days when I am less inspired. This word might seem pretentious, but it is simply one of the realities of our profession. All actors are familiar with those pleasant times when everything works on its own, the gestures and intonations are right without any apparent effort from you. Actors also know only too well the moment when nothing comes spontaneously; it is to surmount such times that you need a sure technique.

I liked this Gertrude who was going to take on my face. Passion blazed beneath her restraint, her conflict was inside. But she could only use her mouth, and no eyes to express that conflict; a face without eyes says much less. What is the world round you like when you can't see it? How do you walk, steer yourself, go towards objects and people? Is running completely out for you? What are the passionate movements a non-sighted person can allow herself? My character was closely bound up with this network of questions. Intuition was not sufficient here, but Jean Delannoy had already thought about this problem, and advised me to go to the Institute of the Young Blind, to talk to them, familiarise myself with their gestures and reactions, learn to think as a blind person.

The first days were pretty disappointing. We spoke different languages, they couldn't 'see', and I didn't know how to find my way into their night. Then the key clicked when I realised that their vision was interior. I couldn't imitate them from the outside. I must completely stop seeing. It was not a question, however, of my closing my eyes or wearing dark glasses—I must find a mechanical 'trick' to wipe out my vision. I decided to look at things and people without focusing—without adjusting, as ophthalmologists call it. It is a very painful form of defective vision, in which things tend to double up, and the world becomes a blur. I decided that if I deliberately took on this defect, my gestures and walk would more easily become authentic and my eyes would have the desired unseeing look.

Apart from these very important sessions at the Institute,

I visited the dressmaker's, both for my own pleasure and for the needs of the production, and found that my impression in America of being old-fashioned was all too accurate.

It is a strange factor in my destiny that I met the two most important men in my life well before they really entered it. Gérard Oury at the Simon School, and now the second on one of my visits to the dressmaker's. Lydia Bercholz, my producer's wife, took me to see Germaine Lecomte's collection. We had watched the parade of the models for some while when Renée Saint-Cyr came in escorted by a faithful knight whose name, I gathered, was Henri Vidal. Smiling, exuberant, witty, he seemed nice enough, though rather anxious to attract attention with his comments on the models and the jokes he made. He was quite near us, and several times tried insistently to catch my eye with a rapid glance. He seemed ready to risk everything for that fleeting second's pleasure, and I could not help smiling despite myself. What interest could I have in the look of a complete stranger when I was choosing a dress at a Paris dressmaker's after an exile of five years?

Hollywood had not ceased to exist for me. Bill and I wrote to each other and sometimes 'phoned. I found it a happy separation. At a distance I could wipe out the painful scenes, and when I thought of him, it was the big guy with the revolver, then the Air Force Cadet, who stirred my emotions. I pictured again our stay in New York, which was responsible for Mike's birth. It was my son I missed most. I put the photos of him on my bedside table. I always had one on me, and I beamed when my friends had the good sense to go into raptures over it: what would they think when they actually saw him! His dimples, his laugh, his eyes now confident, now surprised—I was dying to see them again, and kept pestering Bill to send me new photos. He, on the other hand, was already becoming impatient for my return.

For reasons unknown to me, the preparations for the film dragged on and on. The winter would soon be over, and we had not yet started shooting. My joy at seeing Paris again gradually melted into discomfort. I had lived too long in a hot climate; now I was always cold. Maman heaped blankets and eiderdowns on my bed, topped with a fur coat, but I seldom managed to really warm up. Rationing and the black-market still existed; the Occupation had left painful scars; and as a sequel to its dramas, the purge of former collabora-tors, real or alleged, was raging. It is hard to understand hatred when you have not been living with it. Where was the lighthearted, care-free society of my late teenage years, that Paris which refused to believe in a war? I could not help looking for it, for although the capital had not suffered much damage, it seemed to me a sad place, its inhabitants marked by their suffering. Naturally I was less affected; how lucky I had been to spend those terrible years in America.

The story of *La symphonie pastorale* was set in the Alps, and at last it was time for us to leave for Château-d'Oex in Swit-zerland where the exteriors were to be shot: our company included Pierre Blanchar, the Pastor (minister), Line Noro, his wife, and myself, Jean Desailly and Andrée Clément, Jean Delannoy and Armand Thirard, the chief cameraman.

The day after our arrival, my feet in the snow, my eyes lost in a sightless infinity, I listened to Jean Delannoy, and I acted—*in French!* I felt as if a whole period of my life had just been put between brackets, that I was returning to my profession after an absence of five years. God, how I had suffered with Michael Curtiz, more even than I had thought!

Directed by Delannoy, I found everything easy and straightforward. I appreciated his way of explaining and showing things, precise, without surprises or risks. Each scene had been carefully prepared in advance. I liked his way of working, it was restful and efficient.

I experienced once more the life of a team on location, the evenings in the hotel, the little wood-panelled bars, that time-less atmosphere. I was as happy as I could be, so far away from my son, until I got a 'phone call from Bill in the early hours. Not allowing for the time change, he had woken me up, and in fact greeted me with a gruff 'Morning', although for me it was still night-time. 'When are you coming back?' he demanded bluntly.

'As soon as the film is finished. In a few days we shall finish the exteriors.'

The voice which reached me was the voice of his bad days, sharp and too calm. 'How many days?'

'Eight or ten.'

'And then in the studio?'

'Three to four weeks.'

He exploded. 'Listen, I've had enough of your film and your excuses. I demand that you repay all the money you've had and return home.'

'Pay it back? But, Bill, that's impossible. I'd be sued, and besides we need that money.'

Silence at the other end of the wire.

'Be reasonable, darling, I'm as impatient as you are. I'm missing you both.'

He grunted something like: 'No one would think so.'

'Tell me about Mike,' I said.

'He's all right,' Bill answered drily. 'Growing up, you know. All the same, I'd like you to see him again before I have to teach him to shave.'

This touch of humour seemed to herald a relaxation of tension.

'I'll do everything I possibly can, darling, to get home very soon. I'll have a talk with Jean Delannoy, and ask him to change his working schedule.'

He was not very convinced, nor was I.

'Sort it out with them as you like. But if you're not back here in four weeks, I'll ask for a divorce.'

A divorce! It was the first time he had uttered this word. I couldn't get back to sleep. There was a certain irony about that scene: just at the time when I was thinking of Bill with more and more tenderness.

Next morning—good heavens! Opening my window, I found the sun already very high and a landscape shining with new grass. It was poetic, delightful and completely out of keeping with yesterday's snow, though even that had not been very thick. I looked in consternation at this explosion of spring. 'A nuisance,' Delannoy remarked calmly. 'As you know, Michèle, the weather is one of the aggravating things about our job.'

The idea of confronting Bill with a further delay was most

unpleasant, but it was clearly not the moment to share my conjugal anxieties with Joseph Bercholz, whose imprecations resounded through the hotel rooms, now transformed into production offices. Having come out here in haste, he saw the money for his production melting away at the same speed as the snow.

'Something must be done. We can't stay here till next year! If there's no snow at 4000 feet, let's go up to 5000.'

'There isn't any at 5000 either.'

'Then we'll try 6000.'

This bidding in altitudes raised further difficulties. 'What about the scenery? What are we going to do with the church, built on our shooting site?' It was shining beneath the sun with all its varnished tiles—that sun which is only out when you don't need it.

'Dismantle the church, pack the equipment, and let's go to Zermatt,' ordered an undeterred Bercholz.

'Are you sure there'll be snow there?'

'Get them on the 'phone.'

The assistants returned in triumph: 'There *is* snow there.'

A few hours later we were in the little Swiss rack-train, climbing without haste towards the heights of one of Switzerland's prettiest winter-sports resorts, inaccessible to cars. Half-way there the snow reappeared; Bercholz and Delannoy looked delighted.

The higher we went, the more plentiful was the snow. So I went and sat down by them, having made up my mind to talk to them, to touch their hearts with my danger of divorce, and to suggest tactfully: 'Since we're going to have enough snow, perhaps by changing the order of the scenes ...'

There was a sudden shock, and the train ground to a halt. We were all at the windows. A station? No. We were blocked by drifts. This time there was too much snow. The guard told us serenely: 'The line is cut going up the mountain, we'll back down again.'

'Well, we'll get off here,' decided Bercholz. 'We're only a mile or two from Zermatt, we'll go up there on foot. Wait!' he shouted to the amazed guard. 'We have to unload our baggage.'

All the Swiss were bewildered and clearly doubted our sanity as the operation was carried out. With the equipment on the backs of the cameramen, technicians and cast, our column of Sherpas plunged into the snow like a scene from Frank Capra's *Lost Horizon*, Zermatt becoming our Shangri-La.

At the head of our convoy, guiding it, was Bercholz, a somewhat incongruous sight: in a black suit, with a grey overcoat and a trilby hat, umbrella transformed into alpenstock, he encouraged us in our efforts, with loud voice and grand gestures, up to his knees in snow. After a few hours of walking, exhausting but glorious, we made our entry into Zermatt, under the astonished and mocking eyes of the tourists.

Neither that evening nor on the following days did I dare ask Bercholz and Delannoy to change their work programme. Bill continued to telephone me, and I did not try to explain to him our Zermatt adventure. For an American it would have been incredible, a bad joke; he would have doubted the reality of the production itself and the whole film.

My return to Paris calmed him for the time being, and it was without too many affrays on the 'phone that I came to the end of the film. The Neuilly studio was not heated. The cold was getting me down. I longed for the Californian sun, and counted the days which separated me from my son. And yet—on one of the last mornings I spent in Paris, I crossed the studio courtyard, and stopped to look at a tree, a chestnut. Its trunk was black, its branches were adorned with little tender green leaves carefully unfolding. At this sight, for some reason, my heart melted, and a flash of intuition shot through me like a revelation: I had to return to France for good, my life was here.

'How you've grown!'

These were the first words I said as I took the little man into my arms.

'In six months he's had time to!'

There was no point in picking up Bill's remark. We had

to find a way of life that suited us both and above all would bring us together. If I worked out the time of our understanding, totting up separate weeks and months, it hadn't lasted a year; but it *had* managed to exist, so it must still be possible. The first days that passed made me believe in it. Admittedly I saw little of Bill. I was so 'hungry' for Mike that I spent my days entirely with him. He called me 'Mammy', and I taught him 'Maman', though both were equally sweet to my ear.

But if Mike could listen to me, Bill couldn't. From that first evening, what I already knew had become still clearer to me: the love-romance between us, and that was all it was, had finished. To replace it by a deep affection which could give Mike the father and mother he needed, we were going to have to find in ourselves the necessary qualities of patience and understanding. That was indispensable, and I was determined to try my best. We should have to make mutual concessions, but I was prepared for them. The most important question, it seemed to me, was geographical; and here it was Bill who would have to give some ground. All sentimental reasons aside, I felt it would be hard for me to live permanently anywhere but in France—that was a necessity for me. Here, too, we *ought* to be able to find an arrangement.

After three weeks I had still not been able to talk to Bill about anything. He stopped me either by not being there or by silence. He was playing golf, he was going to meetings, he would only be back in the evening: anything to avoid what he would see as futile arguments. Perhaps he was right, and they would have been. I became cowardly myself, and if we were alone together after putting Mike to bed, I kept quiet too, taking refuge in an artificial tranquillity, which I knew was extremely fragile. Those evenings were saved from heated arguments, but they were fairly dismal. What had we to say to each other? There had been a time when we found so many things to say there weren't enough hours in the day. Now we remained silent, distant, withdrawn into ourselves.

How could we build ourselves a future? We had nothing in common; country, religion, ideas, upbringing, tastes—all

were different. Only love had united us, and its ashes seemed
to me very cold.

How could we tackle the real problems of our life when
my husband showed a complete lack of interest in mine? I
had tried to talk to him about *La symphonie pastorale*, but for
him it was only a 'little film' in a 'small country'.

Then news came which disturbed the false calm of my
Californian life: *La symphonie pastorale* had just been selected
to represent France in the first post-war Cannes Festival. Bercholz and Delannoy insisted that I had to be there, an opinion
which Bill did not share. 'They can do without you—I can't.'

'Bill, it's a matter of professional obligation. I can't shirk
it, I owe it to the producer and to those who had confidence
in me to help them at the film's public launching.'

I refrained from explaining to him the importance surrounding this festival, the first after the black-out of the war.
For him Cannes was not even a village, and the festival was
no more than some country fair.

Why had he become like this? I imagined the event taking
place during our engagement—what enthusiasm he would
have shown then! Oh well, it was no good painfully harking
back to the past. I had to come to terms with today's Bill.
I told him: 'I shan't be long, only a few days, less than a
week ...'

Finally he gave way.

The festival was a whirlpool which caught me up in it. It
was both a film fair and a great cinema circus. Journalists,
stars and starlets, producers, directors, distributors, sellers and
buyers, came and went, met on the Croisette, in the hotels
and corridors, in the Palais du Festival, over cocktails; din-
ners, receptions and gala evenings followed each other in
quick succession. An incessant frenzied motion. Films were
bought and sold and 'packaged'—that is to say, a package
was put together with combinations of finance and stars in
order to set up a production. Dominating these commercial
operations, the festival judges maintained their serenity under
the assaults of press notices and gossip. This made for a few
days of extraordinary intensity, and with some very positive

results. For there were very good films shown, and even though the choice was sometimes controversial, they did provide exposure for different trends in the international cinema.

In the midst of this sound and fury, I did not lose my critical sense, and I found it hard to suppress my laughter on the evening of the showing of *La symphonie pastorale*, when a black limousine of official type, with chauffeur and escort motor-cyclists, stopped outside the steps of the Carlton to drive me to the Palais du Festival little more than a stone's throw away. It reminded me of a famous sequence with Buster Keaton at Monte Carlo, taking a Rolls-Royce for a twenty-yard drive from the Hotel de Paris to the Casino.

The crowd was so dense that I would have been glad of my motor-cyclists to help me climb the steps of the Palais. Jostled, photographed and assailed, I had no time to feel astonished at such great popularity before I was ushered to a seat between Jean Delannoy and Lydia Bercholz. When the hubbub subsided, I was overcome by a stage-fright which constricted my throat. I had left France in such haste I hadn't been able to see the film in its finished version. That my first viewing should be here, in these conditions, seemed to me a tough test.

As the scenes succeeded each other, I gradually forgot myself, spellbound by the beauty and poetry radiating from that white universe. I knew that Gide had liked the film and found it faithful to his ideas, but for me it seemed more than that. Through the magic of the cinema, that art which combines the arts of lighting, pictures and language, the work became transcendent. It had ceased to depend on the words and images, beautiful as they were, and had become reality.

On the screen, the movement was transformed into a fixed image. It set the seal on my death, making it permanent; my face slowly faded out, the word *Fin* appeared. I had no time to gather my wits: when the lights went up, the whole hall rose with one movement, turned towards us, and applauded.

To experience that moment was a great joy. The evening finished in a kind of intoxication, the wine of success. How

I would have loved to have a proud husband's arm round my shoulder.

The next day I told Delannoy and Bercholz I would be leaving.

'Oh no, Michèle, you can't. We've heard some rumours in the corridors: you might be awarded a prize.'

The few days which followed passed in a curious atmosphere of tension, alternating between hope and resignation. At last the results were announced: Golden Palm: *La symphonie pastorale*. Best actor of the year: Ray Milland in *The Lost Weekend*. Best actress of the year: Michèle Morgan in *La symphonie pastorale*. I was also awarded a *Victoire* (the winner received a statuette representing the Victory of Samothrace) for the most popular French actress.

My country was heaping honours on me. Success was wonderful. I didn't feel at all haughty about it—I admitted my pleasure and, after the effort, appreciated the reward.

So ended *La symphonie pastorale*. Not quite, though; it was still to have, as they say, important repercussions on my life.

This time my absence had only lasted ten days, and I found Bill full of smiles; the news of my success had preceded me. On the plane's arrival we again presented the perfect image of a happily married couple. The film journals had devoted their front pages to me, the national press had echoed them, and I had been asked to hand Ray Milland his French 'Oscar' at a party in the French Consulate at Los Angeles. All of which was pleasing to Bill.

Curiously enough, my success in *La symphonie pastorale* was considered in Hollywood rather as the success of an American star in France. Press cuttings and invitations piled up. Very opportunely Bill advised me: 'Oughtn't you to take advantage of this interest to try and make a new breakthrough here?'

I had been thinking of it a great deal, in case that might be the solution: alternate films here and over there.

Once more we were talking to each other. Bill asked me questions about this little European film which was having such a good press in the United States. 'Why don't I get busy placing it in America?'

'Sure—that's an excellent idea. I'll put you in touch with Joseph Bercholz. But you'll convince him better if you meet him in the flesh. We could have a little jaunt to Paris.'

Had I pushed my pawn too far? Bill didn't reject the idea. Better still, he seemed to be considering it seriously. 'Obviously on the spot it would be easier. I'll make some approaches here to start off with, to see what I can do.'

What could he do? I realised that I no longer knew anything of his activities. He wasn't in any films yet he was always at the studios, and here he was, offering to help with film importing. He had stopped singing and taking vocal lessons. Why that sacrifice, which must have cost him a lot? I could still hear him telling me about the position he hoped to achieve in the singing world. So what were his new ambitions? I had complained that he didn't ask me questions about myself, but had I asked him enough about himself?

That day I stopped my car outside a big piano firm. When Bill came home that evening, he stood riveted by the sight of the baby grand which had appeared in our living-room. Then he turned towards me. 'You've rented it?'

'No, my darling. It's a present so that you can work on your voice.'

He went pale, and we looked at each other. I told him he must resume his exercises, that he had a special talent; I so much wanted to convince him, I ended by insisting he would succeed. 'I have confidence in you, my darling.'

He embraced me warmly. I remained there with my head against his cheek, and could not help feeling a little melancholy. I sensed that I had not really found my old place in his arms.

'Thanks a million, darling. I'll start again tomorrow.'

The piano remained closed the next day. It was never opened.

Were we going to make that trip to France? Bill spoke no more about his project, and I was offered a part in *The Chase*, a gangster film set partly in a prison, with a little-known director, Arthur Ripley.

I accepted without many illusions. The film left me with some useful dollars, no memories, and the sad conviction that I was never going to find myself over here. The American cinema was producing some first-rate films, but unfortunately I didn't seem to meet up with them.

Just then, however, I was offered a new experience, a film in London: Alexander Korda wanted me for *The Fallen Idol*, to be directed by Carol Reed. The film was based on a short story by Graham Greene, and concerned a small boy, a diplomat's son, who, while his parents are away, makes friends with the butler. The butler is suspected of killing his wife, and in trying to help him, the boy only succeeds in further incriminating him. I was to play the other woman in the butler's life, a very sympathetic part.

Adult actors and actresses are inclined to fight shy of a film with a child playing a big part; inevitably the child will steal the show. But it was not this which made me hesitate before accepting. Bill and I seemed at the moment to be living in something approaching harmony. We kept clear of dangerous subjects, and we could even enjoy being together. I knew this state of affairs might not last long, and was worried at the prospect of going away again, in case it led to more discord. Still, I couldn't stay here for ever.

To my surprise, Bill said: 'You ought to accept. Carol Reed is a very good director, extremely talented. I'll gladly come with you to London. Did you know my family was descended from Cromwell? Anyhow it was my mother's maiden name. So it will be fun to return to my ancestral haunts.'

Unexpected but pleasant. 'Let's take advantage of it to go to Paris,' I suggested. 'We might even start there.'

He agreed, on one condition: in our absence Mike should be entrusted to his mother. With her the boy was happy and secure.

I don't know how Bill imagined his French in-laws, but they must have been quite a surprise to him. The Roussels, in their Neuilly flat, were perhaps rather unusual, I could see, by my own acquired American standards. Introducing my American husband to them was a bit like a G.I. taking his French bride home and introducing her to his folks in the Mid-West.

Papa, still obsessed by politics, delighted to be able to demonstrate to us the excellence of his English, set about explaining to Bill how President Roosevelt had let himself be taken for a ride at Yalta by Stalin. My brother Paul, shouting so as to drown the chords of Pierre furiously scraping his guitar, interrupted my father's lecture to launch into a virulent diatribe against Methodism as a religion compared to the one true Catholic Church. In a corner of the room my sister Hélène, as mad on the theatre as I had been on the cinema, was reciting a poem *sotto voce*. It was the moment chosen by Berthe, the half-deaf maid, to yell, 'Dinner is served' before departing for her kitchen with her crab-like gait, paying no attention to anyone. Bill and I were overcome by uncontrollable laughter.

When she placed us at table. Maman murmured to me happily: 'You made a good choice, darling. He's a very good-looking boy, your American husband, nice fair hair and blue eyes—like your father, before he lost his hair.'

My American husband was certainly at his most charming and, like me five years before, the whole family succumbed to so much charm and good nature. That evening at my parents' was a wonderful moment for me. I was already convinced I had found the real Bill once more, that everything would be possible again. I felt very grateful to him. But an hour later, back in the George V Hotel, he suddenly found the accommodation 'disgusting', adding that it was typical of France, 'depressing'.

The charm number was over. How could I have fallen for it? After inveighing against the heat—it was August and Paris was certainly very hot—and against this country which had no iced water in its rooms, he dashed under the shower, soaped himself, turned the mixer, and—disaster—not a drop of water.

He burst naked into my bedroom, cursing and pointing at the 'phone with an accusing finger. I was informed by reception that the water had just been cut off for urgent repairs to be made. I ordered two bottles of Evian to rinse off Bill in his froth of fury and soap; but it took half an hour to reach us. His conclusion was that you couldn't trust such a disorganised country.

The sequel, I fear, only confirmed his judgment. We were woken at six, the porter having made a mistake: there were three Marshalls in the hotel. When Bill opened the door, his shoes had disappeared. Our breakfast seemed uneatable to him, and the milk was watery. As to the food generally, he said it was too heavy and he couldn't digest it. I didn't know whether to laugh or cry, so I laughed, but not in front of him. I enjoyed the funny side with Joseph Bercholz, who was ready to give him the rights in *La symphonie pastorale* for the United States. That at least would be one success Bill could chalk up on his first visit to France.

Old England, cradle of his mother's family, seemed more civilised to him, if only for its breakfasts! We spent ten days there without any trouble. He saw the sights while I was involved with preparations for the film.

The evening before Bill was to sail on the *Queen Mary*, as we were entering the Savoy bar, I heard someone calling 'Michèle!' I turned round: it was Micheline Presle!

We kissed joyfully. We hadn't seen each other since *Grand-hotel* in '40. I introduced her to Bill. Accompanied by the producer Paul Graetz, she was going to Hollywood; after her sucess in *Diable au corps*, Fox had signed a very handsome contract with her.

'When are you leaving?'

'Tomorrow.'

'Like Bill. You'll be travelling together.'

She was really a very beautiful woman. When she left us, I remarked on the fact to Bill, but it turned out he had noticed it himself.

Again I was alone, and not sorry about it. I almost considered this picture as a rest-cure. Filming with the British was very different from working with the Americans or the French. The atmosphere on the set here was quiet, discreet, polite, with never a word in anger; and there were breaks for tea at eleven and five. But the studios were outside London, and getting there took time. Adding this to the time for making-up and taking the make-up off, it made a long working day. I left the Savoy early, and returned just in time to have dinner in my room, after which I was almost ready for bed. Bill was still at sea, and I postponed indefinitely any attempt to take stock of my marriage. The first week passed. I used the weekend to go back to Paris and see my family and friends.

The film was two days behind schedule. Would Bill object; should we have more telephone arguments as with *La symphonie pastorale*?

Not just yet, it seemed. For he hadn't called me at all, although he should certainly have been back in Hollywood. I 'phoned home. His mother sounded a little embarrassed. 'No, Michèle, he's not here.'

'He's back, though?'

'Not yet.'

'But he's given you all the news?'

'Of course, and he'll be here at the end of the week. He had to make a trip up country on business. Like to talk to Mike?'

How marvellous to hear that little voice, saying: 'When are you coming back, Mammy?'

'Soon, darling, directly the film is finished. Maman is working, and she thinks of you lots and lots.'

I thought of Bill, too. What did his delay mean? I would have understood if he had stayed in New York for we had friends there. Or he might equally well be doing something about *La symphonie pastorale*. But then why didn't he 'phone me? You can do that from anywhere.

It was now nearly a fortnight since I had heard from him. I called several times, and each time his mother sounded more and more ill at ease—was she hiding something from me? And if so, why? An accident? She would have *had* to tell me that. I needed to be reassured, and also to talk to him about a new project, *Fabiola*, a Franco-Italian co-production directed by Alessandro Blasetti who had just achieved a big success with *Quattri passi fra le nuvole* (*Four Steps in the Clouds*).

I didn't want to accept without consulting Bill. According to my calculations, I could hope for two clear months with Mike at home between the end of *The Fallen Idol* and the time *Fabiola* was likely to start. But if this didn't work out, I decided not to sign without an assurance from Bill that he would bring my son to Europe. I delayed my answer, but the Italians were impatient, and their telephone calls became more and more pressing. I became nervy and slept badly. In the end I decided to sign the contract.

Next morning the chambermaid bringing my breakfast opened the curtains to reveal a clear blue sky. As I drank my tea, I skimmed rapidly through the paper, lingered a moment or two over the headlines, and like all actors and actresses wherever they are staying, looked for the show-business page. There I found an astonishing photograph: a smiling Micheline and Bill, side by side, leaning against the rail on the main deck of the *Queen Mary*. The would-be playful caption read: 'The producer—a new rôle for Bill Marshall. He gives English lessons to the delightful actress Micheline Presle on the *Queen Mary*.'

Curiously enough, I felt reassured. As it happened, he 'phoned the same day and apologised for his silence, without much attempt at explanation, said he had been in New York, and had stayed there longer than he expected. I didn't mention the photograph, he approved of my signing for *Fabiola*, and after some not very flowing conversation, he gave me Mike, whom I was now dying to see again.

Unfortunately Carol Reed, an excellent actor's director, a skilful and meticulous technician, was ready to take his time—and mine! The shooting dragged on, and soon I should have no more than a month at home as doting mother, then only three weeks, then only a fortnight. There was nothing to be done about it. I couldn't go back to Hollywood; I couldn't see my son.

For the first time, Bill did his best to calm me. He assured me he would come to Paris with Mike in the middle or at the end of the shooting of *Fabiola*, in three months, or four at most (not all directors were like Carol Reed).

I didn't cherish too many illusions about this very unusual gentleness. In Hollywood, Bill was seen a lot with Micheline Presle, echoes of all sorts had reached London, newspaper reports, gossip columns . . .

I didn't ask many questions about it. I remained more or less indifferent. Only I didn't want Bill to consider me a complete idiot, so I talked about it to him just before leaving for Rome.

He burst out laughing, a good spontaneous laugh, then became very serious, and asked in a tone of great solemnity: 'You remember we swore to each other we would confess everything the day either of us was about to succumb?'

An odd choice of word. Our oath now seemed a bit ridiculous to me, but still . . . 'I remember,' I said.

'Well, that's still binding. If I had something to tell you, I'd tell you. And don't you ever forget, either.'

I believed him, and I didn't forget.

In Rome I made a superstar's entrance. The press was waiting
for me at the Castello Sant-Angelo, and the Italian press is
really something: turbulent, tumultuous, totally indiscreet.
They were already headlining: 'La Morgan, after long stay
in United States, to make a film in Rome'. 'Blind heroine
of *Symphonie pastorale* to become *Fabiola*, Christian girl
devoured by lions'.

Angelo, our producer, certainly had a strong sense of publicity. He had established his office at the top of the 320 steps
of the Castello (with no lift); and two planes were tracing
my name, which dispersed in smoke over the blue of the
Roman sky. It slightly suggested a detergent advertisement,
but was rather pretty all the same.

'Signora, dica—what are American men like?'

'Signora Morgan, what do you think of Italian males?'

'Signora, e lei felice de essere a Roma?—Are you happy
to be in Rome?'

Dark-haired, dark-eyed, a flurry of hands, gestures and
cameras, their Latin effervescence made me giddy.

'E il suo filio—and your son, where is he? Will you have
him brought over? When?'

'Soon, I hope.'

'E il suo marito?—They say you're getting a divorce.'

'Really? Well, you know, he hasn't said anything about
it to me yet. I'm going to join him in Los Angeles immediately after the shooting of *Fabiola*.'

They stuck to their guns. 'He's seen a lot with your
compatriot, la Signora Presle. What do you think about
that?'

'Micheline is a friend of mine. They travelled together on

the *Queen Mary*. Do you think that's a good enough reason for a divorce?'

I tried in vain to talk about my part in *Fabiola*, but really they hadn't come for that.

A bit further on, slightly away from the noisy jostling crowd, I noticed my friend Michel Simon, chatting with Louis Salou, Gino Cervi, Massimo Girotti and Henri Vidal. It was impossible to go and join them. The journalists would not release me.

Henri Vidal, who, as I had heard in London, was to play opposite me, was the animated young man who had caught my eye in the salons of Germaine Lecomte in Paris, and whom I had glimpsed even more fleetingly on the steps of the Palais du Festival in Cannes. 'He's very attractive, you'll see,' Edwige Feuillère had warned me with a laugh, 'and he'll try to seduce you.' Olga Horstig had been even more concerned to put me on my guard: 'Look out, he's a play-boy—all the women fall into his arms!' I merely smiled, and was continuing to do so; at least this eventuality would not be one of my headaches. Bill was a difficult husband, but I had never felt like deceiving him. As to him, his flirtation with Micheline, which I really couldn't ignore any longer, seemed to me without danger, and after all, why shouldn't it be public? I thought it sensible to close my eyes and ears; so Bill for me was still a firm and faithful husband.

I looked at Henri Vidal from a distance: a handsome chap, healthy and full of *joie-de-vivre*, but certainly not a man to break up my life.

Blasetti realised I was in difficulties, and charging through the crowd like a bull, carved out a path for me. 'I must introduce you to your partner, Henri Vidal!' We were close to each other, and for some reason, to my confusion, I felt myself blushing. The heat and the crowd, no doubt; there couldn't be any other explanation.

'Ah! To be in a film with you,' he said, raising his glass with a superb gesture. 'It's the dream of my life!'

A movement in the crowd, and swish, his port was spreading over the taffeta of my turquoise blue dress! Blasetti,

Michel Simon and I burst out laughing, and our laughter only increased at the sight of Henri's confusion. He snatched up a towel from a passing waiter, bent down, sponged my dress, and apologised for his clumsiness, repeating: 'It's the excitement . . . I was so happy!' There was a rush of photographers: 'Stay like that, Signor! Per favor!' There were flashes galore. 'At the knees of la Signora Morgan! Grazie . . . grazie . . .'

That first encounter had really no connection with the romantic description given later in the popular press: 'Half naked, handsome as a god, Henri Vidal stepped forward towards a Michèle trembling with emotion in her patrician woman's peplum.' The incident did, however, place our meeting under the sign of laughter, and that was much more important. For years now I had not laughed with Bill, or very seldom.

Of course, the next day, and the days after, the papers and magazines published from all angles the photograph of Henri Vidal at my feet. Here we were, a film-star couple: 'Henri falls on his knees before Michèle!' and other stupid captions along the same lines. It was idiotic and irritating, and might be worse than that. If Bill read this kind of news, how would a morbidly jealous man like him react? He would consider a flirtation with Henri Vidal different and much more serious than his escapade, if it was really that, with Micheline.

I loved Rome, first of all for its luminous character—a sun-bleached city—then for its life and movement. I was staying at the Hotel Hassier, at the top of the steps overlooking la Piazza di Spagna, rich with colour, its flower-sellers sheltering under large red, yellow and green umbrellas. The view from my room was very beautiful. The Pincio was only a step away, and I went for walks beneath its umbrella pines with Aunt Yvonne: from there, as from a balcony, you discover la Piazza di Venezia, which was the forum of Mussolini's Italy.

What was Aunt Yvonne doing here? She had accompanied me. I was afraid of the loneliness I had known during *The Chase*, or anyhow that was the excuse I gave myself. In fact it was the fear of 'scenes' with Bill on the 'phone which left me so demoralised. At least I should have someone to talk to about them.

The shooting went off without trouble, quickly and well. Already four weeks had passed. The atmosphere was excellent in its two aspects: *tragediente* during the scenes of love, violence and despair, *comediente* with Blasetti, dressed like a 1925 Hollywood director, in riding breeches and boots, with a recalcitrant lock falling over his brow, his black eyes full of animation, his methods paradoxical to the point of absurdity. He would go into fits of Homeric fury, yelling for silence, and when he had obtained it, inveighing with all his considerable vocal powers against the wretched camera-man who dared sneeze up there on the steps; then urbanely coming to whisper in my ear some points to remember. He was more eccentric than the Roussel family put together: solemnly sticking his eye in the microphone to frame the movements of his 2000 extras, he then gave them orders through his viewfinder. This did not stop him declaring, confronted by the jokes and tricks of the effervescent Henri, that 'the French will never be serious'.

In the evening, we would all go off together for dinner. At the back of courtyards, beneath vines, we would sit at long tables more or less at random, but Henri and I always found ourselves next to each other. We had lamb *à la Romaine* still roasting on a spit, and tagliatelli, which you rolled round your fork; the chianti flowed, light and treacherous, like the love which was gently growing between us without my noticing.

How deceitful was that starry sky of Italy, that danger I did not see coming. Between Henri and me everything was so natural and simple, nothing seemed too important. One flirted a bit, but that was only for the duration of the film, with a burst of laughter or a special look. How could anyone take seriously those nights in which mandolins joyfully thrummed their tarantellas, *o Sole Mio* and *Santa Lucia*? During the day the artificial and the authentic blended. Orange and eucalyptus trees and honeysuckle had been replanted: superb gardens lay round reconstructed Roman villas on the immense sets of Cinecitta (the Cinema City, a vast complex of studios near Rome created by Mussolini) in front of a mock-up of the Seven Hills. You could lose yourself in it all the more when you were wanting to.

One afternoon the atmosphere was very serious. The scene Blasetti was explaining to us was particularly violent: Fabiola gets brutally slapped by her gladiator.

Blasetti wanted the real thing, and Henri resigned himself to producing it. Once, twice, three, four, five times. My cheek was swelling visibly.

After each slap, our director fiercely ordered another.

His terseness brooked no repartee; we started again. Henri was very distressed. After the seventeenth slap he said: 'Michèle, I'm terribly sorry. Have I hurt you?'

'Oh no, don't bother about it. Just hit me—as he wants you to.'

'Fabiola, 307, take 18.'

If only this could be the right one!

The slap came, fierce, sharp, violent. I staggered. My cheek was on fire, my nose smarted, tears came to my eyes.

'Cut! That's it! Excellent, bravo—thank you, Michèle, thanks, Henri.'

At last we had satisfied him. We were exhausted.

'Michèle, to beg your forgiveness—I invite you to dinner this evening.'

For the first time we dined alone together, at a little *trattoria*. When we left it about eleven, the air was heavy with a storm grumbling in the sky, and then the rain came pelting down. We dashed for Henri's little Lancia, and took refuge there, out of breath and soaked. He put out his hand towards the ignition key, but did not turn it. The rain drummed on the metal of the roof, slapped heavily against the windows, streamed over the windscreen. The world all round us was drowned, and we were isolated. It was warm. Damp steam rose from the ground. We stayed close to each other in silence. Time had ceased to exist, and suddenly I found myself against Henri's chest, his lips resting on mine . . .

After this nothing would be the same. It was a moment which changed everything, threw everything into confusion. I was aware of it, but didn't care.

Alone in my room I stayed there dreamily, incapable of taking off my make-up or undressing. My window was open and the pink light of my bedside lamp made the night bluer. It drew me out and I went onto my balcony; muffled sounds were rising from Rome. I leaned against the stone balustrade; bent sideways, towards the façade of Henri's hotel right next to mine, I could see nothing, only a rectangle of light, three floors lower. Was that his window? Was he asking himself questions as I was, or was he already asleep? Was he happy like me? He had the right to be. I didn't.

By now it was no longer a flirtation. I knew it was more serious, but didn't want to admit that to myself.

I found the lucidity of mind one often has on sleepless nights. Stretched out on my bed, I thought things over. Nothing irretrievable had passed between Henri and me, only a long kiss, and that could easily be forgotten. Should I call Bill to my rescue, to come and protect me from myself? If that was to work, he had to love me very much and I had to love him still.

The Roman night had been freshened and lightened by the storm. I decided our marriage was on trial. If we had been capable of facing each other at the precise moment when we needed to be together, I could indeed have appealed to him for help; but I knew that was not the case. Bill was the kind of man who saw his wife chiefly as a mother. Anyhow it was no good spending the night reasoning about what I ought to have done and hadn't, what I should have been and wasn't. The facts were obvious, and I recognised that reason couldn't touch me because I was no longer a free agent. I was madly in love.

So what was I to do? I refused to live a lie. Bill must know the truth. He didn't need to remind me of my vow; I had always meant to keep it, and now more than ever.

Far from calming me, this resolve served only to make me more wide awake. How would Bill react? My brain raced ahead, right through all the stages. I knew practically nothing about the American laws concerning divorce. Already this was the only solution possible, and I let my thoughts drift towards a future which, by and large, was not at all disagreeable. It would certainly be a little difficult for Bill to come to France to see his son; when Mike was older, he would be able to go and stay in America sometimes. I did not doubt for a moment that I should be given custody, and I made resolutions that I would be understanding towards Bill, he could see Mike as much as he wanted and spend his holidays with him. I made plans. I would take a biggish flat, with a room for the little boy and one for the nurse. Impatient to see him again in August, I rejoiced at the thought that he would not be leaving again. We should stay together, he and I. Before that I should have had a talk, several talks, with his father and everything would be clear-cut . . .

I must have dropped off to sleep. In the morning, directly I woke, I eagerly called Bill. 'I need to see you . . . I . . .'

He broke in casually: 'As it happens, I'm flying to Paris tomorrow.'

'You'll have to come to Rome. I must talk with you. I've got something special to say.'

His voice became sarcastic. 'To do with Henri Vidal? I've seen your pictures in the press.'

It was less easy than I had imagined during the night. 'That was nothing to do with me. The photos were a publicity thing, like yours with Micheline.' (I couldn't have chosen a worse example.) 'The truth is different. I . . . I'm afraid, well, I think . . . that we're in love.'.

'O.K. I'll come.'

That was all. I didn't even have a chance to ask him for news of Mike. He had hung up.

It was done, and I felt a little better but just as uneasy. His calm, his manner of being apparently in full control, worried me. I thought I would have preferred one of his rages. But perhaps he too had discovered he was in love, with Micheline, and hadn't the courage to tell me first; men are often more cowardly over this sort of thing than women. Anyhow, I could only wait and see what happened.

A week passed, and Bill had still not come. I called our house, and heard he was in Paris. I 'phoned Paris. He would come a bit later, he assured me in a colourless tone, but he was very busy trying to obtain the rights to *Fabiola* for

America. The success of his efforts over *La symphonie pastorale* had given him an incentive to try with other films.

Another week, and he still hadn't shown up. I was surprised, rather annoyed, and couldn't understand why he was delaying. This unexpected indifference was perhaps the best of answers, though, to the question which was concerning me so much: did he still love me? Unless he wanted me to go to the limits of what was not yet an affair and might never become one? That would be too detached to be true.

I made hundreds of suppositions and imagined all sorts of reasons, everything except the truth. Henri and I got into the habit of walking along the deserted beach of Ostia, miles of sand bordered by long grass in which we could lie in close embrace. One Saturday I was very surprised to see two men walking in our direction. 'Look, there are people over there. I hope to God they don't come here. Suppose they're photographers!'

'Don't worry, they're out shooting, I expect—they're staying in the grass. They're too far away so they can't recognise us.'

The next day the 'sportsmen' were there again. What game could they be tracking here? Our innocence was such that we found nothing abnormal in the sight of their using binoculars but never firing a shot. I never dreamed that these sportsmen were private detectives and I was the game. I was soon to find out that I had been left my liberty in the hope that I should abuse it. I was quite incapable of imagining so tortuous a strategy.

From these walks we returned happy though unsatisfied, catching each other's eyes, convinced we were exercising the greatest discretion, not even noticing the affectionate glances of Michel Simon. How could we ignore the fact that we loved each other? We saw scarcely anything of the rest of the company.

A few years ago, the Italian guides showing tourists round Rome, when they reached the Piazza di Spagna, would point out our two windows, tell the tourists about our idyll, and throw in a quotation from the balcony scene in *Romeo and Juliet*.

One night Henri had come to my room. 'So as not to compromise you,' he said, 'I'll come in by the window, so leave it open.'

What woman would not have been charmed by these romantic suggestions, very much in his style! And soon after midnight anyone looking up that way could have seen a man come out of a window on the fourth floor of the Hôtel de la Ville, climb along the front, from ledge to balcony, right to the sixth floor of the hotel Hassler, and disappear into a room.

At 2 a.m. we heard knocking at my door.

'What is it? Who's there?'

In the best Feydeau tradition I heard Bill's voice. 'Open up! It's me.'

Henri grabbed his clothes, dashed for the window, and to gain time, instead of going down by the balcony ledge, jumped from that directly on to the balcony on the floor below. He landed badly, and there was a terrific noise, lights went on, voices were heard. Was he hurt? He might well be.

Bill knocked louder at my door. I leaned out of the window and thought I could see Henri's figure hobbling along, but couldn't be sure. With increased anxiety I opened the door.

Never had Bill seemed to me so tall as framed in that doorway with fury in his eyes, his teeth clenched. He came in, almost pushing me in front of him, and there was a revolver in his hand. Was it the one from our first meeting? I don't know why, but I had no fears he would use it, that this bedroom scene would turn into a black comedy; I felt sure we should merely descend into farce. He looked round him suspiciously.

The dialogue was typical.

'I was asleep.'

'With that noise?'

'It woke me up.'

He didn't dare to open the bathroom door, and refrained from listening at wardrobes and curtains. So in a nonchalant manner I opened them for him.

We said everything a man and woman in our situation are likely to say to each other. Bill's aggressiveness had suddenly subsided, but he kept repeating: 'If you hadn't come to Europe, nothing would have happened. We were getting on so well in America.'

Did he believe it? Had he forgotten our scenes? I didn't know whether he was really chagrined, angry or jealous, how much was acting and how much sincere feeling. But it soon became clear that he had initiated a contest between us, and that the stake was our son. Even if I didn't know what Bill's feelings were towards me, I realised that he wanted custody of Mike.

He tried to make me admit my guilt until morning. Unafraid of appearing ridiculous, he became very melodramatic: I was the adulterous woman who had terms imposed on her. At the time, as I have said, I knew nothing about American laws, and I still had a certain confidence in Bill. I did not believe he would deprive a child of its mother, and to avoid losing my son, I was ready to accept anything. How was I to know that in such a case either parent may be capable of anything to get possession of the child they adore, the child they have conceived together?

Bill left later that morning. In a few minutes his plane would be taking off. I had accompanied him to the airport, pursued by the photographers. For them his visit gave scope for new articles on our happy marriage—they were to be the last of such articles. We had decided to divorce. I was feeling a little calmer, and partly reassured, as I watched the plane disappear.

It had been an exhausting night. Towards morning we had reached an agreement, a sort of formula with terms dictated by Bill. They seemed fairly vague to me: it was a matter of sharing property, committing myself to letting Bill bring up Mike as a good American, with references to privileges and rights of access for me. I was worried about the importance he attributed to his private detectives' report, proving what he called my guilty relations with Henri. According to him their testimony would ensure the divorce being in his favour. I did not know that the law would consider them only as presumptions of proof and that they wouldn't stand up as documents for a court. I had continued to feel some confidence in my husband, convinced he would see 'fair play'. I had to believe in his honesty over this—it was the only guarantee of my future with Mike, a future far less rosy than I had pictured it in my optimistic reveries of a few days before.

Bill's last words were: 'So long. In three weeks I'll meet you in Paris with the boy.' They were spoken in front of the journalists, and definitely sounded reassuring.

During the last days of my work in Rome, Henri and I kept up appearances. The popular press wasn't as virulent at that time as they became later, but both in France and in Italy many of the papers were sufficiently unscrupulous, and on the look-out for private-life scoops, to justify our taking plenty of precautions.

Paris on the eve of the Quatorze juillet was decked with flags. There were barriers put up for next day's parade, and the city had the cheerfulness of a country fair.

I had already been there a fortnight for the shooting, under Jean Delannoy's direction of *Aux yeux du souvenir*, with Jean Marais and Jean Chevetti partnered.

After the vast mechanics of Blasetti's film, with hundreds of extras continually in movement amidst rocks blazing in the sun, after all the noise and shouting, to be in a film directed by Delannoy was restful; and the intimacy of this story of love between an air-hostess (me) and an airline pilot (Jean Marais) couldn't have suited me better.

Henri was still in Rome, with *Fabiola* not yet finished. The scenes in the arenas, the positioning of the wild beasts, the crowd movements, had taken longer than was foreseen. Every week he hoped to come back the week after, but had to be content, when not shooting, to join me for twenty-four hours; the rest of the time we wrote each other letters as mad as our love. Almost directly I had slipped one into the post-box, I was starting on another.

At last Henri told me he had a long weekend of freedom coming up. I was to meet him at Orly and we would take refuge in a flat belonging to one of his friends, on the seventh floor of a block in the Champs-Elysées. At dawn, indifferent to the tramp of troops massing for the parade, we were asleep. I was the first to wake up. I shook Henri. 'Wake up, there's someone here . . .'

'Who's there?' shouted Henri, surfacing with difficulty.

'The police superintendent. Open up in the name of the law!'

'It's a joke,' Henri assured me. 'Some friend playing a trick.'

Behind the door, the authoritarian voice began talking about fetching a locksmith.

'No, no,' protested Henri, 'I'm coming.'

Draped, Roman fashion, in a blanket snatched up in passing, he opened the door to the superintendent of police of the 8th *arrondissement*, who came in, followed by his clerk and a moustached usher. 'Madame, this is a certified statement of adultery. Your name, please, and yours, monsieur,' the superintendent demanded, displaying his tricolor sash, just as the Foreign Legion band blared forth.

Hastily wrapped in a sheet, I caught Henri's eye, and we both burst into slightly hysterical laughter under the reproving eyes of the representatives of the law who saw nothing to laugh at; and they were right.

When this nervous hilarity had passed, I realised that I had just been trapped by Bill. He had assured me of a divorce by agreement. The formal document, a certified statement of adultery, completely changed the situation. Why hadn't I had a similar document attested against him? Everything would have been different then, but I would never have thought of such a thing. I realised I had just lost the match; I was disarmed. But I didn't know what that was going to mean for me.

In the whole of this painful affair, which was to last for years, Bill kept only one of his promises: he did come to Paris, with Mike, Mrs Marshall and a nurse.

We installed ourselves at La Malmaison in a pleasant villa I had rented from Roger Hubert, the chief cameraman from *La loi du nord*.

I had not seen my little boy for a year. It was wonderful to feel his arms round my neck, his cheek rubbing against mine.

'Mammy, why haven't you come back home?' he asked me a little later.

'I was working, darling.'

In a shrill, imperious little voice he objected: 'You weren't working. You were making a film.'

'But it's the same thing. Maman's job is to play parts in films.'

'You see,' he triumphed, 'you were playing!'

A suspicion crossed my mind: what did Bill tell our son while I was not there? I chased away this ugly thought, and explained to Mike what my work consisted of. 'Papa goes away, too. He goes to work for you as well.'

Mike was very surprised when I introduced him to his grandparents, and his very big blue eyes contemplated in astonishment this lady and gentleman, the lady being, as I explained, his second Granny, only it was very complicated. But he accepted with good grace the admiration of Papa and Maman. It must be admitted that at that age he was particularly good-looking!

I did not see as much of my son as I had hoped. His life, very carefully regulated by his grandmother and his nurse, had a timetable very hard to fit in with the one imposed on me by the shooting of *Aux yeux du souvenir*. When I got back in the evening, I noiselessly opened the door of his room and looked at him sleeping, but dared not kiss him; I hardly even dared breathe, for fear of waking him. The nurse had declared that a child must not be woken during his first sleep as it might have traumatic effects. This woman was arrogant and uncompromising and I immediately realised that in her eyes I represented the artistic and therefore negligent mother. What did she know of my quarrels with my husband? Certainly more than she should have done. She had a supercilious way of staring at me and taking Mike by the hand. 'Come along, it's time for your bath.' Or for his meal, or to go to bed, time for anything but me. It was very frustrating for me.

Bill found her perfect. His mother, who had different ideas

from her son, was more discriminating. She made few judgments anyhow, and during that difficult period she showed great tact, moderation and even friendship towards me. Being both very reserved, we only exchanged general remarks; but we sometimes caught each other's eye in understanding. I had been only twenty-two when she opened her door to me, and for three years she had been my only family. I remained fond of her. I knew she was upset at the failure of her son's marriage; that she worried about Mike despite the pleasure she felt in keeping him near her. I was well aware that what would have made her happy was for me to return to Hollywood and have everything wiped out.

That was not what happened.

A real battle started with Bill over the drawing up of a form of agreement. Armed with the certificate of adultery and relying, too, on the statement he had made me sign in Rome, he offered me extremely harsh conditions which Mr Izard, my counsel, called inhuman: he would ensure the care of the child, authorising me to see him in school holidays, on Thursdays and on certain weekends. This was equivalent to separating me from Mike. With Bill living in America, how could I 'profit' by these conditions, which would be very hard to accept even in the same country? I told Bill this, and he replied with a malice which disgusted me: 'Come and live in California, and you'll see your son every day.'

'In Rome you promised me we could find an arrangement on a basis of six months each.'

'Everything has changed since then.'

Obviously, because in Rome he didn't have the certificate of adultery.

'Besides, I'm bound to think of Mike's health. He's delicate, not very strong.'

Before I could object, he was continuing imperturbably: 'It's a bad thing to expose him to the shock of two such opposite climates. France just can't give him the food he needs. Your solution is absurd. What about his schooling and his future?'

'But he's only four. At his age the most important thing is not to deprive him of his mother.'

'You should have thought of that before,' he said scathingly.

I protested at his hypocrisy. 'You know very well that you're the one who deceived me. I respected your promise, but you didn't. Did you call me up the day you met Micheline.'

'No. Because there's nothing between us.'

'Tell that to the marines. Everybody knows about it.'

'Prove it. As regards you and Vidal I've done so.'

'Bill, be understanding. Let's adopt this arrangement until he's seven. I'm not an alcoholic nor a drug addict, and my work will let me give him everything he needs. I lead a balanced, respectable life and I can perfectly well bring him up.'

'All you have to do is convince the jury.'

'All right, we'll go to court. No court will be ready to separate a child of four from his mother.'

'The hearing will take place near my home, in California. Don't forget you have an American passport, that we were married in my country, under its laws, that my son is a citizen of it. In our state, juries aren't very favourably disposed towards an adulterous woman.' (It would have been laughable had the stake not been Mike; obviously he was already addressing the court in his mind.) 'I shall tell them that I want my son to be brought up according to our traditions, that I want to make him into an American!'

My lawyer was continually warning me: 'That certificate of adultery has really put you in the soup. It's absolutely essential we get agreement to have your divorce decreed by the French courts for they will do better by us. Especially if we can present an advance agreement by both parties. For my part I will try to obtain the best possible terms from my colleague, and you should try to do the same with your husband.'

From these consultations with Mr Izard and the discussions with Bill, I came out exhausted; and whenever I could, I took refuge with Henri. I hardly saw him except to cry on his shoulder. Like all women in love, I thought: how lucky I am to have *him*! But he was discreet and patient, could even be self-effacing, against the grain of his character—but then he loved me.

The moment when Mike was to return to California was approaching and there had to be some solution before he left. Bill had modified his attitude. He seemed to have become considerate, even understanding. He fixed a date with me in a little restaurant near the rue Francœur, where I was shooting *Aux yeux du souvenir*. There, deploying all his charm, he declared that he felt nothing but goodwill towards me: when I said to him, 'Why must we hurt each other? Let's keep our affection intact through love for our son,' he assured me that he would never use against me the form he wanted me to sign. 'This compromise is only a precaution. How could you think I would stop our son from seeing his Mammy? You can and you must have confidence in me.'

'He'll come here?' I pressed him.

'Of course. Be reasonable, you've no other solution. You can't prefer the scandal of a court case.'

This remark hit me hard. The mere thought that Mike's photograph might be displayed in the papers, beneath blaring headlines, revolted me. If I had been an unknown name, this argument would not have affected me as it did. It was the time when Ingrid Bergman's divorce was prominent in the whole world's press. Everyone was taking sides, either for the Swedish star or for her husband, Dr Lindstrom. They were judged and blamed. Trailed about by both parties, their child ended up in front of an American court; and when asked, 'Do you want to go with your Daddy or your Mummy?' the little girl answered, 'With my Daddy.'

I would do anything to stop Mike ever being in this situation; anything to keep friendly relations with his father. Also, I didn't want our child to be able to think his father and mother hated each other.

I still had great illusions.

I felt like those wild animals which, on the way to their water-hole, fall into a pit. They try to get out by themselves, to reach a branch; their claws touch it but can't get a hold on it. Then they realise they are in the hunter's hands and will suffer the fate he has reserved for them.

It was in this frame of mind, with my nerves and morale exhausted, that on 19 August, 1948, I signed the document of agreement which Bill had had drawn up.

He agreed to send Mike to me in France every year for the school holidays, and I enjoyed the fullest rights to have him with me every time it was possible for me to go to Los Angeles. In return I abandoned to my husband all our common property. That seemed very unimportant compared to seeing Mike.

Bill never kept his word. He never sent me Mike as had been agreed.

Mike kissed me once more, and I said to him: 'See you soon, my darling'—without knowing how many months that 'soon' might mean.

It was over. He was gone—and it was years, not months, before I saw him again. Not soon at all.

For weeks I had watched eagerly for the postman's arrival, but the envelopes bearing an American stamp were rare. I sent Bill ten letters to get one reply. He insisted that he was writing to me and it was the French postal system that was responsible: they just didn't distribute the mail! When I telephoned, weary of waiting, he wasn't there. Most of the time it was the nurse who answered: 'Mike's fine.' She wouldn't put him on the 'phone, though. It didn't occur to me she might have received instructions on this subject; at that time such an idea was unthinkable to me.

I tried to rearrange my work schedule, but never found a blank period when I could visit Mike in America. The shooting of one film was followed mercilessly by another. To have a run of films, the dream of all actors, had for me become a form of slavery: *Aux yeux du souvenir, La belle que voilà, Maria Chapdelaine, L'étrange Madame X.*

I felt the victim of an unvarying, almost conveyor-belt process set in motion by the signing of a contract: costume tests, hair-style and make-up tests, then the turn of publicity and the press, the shooting, exteriors and interiors, then the showing of the rushes, accompanied by doubts and anxieties, which increased on the release of the film; the first public showing became a new ordeal. And when I read the reviews, I was already on the next film. For thirty years I have had this sort of existence—coming to date events not by the year but by the film I was in at the time.

Professionally, it scarcely seems a thing to complain about and I have adapted to it, but with resignation more than enthusiasm.

Only on this occasion, in the comparatively early days,

there was one very different circumstance to the syndrome. I could not accept life without Mike; everything inside me rebelled.

I kept on going to see my lawyer, protesting: 'It's a whole year since I've seen my son. Really, his father could bring him to see me. Isn't there anything be done to make him?'

'Nothing, madame. An agreement was signed on 19 August, drawn up in English, deposited in the American Embassy. We must respect it.'

'But he's taking no notice of it. Look, Mr Izard, I read here: "... the wife shall be entitled to have the child with her, with the husband's consent, during the holidays or at any other suitable times, the wife being responsible for the child's maintenance and the expenses incurred during the periods while he is with her." "Shall be entitled ..."—that surely means that I can have him over here. It gives me rights.'

Mr Izard smiled sadly. 'Don't forget that it specifies, "with the husband's consent". You signed this document of agreement, and it governs your relations with Mr Marshall in respect of the child.'

'But I had no option.'

He made a fatalistic gesture with his hand. 'Be patient. Wait until the divorce is decreed and everything will change. We shall be able to act.'

During the shooting of *Maria Chapdelaine* in a little village in the Tyrol, my isolation added to my distress and tension as I waited for letters and telephone calls. If it had not been for the visits Henri and I made to each other by charter plane whenever time permitted in either direction, I should have had one of the worst periods of my life.

On 3 May, 1949, my divorce was decreed by the French courts in my favour. Part of the agreement of 19 August was maintained, and it was explicitly stated that I should have free access to my son. Not having hoped for more, I was ready to settle for this semi-victory.

In the evening, we had dinner at an inn near Paris. The flickering candle-flame lit Henri's face with a shifting pattern of soft lights and deep shadows. The strongly marked planes emphasised its tender and virile aspects; almost primitive, with the high cheek-bones, the set jaw and brow. I felt happy.

Chickens were roasting on spits over an immense fire-place. The light wine was warming. The time to relax had come at last. This divorce had delivered me, and Henri's optimism carried me with him. As usual, I indulged in plans: 'It would be more convenient if I took a flat with two more rooms, one for Mike and one for his nurse. The little man will be able to stay here during the holidays, that's three months, and perhaps for Christmas and Easter. I don't know anything about school holidays in America, but there must be some. When I come back on an evening like this, a happy evening, I'll tiptoe up and open the nursery door, as I used to do last summer at La Malmaison, and look at him sleep-ing ...'

Alas, this was one more empty dream.

America was far away, and Bill was quite unconcerned about the French laws. When I invoked my right, his lawyer took refuge behind the famous phrase 'on condition that the husband has given his consent'. And Mr Marshall did not give it. 'Any long trips would be harmful to the child. But he does not object to the mother coming to visit him.' Bill's reactions had not altered since the beginning of our discus-sions. I felt an impotent disgust.

So I made my decision; I would have to go to Mike. Olga listened to me patiently. She knew that I was 'tied up': between 1948 and 1949 we had signed for five films.

'For the first time,' I declared, 'I'm ready to break my con-tract if need be, to renegue on my signature, to pay a forfeit. Nothing in the world, not even Bill, will stop me seeing Mike.'

Olga calmed me down. Like me, she had a child so we understood each other. Despite her efforts, I was going to have to wait a few weeks before I could leave. But only a few weeks, she said. Her confidence soothed me.

The announcement of my impending departure had an un-foreseen effect on Henri. First he was delighted and my joy was his. Then one evening he asked anxiously: 'You're not going to stay in California?'

Above: La minute de vérité the fourth and last film with Jean Gabin. *Below:* After being Jean Gabin's dresser for many years, Micheline Bonnet ('La Miche') became Michèle's on Gabin's death.

Above: Maxine Michèle's second film with Charles Boyer was made twenty-one years after their first, *Orage. Below:* Michel Deville's *Benjamin* had a fine part for a 'new' Michèle who felt she was being type-cast.

Above: André Malraux after investing Michèle Morgan with the *Légion d'Honneur* for services to the Arts and Letters. *Below:* Left to right: George Clouzot, Michèle, Henri Vidal, Charlie Chaplin, Jean Cocteau.

'With those eyes ...'

'You must be joking, Henri.'

'Well, it's a bit your fault if I got that idea—you love your son so much. I mean, you . . .' He floundered and became confused, then created a diversion by kissing me. A few days later he started again, and I took it more seriously. This time I convinced him for the moment; but he had not given up his fears. He monitored everything I said for references to a long absence; even the dresses I was buying for the trip worried him. 'You don't need all that for a month.'

I realised then that, since I had come to love Henri, we had never had any quarrels; these were the first. They astonished me. I tried to imagine what could be going on in his head. Did he think that through love of Mike I should stay over there with Bill?

'Really, Henri, my life is here, at your side.'

'What proof have I of that?'

'What proof do you want me to give you?'

'Let's get married.'

I do not guarantee that the conversation took place in exactly those words, but this was certainly the gist of it.

To get married? To say 'yes' in front of a registrar or a priest. That was easy enough, but suppose you no longer got on together? I had just been through a painful experience. I tried to explain this to him, but he could not accept it. The discussion went round and round, each of us repeating his own arguments, always the same ones, opposing everything the other said.

I had never thought of remarrying. Already I preferred free love to marriage, despite the still rigid traditions of the times. Happily, a different code has evolved since then; but in 1949 to live with a man 'in sin', as it was often called, might have seemed scandalous. It was not the case with me, however: I had been married, divorce proceedings were taking place, and I was deeply in love with Henri. In France much is forgiven in the name of love. My family, my parents, whom I would never have wished to shock, understood this very well. No one was surprised, not even the journalists, that I should be living with Henri in his flat in the rue Fabert.

So I didn't see any reason for this marriage. In the end,

though, I said 'yes', and when I had done so, I realised that I had really wanted our union, that only my reason had opposed it, and that in face of love, mere reason is not so important. Henri's joy was tremendous. I let myself be won over by his happiness. It became mine.

The ceremony took place in February 1950 in the Town Hall of the 17th arrondissement, shortly before my thirtieth birthday. All publicity was avoided.

Three weeks before I left, Bill, learning of my approaching arrival, informed me that he was not disposed to let me take the child away with me. I could see him only in the presence of my ex-mother-in-law or the nurse, 'within the limits allowed by the regulation of the child's life and the spending of his time'.

I left Henri sad and uneasy. Yet since we had loved each other we had been separated very often. He joked amiably about it. 'You realise this time it's a bit far for a weekend.'

Then, when we were saying goodbye, he remarked: 'I'm not a person who ought to be left alone.' Why did he say that? I quickly forgot about it, and it was only later on that it came back into my memory.

My stay in California was a mixture of light and shade.

It was so wonderful to see Mike, to find a little boy of five asking lots of questions, so very curious to hear all about me; to be able to talk to my son, to see a mind opening up, an attitude to life. Nothing could replace that.

These moments, though, were numbered. In this house, which had been mine, I went to find my son as some distant aunt might do. Mrs Marshall was embarrassed and this feeling further increased her reserve. In her eyes I was no longer her daughter-in-law. What part did she attribute to me in the break-up of the marriage? It was hard to assess. I sensed that she was worried every time I picked Mike up, let alone took him out with me. Progressively, and I could understand it, this child had become hers. She was bringing him up; she had coped with his colds, his chicken-pox, his mumps. She was teaching him all the things he needed to know about daily life. It was to her that he ran when he was unhappy, to her he told stories about school.

A shy child, with his own secret life, he gradually began to look at me with more and more confidence: I was his redis-covered Maman or Mammy, it didn't matter which. The sense of this new serenity was rather shattering, for I knew I should soon be leaving again, and I realised through his remarks and questions that what he was being told was very different from what I was telling him about my profession and my country, which was also his country. Who was I to blame for this cunning, undermining work? His grand-mother? If she was doing it, it couldn't be directly to hurt me. Perhaps she had been convinced that I was the villain of the piece.

When I brought him back to her, she looked at us suspi-ciously. What had I given him to eat, to drink? Had he over-tired himself? Behind these harmless questions, I guessed at others that were less so, but preferred not to imagine what they were. I think she worried over what I might have told Mike, might be telling him, about his father.

If that was so, she was misjudging me and didn't know me properly. I had no intention of 'knocking' the man who had been my husband. My most serious complaint against him was his wish to separate me from Mike, to keep him to himself. I took good care not to trouble the heart of a little five-year-old boy with grown-ups' quarrels. I believed, and believe, that when parents divorce, their first and main duty towards their child is to do everything to stop him suffering from it. A small child cannot understand the reasons why adults may have to separate. For the child they are his mother and father and he loves them equally—or should do so.

It seemed to me bad enough to break up Mike's home into two parts without trying to fill him up with resentments which were quite alien to him.

I gradually came to realise that I didn't know Bill, or what he was capable of doing in order to capture Mike's affection. I didn't know, either, how devastating it can be to hate some-one else and want to take revenge.

My fears were justified. In spite of everything that has happened since then, and all the tenderness and love I have given Mike, I have never been able to change the way he feels about his childhood. I had the proof of this very recently, hearing him declare during a conversation: 'Personally, I had a ghastly childhood.'

'Look, Mike,' I broke in, 'how can you say such a thing? When you were so much loved?'

'Yes,' he answered, 'but I didn't know I was.'

Nothing can ever wipe that out.

It was about this time that the papers in France began to make references to my son: the divorce did not explain everything, and it was hard for people to understand why Mike should not be with his mother. This might have been held against me, but it wasn't. I dreaded these articles which were so friendly towards me. Each time, Bill complained of them through his lawyer as if they showed disloyalty towards him on my part—and I was in his hands.

I received many letters just then from men, and even more from women, writing to tell me that they understood me and expounding their own cases. For most of them, hatred of their former partner added to their despair at being separated from their son: a hatred which, to get their own back, they tried to communicate to the child, without realising it was him most of all they were hurting. Unfortunately, anything one may think or say on this subject is without effect if the other person refuses to understand it—and separated parents seldom agree on this point.

I don't know if later generations have reached a happier development, if their attitude to divorce has been modified in depth. I am inclined to think so, especially when I see the relations which have been established between my son and daughter-in-law, now divorced, with regard to their child, Samantha, my grand-daughter. Mike has remarried, his daughter lives with her mother, and neither of them has ever said anything malicious about the other—it would have come through, if they had, in remarks the child made. Samantha has suffered absolutely no traumatic effects from that divorce; the situation doesn't seem abnormal to her, and doesn't embarrass her in any way. On Wednesdays, when she comes to stay with me, or in the summer holidays, she speaks of her father and her mother with the serene confidence of happy children. Even better, it has not been concealed from her that Papa was going to have another little girl and she is eager to see her new sister. It is the attitude of grown-ups which makes children wonder about things; to start with, everything is simple for them. It is we who complicate their universe. One of the laws you must impose on yourself when you have a child is to love him enough to rise above your own resentments.

When I said *au revoir* to Mike after a month and a half, I was filled with an almost animal desire to stay on. I was going to lose that trusting smile, that look full of love. When I saw him next, perhaps the whole process would have to start all over again.

On my return to Paris, I sensed an indefinable cloud behind Henri's joy.

I wasn't able to devote all the time and attention to him that he perhaps needed. No time: how often have I used these words and invoked this excuse to postpone things or regret them! As I write, I can see how incomprehensible such a reason may seem to those who do not live the sort of life that Henri and I, like most actors and actresses, were obliged to do. Not to be able to show sufficient concern for one's partner may sometimes seem a basic neglect, especially if that partner is frail. I was to find this out by bitter experience. *L'étrange Madame X*, which I agreed to be in out of friendship for Jean Grémillon, the director, and to be with Henri, had a certain importance in our life: it was during the shooting of this film, paradoxically, that Henri and I decided not to act together again.

It is sometimes believed that being in the same production brings you together. Not so, or only in rare cases. I wouldn't claim that this statement is an infallible rule. There are married couples, especially in the theatre, who get on as well at home as on the stage; but they are the exception.

Professionally, as far as I am concerned, I would rather my

partner were not my husband. I play passionate love scenes with more ease in the arms of a man who is indifferent to me. Modesty, reserve, the exhibitionist side of expressing very private feelings in public, all make me uneasy, and in fact are inclined to paralyse me. But this very personal reason was not the main factor in our decision to separate our careers. Till then, of course, we felt we couldn't act together often enough. Already in three out of the five films I had just been in, I had had Henri as my partner.

It was during the shooting of *Madame X* that a remark of Grémillon's struck home. The story was of a woman of the world who falls in love with a cabinet-maker (Henri) and, so that he should not feel any inferiority complex towards her, passes herself off as her own chambermaid: a real hoary melodrama. Even the great directors can make mistakes.

Grémillon was meticulously arranging the scene at the wedding reception of one of the cabinet-maker's mates. 'You, Henri, don't notice at first that she's ill at ease. You're cheerful, you've had a bit to drink, and it's when you turn slightly on your chair to look at her that you notice it. Seeing her so different from the others, you realise everything that separates you. You explode: a mixture of despair and anger. You, Michèle, are following an identical path, you feel out of your element, you resent being at this table; you find Henri's anger unfair and misplaced, and you pass judgment on him ...'

The shooting started. Listening intently and watching critically, I was surprised by a particular gesture of Henri's; an intonation disconcerted me, I hadn't 'felt' it like that. I mentally applauded a happy moment, the rightness of an expression. I was approving and disapproving in turn. I became too concerned with Henri, in fact—and a spectator myself.

'Cut!' cried Grémillon. 'It's fine for Henri but, as for you, Michèle, you're underplaying it, as if you were thinking of other things.'

We started again.

'No, Henri, now you're doing it.'

After three takes, Grémillon took us aside. 'Listen, stop bothering about each other. Each of you act for yourself.'

These words had the effect on me of a revelation: directly Henri came on the scene, I became completely concerned with him and forgot my own rôle. I had ceased to react as an actress, I was a wife keeping her husband under surveillance because she wanted him to shine. It couldn't be denied that this attitude was equally detrimental to Henri, that it embarrassed him and took away his spontaneity. His impulsiveness was one of his strong points. He was a creature of instinct who worked best in the heat of the moment, and had difficulties in repeating the same scene twenty times 'from cold', preserving gestures and intonations. Wanting to help him, I worried him. Consequently the scene took a long time to get right and had us all on edge.

That evening, talking over the incident during the shooting, perhaps a little hastily, we made up our minds not to accept any more contracts which brought us together.

I had the impression that this resolve satisfied Henri and relieved him. We were neither of us taken in by the manœuvres of producers who came to Henri, offering him an exceptional part and adding, 'It would be perfect if Michèle agreed to be your partner.' Conversely, I would be offered a film with the additional carrot that Henri would be able to play such and such a character. These crude and childish little contrivances amused me. Henri was affected differently: being very punctilious, not tolerating the idea of being the object of bargains and pressures, still less of being 'merely' my husband, they irritated him.

I loved him too much not to take great care to avoid putting him in an artificial or embarrassing situation. Even so, I was well aware that for a man as virile and sensitive as Henri, to be Michèle Morgan's husband was not easy. First of all professionally: was he being offered a part as himself or as her husband? Then there was the fear of being a sort of prince consort. I wasn't the one to bring this fear into being—it was the people around us, some from malicious intent, others without thinking. Sometimes his sensitivity alone was responsible for it: one day when the telephone had been ringing almost continuously, he said to me plaintively at the end of the morning: 'There hasn't been a single call for me.' But what could I do about that?

Henri was a very secret person, and it was one of the very few times he expressed his disappointment even to me. Retiring into himself, my husband was a 'phoney' extrovert, whose apparently extravagant actions often surprised me. This man I loved remained for me in part an enigma. I kept wondering things about him; wondering, too, how we could be so close and yet so distant.

When he courted me, he had perhaps been more interested in the famous actress than the woman. Later, when we had lived together, when we had got married, I was sure everything had changed, and that it was then he began to really love me. It was then too that he suffered from his love.

'Bill Marshall has just married Micheline Presle.' At first this news, which had nothing astonishing about it, amused me. It brought me a brief flashback of two memories: the photograph of Bill and her on the *Queen Mary*, and my exhusband's voice assuring me that there had been 'nothing between them'.

Henri for his part was delighted. 'Well, you won't be going off to California any more.'

'Why's that?'

'Micheline certainly won't go and live in Hollywood. So—he'll be coming here.'

'That would surprise me a lot. Bill will never agree to live in France. I don't think this will make any difference.'

In the short run, I was right. Still, I consulted Mr Izard, who thought there was a basis here for starting negotiations. 'It's quite clear that it would be preferable if Mr Marshall came to live in your city, but the mere fact of this remarriage may allow us to try to establish a form of agreement with the other party regulating your son's coming to and staying in Paris.'

So we were back again in proceedings which caused me new nervous tension. I changed my lawyer, hoping to have a new point of view on this matter. Bill, through his lawyer, accepted the principle, and one evening in the office of the new lawyer, Paul Weill, I was confronted by an 'agreement' which even today I find scandalous. It started promisingly: 'The undersigned parties agree to regulate as follows the child's way of life'—not a very happy way of referring to your child's happiness. The 'as follows', if I signed the agreement, was equivalent to my recognising that 'in the child's interest, he must follow the moral, intellectual and religious direction to be given him by his father', that 'the child, being of delicate health, must be surrounded by attentive care, and his father has always been vigilant that this care should be given him'.

The rest was along the same lines. There was pompous talk of journeys likely to interfere with the child's studies. He was only six, and only the summer holidays were concerned.

As this document merely aimed to get me to accept Bill's arguments unconditionally, offering me nothing in exchange, we remained with the *status quo* till the time when—as Henri had predicted—he did come and live with Micheline Presle (or, rather, Marshall). This time Mr Weill seemed more confident, I thought, and considered there was a new factor that might be exploited. 'Here is how I have written to the other party,' he told me: '"The two former spouses being now settled in France, it seems really absurd, I would even say inhuman, to allow the child to continue to live far from his parents."'

It was the first time I had seen the word 'inhuman' used, and I thought it was high time!

After a few weeks of negotiations I had a new draft submitted to me which still had the general aim of regulating the child's life and the particular aim of jeopardising the visiting rights I had been granted:

'1. While the child is in Paris, Madame Morgan shall be able to take him out with her two or three times a week, on condition that she sends transport to fetch him and to take him back to his domicile. The child's excursions shall be confined to the afternoons from 3 to 7 p.m. except on Thursdays, when Madame Morgan shall be able to keep him with her for lunch, having him fetched at 11.30 a.m.

'2. The child shall follow his father if the latter goes to the sea or the mountains, to any place of his choosing.

'3. For a fortnight Madame Morgan shall be entitled to keep the child with her outside Paris, either by the sea or in the mountains, but only after the choice of place made by her for his stay has been submitted to Mr Marshall for his approval. The child shall be accompanied by his nurse, at Madame Morgan's expense. She shall ensure the return of the child and the nurse to his father's domicile, on the fifteenth day at latest. In case of the child's illness, the father shall be immediately informed by telegram.

'4. At any time, if Mr Marshall so decides, it shall be possible for him to resume custody of the child with a view to taking the said child back to the United States, and this applies even during the fortnight's period reserved to Madame Morgan.'

I didn't know which was the more remarkable in this document, its inhumanity or its hypocrisy. The conclusion was a masterpiece: 'Agreement drawn up in Paris, in duplicate, and established in good faith in the exclusive interest of the child. Dated: —'

Was that how adults, because they couldn't get on together and had separated, conceived their child's happiness? Never had marriage seemed to me a more 'male chauvinist' institution than that evening in Mr Weill's office. I refused to sign anything, but that made no difference: it was the restrictive clauses which were respected.

In 1950, the laws governing divorce were profoundly unjust. There has been much too long a delay before they were reformed, and they are still far from perfect. When I defend the mother's rights as regards the child, it is not in opposition to the father's rights. What divided Bill and me was that for nineteen years he refused to admit that I was only asking to share honourably in the love of our son and not in any way to take him over.

At last Mr Weill announced Mike's coming. He would live with his father. Full of confidence, drawn from some apparently inexhaustible source, convinced that despite the horrible conditions made I should be allowed to have Mike for weekends and school holidays, I moved to the rue Saint-

Louis-en-l'Isle. Mike had his own room there and he would be in his second home. How could I have deceived myself so badly? It was only on Thursdays he was allowed to come to me.

Even then Bill abused his right of veto vigorously. He continued to set himself up as an uncompromising moral supervisor and vigilant father—he was that anyhow—for whom anything was a pretext to say 'no'.

Henri's presence under my roof seemed unsuitable to him, likely to shock this little boy who was now nine. 'He might ask questions.' Ask *me* questions, no doubt? But all I wanted to explain to Mike were the reasons why he was leading a different life from that led by other boys of his age. Only in that way would he be spared any traumatic effects from this.

Bill even went to the point of demanding that when he granted me a weekend, it should be spent outside my house. Twenty times I felt like saying: 'In what way is Henri's presence scandalous? Mike is living quite happily in your wife's house. After all, I might consider that far more serious; that house is his home since you're living there. The woman looking after him is your wife. In the long run, over the years, isn't that situation likely to rob me of part of my child's love? What are you afraid of? In my house it will never be more than a visit.'

This was the start of a long period—several years—during which I had to repeat to myself that as Micheline lived quite near, Mike and I were only separated by a few streets. And luckily, though she was in an embarrassing position, Micheline herself showed great tact and delicacy towards me—towards us.

Ours is a cruel profession. The first time I acted in a film with Jean Gabin, I was only a young hopeful and he was the star; today the situation was different. We were shooting *La minute de vérité* under the direction of Jean Delannoy, my third film with him. Olga said to me: 'I've asked for your name, as the star, to be put before Gabin's.'

I protested: 'But nothing's changed.'

'Yes, it has. Since *Martin Roumagnac* he no longer carries the same weight.'

I realised it was true, and was sickened by the unfairness of it, all because of that one film. *Martin Roumagnac* had been very eagerly awaited: it was Jean's first film after a long absence due to his engagement in the Free French forces during the war, followed by a stay in the United States; and there was Marlene Dietrich's appearance with him in the same film. The producers thought this partnership would bring them in pots of money, and the critics were convinced that the combination of these two outstanding talents would be a dazzling success. They were sadly disappointed. The two talents damaged each other, and the producers' disappointment did especially great harm to Jean. He was not in the trough of the wave, but he was certainly not on the crest of it any more; he had lost prestige. Luckily, he had the toughness and skill needed to face this and regain his position; it was only a brief eclipse. With his appearance the following year in *Touchez pas au grisbi*, he became a superstar again, and remained one till the end of his life.

I hadn't seen him since America. To find him on a set with his smile, his cigarette, his banter, and Micheline—'La Miche', 'Fat Girl'—in his shadow, took me back a decade; we were united by the same shared memories and friendship. I felt as if we had only said goodbye the evening before, and yet, as Jean said, I hadn't been idle—two marriages, a child, a divorce.

When you meet a friend from whom you have been separated for a long time, and he asks you, 'How are things?' you may say, 'Fine.' It's a general answer, taking in all aspects of life. I said, 'Fine, thanks'—I loved Henri, he loved me, I was happy. But as you talk, through your own words and the look in your old friend's eyes, you notice that things aren't quite as fine as all that. I didn't need that meeting to find this out, but I needed it to be able to talk about it. You tell your close friends everyday details, and it's hard to see the wood for the trees. You don't realise that when you add up these minor factors, they produce a total effect, and that total effects have a significance which you have not always

244

wished to register. The more I talked to Jean, the clearer things became. The cracks I had sensed on my return from Hollywood had widened; the man I had at my side was no longer quite the same man as I had lived with and then married. Was the marriage responsible for that?

This time the change coincided also with my absence, and I was more inclined to blame my trip than the marriage although the two seemed linked. We had been separated before, and he had put up with it very well, though admittedly we had come together almost every weekend. During the years of our passion these separations had not done us any harm; they only intensified our pleasure in meeting again. The kind of tranquillity which the marriage had brought Henri, which he said he needed so much, had perhaps, on the contrary, given him a security which allowed him to do anything he liked. He had nothing to fear now; I should always be there. He was right about that.

On my return from California he had come to meet me at le Havre. In our hotel room, looking rather pale, he had seemed a little ill at ease, rather like a small boy who has done something naughty. But what?

Talking to Jean, I tried to probe this. 'You know, he can't resist the desire to please, to make a conquest. He always needs something new. As if he were searching for something he never finds.'

'But with you he's found it.'

'Yes, when I'm there. He's told me I'm the only woman who can give him the tenderness he's missed. And I believed him at the time.'

'Like all women you try to complicate things too much. Wasn't he happy as a kid?'

'I think he had too strict a childhood. Good parents certainly, but severe. Not being able to control him properly, they sent him to a monastery school. He was so turbulent the monks tied him to his bench to make him stay still.'

'He's a chap with an excess of energy, you say it yourself, so let him use it.'

This very masculine reasoning did not console me as much as Jean seemed to hope. Then Delannoy wanted us, and the conversation stopped. But on another occasion I resumed it, explaining: 'I'm more afraid for him than for myself. He's somehow unbalanced.'

'What is it you're afraid of?'

Quite naturally, what I was afraid of, the first thing that came into my head, was another woman, an affair. I was not at all worried by what Jean called 'a slit in the marriage contract'. I had been fortunate enough at a very early age to realise that physiologically men had more imperious needs than ours. I wasn't jealous in that sort of way. What I was scared of was lying, which gives more importance to an act than it would otherwise have. The old story of the forbidden fruit remains true; more especially for the young.

I have always preferred to know the truth, and I was anxious about what Henri's silence might be concealing. What were the grounds for the transformation in him that was taking place? I had a presentiment that it heralded a long period of difficulty.

'The thing that makes me feel calmer about him,' I explained to Jean, 'is his origins. He's of farming stock. You've seen him. He's typical of the down-to-earth country boy with plenty of common sense. In his reasoning and his opinions, his whole way of looking at life, he's one of those reassuring people you can say has his feet on the ground. Yet he seems to have a frantic appetite for all kinds of pleasure, as if he didn't want to miss out on a single one. At those moments it's Mr Hyde who gets the upper hand, and that's what alarms me. That reasonable, well-developed brain suddenly has flashes of unreason shooting through it. Under their influence he can do the most stupid things, because he wants to make people laugh, to appear the funniest and most brilliant person there, to be the chap who dares to do what nobody else would, to be considered the man all the girls fall for. He has to be "the mostest" in everything, and to reach that objective he's ready for anything....'

'When I'm near him,' I went on, before Jean could speak, 'everything's different. My presence gives him balance, it restores Dr Jekyll. Unfortunately our work separates us too often, and now I'm off to film in Mexico while he's got a film starting in Italy. We'll be away from each other for two months, perhaps more. You understand?'

Jean understood. I knew this from his smile, his way of turning his head away slightly. True to himself, to his personality and our friendship, he murmured lightly: 'The important thing is that he loves you.'

We were only at the prelude to the drama ahead.

The Tunnel

My memories of the next nine years are vivid. They were like a dark tunnel stretching far into the distance, with just an occasional gleam of light. During that period I was fighting against hopeless odds; I was really beaten in advance, but refused to believe it.

As often happens in such cases, my conversations with Jean had slightly clarified the situation, or at least I thought they had. While I had been away in California, Henri was on a theatrical tour in Morocco. He had a good friend with him in the company, Bob Dalban, and had been looking forward to it. When I returned a month later, it was fairly obvious, as I have said, that something was wrong. I had left a man in love, overflowing with vitality, and I came back to a listless character without any passion or drive, who obviously had his mind elsewhere, perhaps his heart too. That was what I had thought at first, without attaching too much importance to it. But I could no longer consider things so lightly. I couldn't reassure myself by saying: 'It'll pass. It can't last. He's had an escapade which is worrying him and he doesn't dare admit it to me.' Like all women who find themselves in a similar situation, I showed great imagination in supposing reasons, and was convinced I was taking all possibilities into account, even that he was being blackmailed.

Perhaps I am overstating my feelings for this stage. I still couldn't really think it was anything too serious. If it had been, I was sure he would have told me. But if it wasn't anything to do with a woman, then he was ill. He might even be seriously ill. Why was he hiding it from me?

In the next few weeks his condition had clearly worsened. His periods of prostration, at first intermittent and not very pronounced, became more or less chronic. He had become very thin. His skin was grey and he dozed off anywhere. One evening we were at a premiere and I saw his pupils close. The man who couldn't stay still would now lie apathetically wherever he had flopped.

He was in a film with Maria Mauban, *La passante*, and had just returned from work. I looked at his great body slumped on the sitting-room sofa, saw him vaguely contemplating the glass of Scotch he was holding in his hand. I thought about drink. If he was an alcoholic, I should have known.

'Henri, you're hiding something from me.'

He raised lazy eyes towards me. 'Nothing, honestly.'

'But listen, you're sick. You're getting thinner and thinner. Perhaps you picked up some horrid bug in Morocco.'

'Forget it. Bob and I did rather paint the town red, but I didn't even have a hangover. No, I've been overworking a bit'—he yawned, unable to stop himself—'sorry, darling. It's being so tired, you know. I'm up every morning at six to get to the location. This film is killing me. As we usually go out in the evenings, I can't quite stand the pace.'

It was not a good excuse. I had seen him staying up all night without it leaving any trace. 'Look at you, you're white as a sheet. It's not normal. Go and see a doctor.'

'Oh, no. I know what he'll tell me.'

That was true enough, though I didn't realise it.

I pressed him. 'I'm worried, I need to be reassured. If you love me, you owe it to me ...' I said what we all say in such a situation. But it only annoyed him, he told me again to forget it, and things were left as they were.

I was as concerned as ever, and had to talk about it to someone. One afternoon I went to see Olga and confessed my fears to her. 'Since my return from America I can't find the real Henri. I'm living with a completely different person. I keep wondering all sorts of things. I'm afraid he's ill and is hiding it from me.'

Olga seemed upset, but not surprised. She listened to me without asking any questions. When I stopped, she said: 'Well now, I'm not sure of anything, but what you tell me makes me think of a rumour that's going round Paris. It may be true.'

In a flash, like someone being given a slap in the face, I thought: 'That's it. What I was afraid of is true. She's going to tell me he's having an affair.' I felt my blood run cold. I must have gone all the colours of the rainbow. It seemed to me that Olga was making me wait an age for her revelation, whereas she only allowed herself a slight pause in her embarrassment before continuing: 'Well, it's a rumour in the profession. People say Henri's on drugs.'

The shock was less brutal than Olga might have feared, and I believe I murmured: 'Ah! So that's it! I understand!' It was not the surprise for me she could have expected, and in fact I was amazed I hadn't thought of it before, for it wasn't a new thing but went back to when he was seventeen. His parents—solid, down-to-earth Auvergnat farmers—made him take business studies. Henri was only interested in literature, poetry, art. In complete revolt against his background, the severity shown him, the restraints imposed on him 'for his own good', and the strict financial dependence in which he was kept—he was given very little in the way of pocket money—he decided to become an actor; and having plenty of courage, told his father so. Far from his benefiting as I had from his family's help, his father gave him the classical admonition: 'If, instead of having a solid profession, you want to become a mountebank, I shan't stop you. You can go at once, but as soon as you've left this house, you won't get another sou from me.' He kept his word.

Henri had often talked to me about his early hard times. But only once, three years before, had he told me about a time in his life which threw light on the present situation. 'There I was in Paris, seventeen years old, and without a brass farthing. I had some pals but they couldn't help me much, and I don't know how I'd have managed if I hadn't met a woman who took an interest in me. With her I was quite happy and well. It was when I left her that things changed. I hadn't completely broken with my parents, especially Maman. I went to see them now and then in Lyons. Every time I slept in their house, I felt bad, ill even, with abnormal sweats. I couldn't understand it at all. Directly I returned to this woman, my sickness stopped. And then one morning—what I'm going to tell you sounds incredible, but it's true—when she thought I was asleep but I was half-awake, I could feel she was making me breathe something. I seized her hand. Between her fingers there were traces of a white powder. The bitch was drugging me so that I didn't leave her. She admitted it to me, can you credit it? So, of course, when I went to my family, I was missing the stuff.'

He had escaped from the drug. 'During my military service I met a doctor who became a friend. He got me into a hospital and put me on a cure.'

So I'd known all the necessary facts, but hadn't thought of it. I had found that story strange and psychologically interesting: to drug someone you love in order to keep him with you was a form of *crime passionel* which had remained in my memory. But as something very remote—and I had failed to make the connection.

I had suffered so much from my uncertainty that I was almost relieved. Everything was now clear. Everything could now start again. I didn't know what drug it was. I knew fellow actors and actresses who took drugs, but not many, and they were rather proud of the practice, as if it were the smart thing to do. I only realised it was harmful and dangerous, but otherwise I had everything to learn.

I made up my mind at once: I would talk to Henri that very evening and help him to come off whatever it was. They were brave words which for a time I could believe in.

It often seems best to me to play down situations. I merely said to Henri: 'I know.'

His face lightened, he looked like someone whose toothache has suddenly gone. 'My darling, how marvellous! I didn't dare tell you, but now you know, the nightmare is over for me as well. I'm going to be able to kick the habit. Until you knew, I couldn't do it. A cure makes you very ill, and you wouldn't have understood. At last I'm going to be able to come off it, and you can help me.'

He began to give me a glimpse of the life of a junkie, talking about the pangs of being without the drug, which, it turned out, was heroin; the terrible withdrawal symptoms during the cure; the prison the drug kept you in. I was overcome by a great wave of pity, and also of hope; this calamity was not going to destroy our marriage.

'Look, directly the film's over, I'll go into a clinic. Now we needn't talk any more about it.'

I had no doubts about his sincerity, and I was right not to have: he believed it as much as I did. He was so happy to be able to talk to me about it that he told me about his relapse.

'It's not been going on very long, only a few months. Three days before your return I went to a nightclub in Saint-Germain. I met some pals and they said, "Come with us, we're just going to have a little fix." I'd refused several times, but just this once I accepted. Then I was feeling low before coming to meet you, so I went on taking the stuff to stop you noticing anything. After that I couldn't stop.'

I could see something of the danger of these 'little fixes', which they talked about so lightheartedly amongst themselves, like a booze-up with friends. When they were repeated a certain number of times, they made you into a junkie.

Everything happened as planned. Henri went into a clinic. I took him in, and went to see him. It was the first of his many visits to clinics and every time I was at his side, losing hope more and more of any lasting recovery. He would come out believing he would never start again. 'I've suffered too much,' he would repeat. 'I've suffered the tortures of the damned. Nobody can know what it's like. It would be too stupid to let myself be trapped again by that bloody filth. It's over for good.'

I still didn't doubt his resolution, which was quite genuine. We really believed that resolution was firm as a rock. For me it had just been a bad moment in our life. I watched quite a few remissions of this kind.

In my joy at finding the old Henri, animated and exuberant, I didn't notice immediately that this hectic vivacity was no longer quite natural; a little extravagant, with rather too many Scotches, as if he had to find some different form of drug to compensate for the absence of his former prop. He was not relaxed; he hadn't recovered his balance. All junkies know this state. He was having psychological withdrawal symptoms. To mitigate them, to cheat this need, to forget this form of imbalance, he started going out in the evenings and most of the night, leaving one nightclub to go to another, ordering one Scotch after another, laughing too loudly and too often. The night would drag on and on, a ridiculous waste of time and sleep, morally and physically exhausting. I would show my lassitude, and a certain disapproval, then get to my feet. 'Darling, it's four o'clock. I'm on the set early this morning, so I'm going home.' He would follow me protesting, worked up by the alcohol. Annoyed myself, I would answer back, and we'd have a quarrel. I would get to bed dead tired, vowing to have early nights for the rest of the week.

When the evening came, it was as if a signal had been lit up inside him, setting in motion the same dreary process. Everything started again, and as I was afraid of leaving him alone, afraid of whisperings in the back of cloakrooms and the corners of toilets, the collusion of page-boys and porters, of friends who were often mere acquaintances, of the whole little shadowy society of drug-pushers, I followed him—and we quarrelled—and our marriage began to break up. Not very quickly. There were magnificent recoveries and revivals which made me forgive and forget everything, finding again the love and tenderness and joy which had been ours for two years. But I found them more and more rarely.

One day I told Olga and Tanine, my sole confidantes, that things were better. He was calmer. The night before, we had a very pleasant evening; in the afternoon he had stayed at home.

'You see,' they said, 'the bad moment is over. Coming out of the clinic after the cure, there's always a painful period of readjustment.'

I agreed. This time it was really over. We had started again. I was right there, only it was not the new beginning I had thought.

In the evening I noticed that he was sweating a lot, and

also something curious, that his eyes no longer watered. Since then, I am told, it has been discovered that drug addicts need to be given potassium to provide continued lubrication. Moreover, his pupils had narrowed to pin-heads. They gave him a strange expression, too bright, slightly staring. I realised he had started taking the drug again.

I sat down beside him, and we looked at each other. His distress went right through me. Again he was going to need a cure. Gently, like someone questioning a child, I said: 'Darling, I shan't reproach you at all, but tell me the truth, you've started again.' He first denied it obstinately, then gave in: 'Yes, it's true, but it's not worth talking about. I met my pal who let me have some, just for a little fix. I'm not going to go on with it.'

A junkie's declaration of intent.

I had just come to a profound change in my whole life. For years after this nothing in my personal affairs could be quite the same.

My departure was approaching. It was several months now since Yves Allégret had asked me to be in a film, of which we didn't yet know the title, taken from a short story by Jean-Paul Sartre. The adaptation was to be made by Aurenche and Bost, who had been so successful with their adaptation for *La symphonie pastorale*. My partner would be Gérard Philipe, then reaching the peak of his career. I didn't accept at once but, after Yves's visit, Henri and I had a long talk about it in one of our all too rare evenings alone together.

'You don't sound too enthusiastic,' he observed.

'Yes, I am, very.'

But Henri was not satisfied. 'Don't you like the part?'

'From what Yves has told me about it, it sounds pretty good.'

'Let's hear.'

'I'm a young married woman and go off with my husband to a small town somewhere in Asia. You can imagine the atmosphere, the heat, the sun, the dust, the natives, not many whites. Almost directly we get there, my husband falls ill. I find him in a squalid room and realise that he has had his wallet taken. He is the first victim of an epidemic which ravages the country. I am left without money; in the company of the doctor, Gérard Philipe, who has treated him. The doctor is a wreck of a man, an alcoholic. He comes to love me, and I him, but neither of us will accept it, I from pride, he because he refuses love—he believes he was responsible for the death of his wife while he was delivering her baby. There is a mutual affront to our feelings: I embody the bourgeois virtues, the self-respect he rejects; I despise his alcoholism, though in my love I pity his weakness, and want to fight it ... Yes, it could be a very fine rôle, very powerful.'

Henri had come out of the clinic after his second cure, and was in a good period. The similarities in the situation, fiction linking up with fact, did not seem too near the bone for him; it only increased his interest. 'And how does it end? You triumph?'

'Yes. Love wins the day.'

That victory could be his. 'Wins the day for good?' he asked. 'Or does he relapse?'

'I don't know yet. The happy ending is Raoul Lévy's idea. He's the co-producer of the film with Raymond Borderie, a very go-ahead chap. Nellie is a fairly new type of character for me. They've described her to me as a passionate woman, capable of violence despite her self-control and reserve.'

'And you're in doubt?'

'No.'

'There's a "but"?'

'No, not really.'

Henri was quite right, of course, there *was* a 'but' and he knew it was him—the idea of leaving him at a time when I knew he was frail, capable of succumbing. That evening he was full of tenderness and love. 'You needn't worry about me. I swear to you that I won't touch the drug again. You can believe me. All right, I had a relapse but that was almost inevitable—all the doctors will tell you. This time I'm sure it'll be all right. I can feel it—it's finished.'

So I signed.

The days passed. Neither the date of my departure nor the location was yet fixed. From Asia, the action was shifted to Vera Cruz; Raoul Lévy had cousins in Mexico, and thanks to the finance promised by them on the spot, the film became a Franco-Mexican co-production. This change involved others.

I prepared to leave without having seen the final script. I didn't like not being familiar with it in advance. 'Aurenche and Bost are working at frantic speed and quite brilliantly too,' Raoul Lévy assured me. But I still hadn't read anything. I should have liked to get into my character during the journey, which would be quite a long one. After a traumatic incident on a plane, I couldn't stand flying any more, and to everyone's disgust insisted on crossing by sea to New York, then taking the train.

They laughed at me: 'Boat and train, why not a galleon and a stagecoach?'

'It's idiotic,' Henri protested. 'You'll take five days to get to New York instead of a few hours. I'd be dead bored on a boat...'

'I can believe that, my darling.'

'What on earth do you find nice about it?'

'Taking my time over leaving one continent and reaching another. Savouring my journey.'

'But listen,' said Raoul Lévy, 'you don't realise what's in store for you, three whole days and two nights on the train. It'll kill you.'

'I shall find it pleasantly relaxing. American trains are very comfortable. I shall have a saloon, my own bathroom, a bar, a hairdresser when needed. At any hour of the day I shall be able to order anything I feel like...'

'A ghastly drug-store *cuisine*. Besides, think of what speed means. You leave Paris this evening, and a few hours later you're in New York. It's like magic. You lose the sense of distance.'

'Just what I don't want to lose. The speed you like so much is something I don't enjoy.'

I wanted to watch the clouds from below; the aerial views of land and sea left me unmoved. What I liked was passing through unknown country, seeing the new types of architecture, people who dressed and lived differently from me.

It went against the grain to tell Mike I was going. I no longer needed to explain to him that it was for work; at eight he knew all about it. Sometimes I imagined him being proud of his Mammy, boasting to his school-mates: 'My mother is Michèle Morgan.' I imagined it but had no idea if I was right; he never told me any stories about his friends in which he referred to either me or my profession. When I told him of my assignment, he put on a serious grown-up face, slightly disapproving.

Henri came with me to Le Havre. I said the trite things I was thinking: 'It'll be wonderful when we're back together again!' I didn't ask him to renew his vows for it would have been pointless; we knew this was uppermost in both our minds. His anxiety over being on his own distressed me. 'I'm not like you,' he grumbled. 'I haven't got your patience. Dreaming of your return isn't enough for me.'

'Nor for me, you know that.'

He changed his grounds for anxiety. 'Suppose you fall in love with Gérard Philipe?' Was he putting it on or did he believe in the possibility? A little of both perhaps.

'Don't be stupid. He's married. Besides you know very well that I'm faithful to you. Which is more than I can say for you. Remember in Rome?' I teased him. 'You were falling for those signorinas right and left. Specially the big brunettes.'

I was ready to say anything to make this departure like any other, not to let go and say the words on the tip of my tongue: 'You've promised me!'

'Two months, my darling. It's not such a long time.'

I had used the same phrase to Mike *and* him, not believing it myself. I was already finding the prospect of those weeks unbearable. I would have given anything for them to come . . .

From New York I took the train to Mexico City. I found the journey enchanting. When Bill and I were living in California, we had been to Tijuana, on the frontier, and from the display of souvenirs for tourists I caught a glimpse of the fabled country of the Aztecs and the *conquistadores*. The approach to Mexico City was very beautiful. As we travelled further west, the scenery became spectacular; the Indian crowds we passed in New Mexico were amazingly colourful, and I wished I had brought painting things. The Mexican pink, slightly purple, was the dominant colour, and looked particularly beautiful on their brown skins. The stations were very lively places, and many Indian women had a child tied to their backs. The children had big velvety eyes with thoughtful, curious expressions, and silky, dark blue, crow's-wing hair. The men in their dark felt hats looked as if they had come straight out of a western. They displayed pieces of silver jewellery with turquoises set in them, and offered us these in a lordly way, as if they were a present, for a few dollars. At every stop the grey of Europe became more and more remote, buried beneath this kaleidoscope of colours and shapes.

I reached Mexico City about six in the evening. The station was swarming with a cheerful multi-coloured crowd, everybody talking in loud and rapid Spanish to the accompaniment of bands in native costume playing noisily. It was a picturesque and animated scene.

In Rome I had thought I was having a star's reception; I didn't know what it meant. The full production team of Mexicans and French who had already been here a few days, the crowd, the bands—they had all come to welcome me. There were joyful cries and shouts of 'Viva!' and the inevitable fireworks let off to celebrate the occasion. If they didn't roll out a red carpet for me, it must have simply been because that wasn't done in these parts. Crowd, bands, radio interviewers and journalists escorted me to my car in a pleasant free-for-all.

That evening I wrote to Henri and to Mike describing this boisterous and colourful arrival. Next day I started on the period of preparation before the shooting, which I always found rather exciting.

The Mexican dress-designer and I—nothing had been made in Paris—began taking counsel together over Nellie's *trousseau*. As she was travelling with only a single big case, one of the props in the film, this was obviously very important. It would contain small, light dresses, blouses and skirts. The work of selection could at present be no more than a rough sketch, indicating the general lines of the picture; the character was no more than a silhouette for me at the moment. I realised that I knew scarcely anything about my part, or what scenes I had to play.

It had been agreed that the script of the film would be handed to me on my arrival. I asked Yves Allégret and Aurenche, who had accompanied him, and both seemed rather reticent on the subject. I gradually learnt that the film was to be called *Les orgueilleux*, and that as the action had been shifted from Asia to Mexico, Jean-Paul Sartre had rejected the adaptation, which in his judgment was not nearly faithful enough.

This was disturbing news. The name of Sartre had been an important guarantee for me. It had influenced my decision to accept the part, and I was worried about the repercussions his rejection would have. 'So do you plan to make changes in the script?'

'No. Borderie, Raoul Lévy, Aurench and I all think it's all right as it is. I'm quite sure that when you've read it, you'll think so too.'

'Sartre's name, if I understand aright, will not appear in the credits. I suppose Gérard Philipe knows about this. How did he take it?'

'He was quite happy. You won't see him this evening, by the way. He's gone out somewhere with his wife, and they won't be back till late. You'll be able to talk to him about it tomorrow.'

But Philipe wasn't the person I had to talk to about it.

They had at last given me the shooting script. About midnight I finished reading it. Discouraged, I put it down on my bedspread, snuggled down shivering into bed to think things over—at an altitude of 7000 feet, the nights were cold. It was not the quality of the script which had produced this effect on me. It was excellent, with great dramatic intensity and a consistently impressive atmosphere built up. The dialogue was realistic and natural; it was really a fine piece of work. That only showed up all the more clearly, by contrast, the slightness—not to say nullity—of my part. The film was entirely built round the doctor's role, and very fine scenes he had, too; any actor would have been delighted to play this character, a man whose existence has been degraded by drink and remorse and who no longer finds even drink any help in enduring it. But the woman playing opposite him was a complete nonentity.

This has become more and more the case in the French cinema, but at that time there were still some women stars and I found it astonishing as well as shattering.

It is a significant fact that for some time now few films have been built round a woman's character. Everything suggests that the cinema is the last refuge of the male chauvinist, which is all the more striking in our age of women's lib. Woman claims equality and is becoming more independent, yet she has never had such a diminished and dependent place in films. They are built round men like Alain Delon, de Funès, Jean-Paul Belmondo, Philippe Noiret, Lino Ventura, Jean-Louis Trintignant, etc. etc. This is inevitable, since the choice of subjects is masculine: comic films, politically committed films, films of action and violence—these are all things which are considered rather outside a woman's prerogative.

I was incensed to have been inveigled into coming so far, leaving those I loved, for such a miserable part. Not a single time in the script was I offered any chance of filling out my character, showing by my acting what made her tick. I decided to telephone Olga. We couldn't hear each other properly, the line was full of crackling, but I managed to tell her my problem. 'I don't like complaining. I've no wish to seem like a *prima donna*, but really I've nothing to do. I scarcely exist. All that's asked of me is to weep from beginning to end.'

Olga's tone was firm, and comforted me greatly. 'You mustn't accept this. You must stand up for yourself. But if you like, I'll jump onto a plane and come over to help.'

I was very tempted to say 'Yes, please come', and then stop bothering. I dreaded this kind of discussion, for which I was ill equipped: my shyness and fear of being misjudged always put me in a position of inferiority. But Olga was my friend first, and only after that my agent. I didn't want just out of cowardice to inflict an unnecessary trip on her. So I assured her I would cope alone.

The hours before my protest were painful for me. Although defending her rights is part of an actress's profession, agent or no agent, I have always tried to avoid making personal demands. However, producers, director and adapter were no doubt all aware of the justice of my claims, for they didn't appear astonished by my reaction. Their objections to changing the script at this stage seemed a matter of form, and we were soon agreed in principle. Aurenche assured me he would 'arrange something'. After a few conversations and re-writes, two scenes were added. In one, I am alone with the doctor and have to turn over my husband's body. Going through his pockets, I realise that in this remote spot I am completely without resources, without a peso.

The second was something very different—a sort of strip-tease. In a sordid room, exhausted and dying of heat, I take off my *crêpe-de-Chine* slip, that being the maximum undress permitted at the time. I stretch out on my bed in pants and bra, and to comfort myself with a little air, I pass a small electric fan over my body.

When the film came out, this scene was described as 'sexy'. It was 'about as far as you could go'. 'They didn't need much in 1953,' people will say today who are quite blasé about naked bodies.

Although it may sound otherwise, I have no respect for sexual taboos. When someone has the dubious taste to ask me: 'Would you be ready to perform in an erotic scene?' I say no. But that is not from any prissiness; I merely think there is a right time and use for everything. In my view it is not nakedness which is objectionable in certain films, but the way it is exploited.

A fortnight later we left by car for Vera Cruz, on the south-west coast of the Gulf of Mexico. I had prepared myself for the typical idea of Mexico: the desert, cactuses like candela-bras, big hats hiding face and shoulders, the whole picture-postcard scene. But here we were, passing through Switzer-land: green mountains, peaceful prairies stretching out between pine forests! Just before we arrived, I did have my little portion of burning desert behind the car's carefully closed windows.

Then we were in Vera Cruz. When I got out of the car outside the hotel, I staggered back, choked by the heat; we had had air-conditioning in the car. It was a damp heat, 90 per cent humidity, and as my cases were carried in, I spared a thought for poor Charlotte, Maximilian's wife, the Empress of Mexico—who went mad. Fancy having to reign in a town like this; I would have abdicated at once!

I swept into the foyer, sure I would find there the comfort of air-conditioning. Not so. We were in a small provincial town, and in this holiday hotel such a luxury was unknown. The sheets were damp. They never got dry and they smelt musty. The room was full of insects running about, climbing and flying.

There were wooden bars on the windows. I pushed open a shutter, and in the slit of blinding light could see a motionless town, all its doors and shutters closed, dozing in a fog of heat. I hastily closed the shutter again.

For five months I had to live in this Turkish-bath atmosphere, unable to stomach the food, based on sweet peppers (whereas I had very much enjoyed the food in Mexico City). I took all kinds of precautions which made everybody laugh: avoiding raw fruit and salads, cleaning my teeth in mineral water, living on a few dishes of seasoned rice, rum and coca-cola. This unusual diet took several pounds off my weight and allowed me to retain my figure—I doubt if I have ever been as slim again. Anyhow, I was one of the few people in the production who didn't get ill.

I was very curious about Gérard Philipe. He had come into the hotel restaurant in a white suit, looking immaculate, tall and slender, a Renaissance figure with a boyish smile. It was true that he inspired a maternal feeling in women, and although I didn't feel it myself, I could understand it. I found him attractive, charming, amusing—but our relationship during the whole of the shooting never went beyond a friendly but distant camaraderie. I have tried since then to analyse why we did not come any closer. Certainly he lived in his own very private world, which I didn't know, and then both of us perhaps relied too much on the appearance we presented to each other. He seemed to me a committed 'leftie', while he took *me*, I think, for a conventional middle-class woman.

The humidity was almost as oppressive at night as during

263

the day. In the evenings actors and technicians would take refuge in the bar and sit around over their whiskies having long conversations. There was nothing to stop me joining them, but as the climate was so tiring I preferred as a rule to go up to my room. Micheline would accompany me—yes, she had become my dresser—and we would chat for a bit before she went off to bed. The heat tired her even worse than it did me; I was a bit worried about her.

She and I had met again with great pleasure during the shooting of *La minute de vérité*. I had asked Jean: 'You wouldn't sort of lend me La Miche when you're not in a film yourself?' He laughed. 'As you and she must have arranged things together, I suppose I'd better say yes.' So after that she continued to share herself out between 'M'sieur Gabin' and 'M'ame Morgan'.

I no longer talked to her of M'sieur Gabin, but of Henri and Mike. She would listen to me patiently, smoking her inevitable cigarette, and in reply give me the benefit of her good practical sense, her firm and clear philosophy of life. It was marvellous having her with me. I appreciated her way of stubbing out a cigarette-end in the ashtray before answering—she somehow turned this into a gesture of comfort. She made me laugh, too, exercising her sly, irreverent, Parisian wit over everything and everyone. In the evenings she was usually my only companion.

I found great affinity with the Mexican actors, Carlos Lopez Moctezuma and Manuel Mendoza. That brought me in touch with the real Mexican people, who are a combination of three communities: the temperamental Spaniards, proud of the blood of the *conquistadores* flowing through their veins; the Mexicans of mixed origins, whose rough and rather surly attitude is explained by the suspicion they feel for 'pink-skins', the *gringos* who have oppressed them (but when they give you their confidence, what incomparable friends!) and the Indians, with their aloof and taciturn honesty, lacking the Westerner's easy smile. In their impassive faces, only the eyes, a liquid black, reveal their feelings. When I summoned up the courage to face the climate, I went for walks with Carlos and Manuel. Doors and faces opened up for *them*. These walks, and my times at work, were my best moments.

I think the country and the isolation had something to do with my lack of warm relationships outside these two. We were living on top of each other, without much chance of escape except by seeing the country. This is what Anne and Gérard Philipe did on days when he wasn't wanted on the set: they hired small charter planes which enabled them to go quite a long way in the tracks of the 'Plumed Serpent'. It sounds a tempting way of passing the time, but only if there are two of you. I just didn't feel like making the effort on my own; besides it was so hot! At midday Gérard boiled an egg on the window-ledge, giving it the regulation three minutes—in the sun.

Nearly ninety in the shade, and down by the harbour we were filming right in the sun. From the end of the quay, Gérard and I watched the slow passing of fishing-boats and exchanged a few idle sentences. Carlos joined us. 'You know there are sharks?' said Gérard.

'In the harbour?'

'Yes, they stay in deep water looking out for any trash: fishes' entrails thrown out by fishermen, dead fish, refuse of all sorts.'

Quite close to us a car stopped noisily. Tourists left the overheated bodywork and spread out along the quay. A swarm of small boys suddenly emerged from nowhere, surrounding them and imploring: 'Pesos! Pesos! Señor ... Señora.' Many were good-looking, but quite a lot had bloated bellies like the abdomens of some insects. The group of tourists, surrounded by the imploring band, made for the end of the quay, with their guide at the head; but the seven- or eight-year-old *muchachos* soon pushed past them. The guide threw a coin in the water and several boys plunged in after it; the tourists, delighted, began throwing in more coins. The boys jumped into the water covered with iridescent oil and rubbish. I couldn't believe my eyes.

'Are you sure there are sharks, Gérard?' I asked in horror.

'Yes.'

'Don't be scared,' said Carlos reassuringly. 'We're used to

seeing them here at a distance from the beach. You'll get used to it, too.'

'But they're here in the harbour!' I protested. 'And these children diving for pesos—it's cruel, it ought to be forbidden.'

'They'd still dive,' said Carlos, a profound lassitude in his eyes, a fatalistic resignation. Gérard's eyes showed helpless compassion. He shrugged his shoulders. 'You don't know what poverty can do to people.'

I then caught a glimpse of the real Gérard, and it was probably because of this flash that we made so much better contact two years later during *Les grandes manœuvres* when we were under René Clair's direction. This was a rare pleasure. It was perhaps the lighthearted yet intimate atmosphere which suited us and removed our mutual prejudices. It was Gérard in fact who unwittingly inspired Mike with his 'vocation'. It was not his mother he came to see filming that day but the male star whose charm and nonchalance dazzled him. When Gérard asked him what he was going to be when he grew up, nine-year-old Mike stood up very straight, wearing the peaked cap Gérard had lent him, and to my great astonishment answered: 'An actor. Like you.'

An assistant producer came to fetch us. 'Señora Morgan, Gérard, could you come please? Everything is ready.'

Yves quietly explained the scene to us: 'We're shooting your first meeting, Gérard. You're completely drunk, only just able to walk. You, Michèle, are looking for a doctor—your husband is dying. You're walking as straight as he is crooked. You don't see her, Gérard, and you bump into her. She takes a step back, deeply disgusted. You are smiling, and with a trembling hand you vaguely touch your hat... Michèle, you start from here, Gérard from there. I'll give you a signal.'

Frayed straw hat, dirty native shirt full of holes. A man knocks into me, then looked up at me with eyes that have lost all intelligence. His lips are moist and spluttering. He stammers an apology.

A few seconds before, in the same tattered costume, he could have been a young aristocrat. It was a metamorphosis in depth. Whether it was the remarkable and painful scene where the doctor in his drunken state dances for a bottle of alcohol, sweat streaming from his brow over his face, or the one where he remembers that he is a doctor, Gérard's impersonation was brilliant.

Yet although it was a great pleasure to act with him, he gave me the feeling of working with an illusionist, making me a spectator of his performance; whereas Jean Gabin made me into an actress. When a scene with Jean was over, I continued to feel I was the woman with whom he had just lived out a few minutes of a story. Two different talents and two forms of art!

Despite the added scenes my part remained shadowy compared to Gérard's; but for all that, its importance in the story made it count among the most striking in my career. The grim realism of some scenes, however, sometimes made me uneasy. I alone could know that I was often giving Nellie my own feelings: the cruel, all too convincing study presented to me by Gérard of degeneration through alcohol, another drug, was shattering in its inevitable reminders of Henri.

I couldn't confide in anyone about that, not even La Miche. The time dragged on; we were long past the two months scheduled. I couldn't keep my mind off Mike and Henri. I missed them both so much, and news of them was uncertain.

In the clammy humidity of my room—its corners swarming, as I could guess, with many varieties of insect—I would write to Henri before stretching out under the protection of my mosquito-net. I sent him a daily letter, or rather I handed it to the porter, who would assure me with his best smile: 'It's for the Señor Morgan, it will go at once.' But 'at once' was 'mañana', and 'mañana' might mean several days later. I don't know how many of them reached him; his were also written every day, and reached me irregularly. It was a fragile bond, continually being broken. The telephone worked very badly between Vera Cruz and Rome, and the time difference was a further obstacle to communications; when it was night there, it was day-time in Italy and Henri was at the studio. Reception was difficult, too. I can still hear in my mind his distorted distant voice, disappearing like a diver, swamped by noises of frying, smothered by Spanish and Italian voices, annihilated by silence.

Henri's letters were full of little endearments linking up the trivia of daily happenings. I searched for the truth between the lines. What was he doing? Who was he seeing? And, above all, without me at his side, had he relapsed? That was not a thing you could tell at once from his letters for it was so easy for him to cheat. I scrutinised his signature—nervy, impulsive, apathetic, flabby? It could be any of these things without this giving any real indication. Among the people he told me about, there were many capable of tempting him, and procuring him the drug. I was totally helpless. How could I be any use to him? When I answered one of his letters, it had become a futile exercise. I was discussing a state of mind long past, replaced by others. I had the nasty feeling of being constantly beaten by time, constantly 'missing my connection'.

One evening La Miche was chatting to me as usual, but I found her face drawn, her eyes hollow. 'You ought to go to bed. You need a good night.'

'Yes, I don't know what's the matter with me. I've got a stabbing pain in my back and another in the side of my tummy.'

'The liver?'

'No, I don't think so. But it's getting worse every minute.'

The violence of the pain became unbearable, and she had a terrible night. Nothing we tried relieved her, though she could still joke: 'I'm acting out the film for real.'

In the morning the doctor diagnosed an attack of nephritic colitis, so serious that he decided she would have to be sent home. I drove her to the airport. Pale and feverish, she climbed into the plane with Aurenche and his wife, Lili, an amusing Hungarian whom I liked very much. On my return to the hotel I felt really alone.

This loneliness lasted over two months. I had no company now except my letters to Tanine, Olga, Maman, Aunt

Yvonne, Mike and Henri. I wrote to them as one talks, real diaries filled with little happenings and thoughts and questions. In this activity I somehow filled up the void of times when I was not working.

If Henri had not been an actor, he might have been here, accompanying me as Anne had done with Gérard. We, too, should be seeing the country, sometimes as a foursome, why not? I should have felt more forthcoming with others, readier to share in their lives. Henri would have been dead keen; he loved going out in parties of friends. Instead, he and I were pursuing different lives which the partner knew nothing about, enriching experience with memories which the partner could not share.

I went to sleep, and woke up, and lived with this thought in my mind: what's he going to be like when I get back?

21   *Diversion beneath the Olive Trees*

There was nothing triumphal about my return. Henri was in one of his periods of being determined to cure himself, the dream of all addicts. They all believe it; they think it will be easier and they will suffer less; and they all fail. Of course, being new to this experience, I let him convince me that it would be better for him, and for us. His doctor friend, though sceptical, had told us the doses required, and the rate at which they should be gradually reduced. For the first days everything went well. I felt almost euphoric; at least I began to recover hope. I became like him: every time it was just the right amount. I don't know how far I deliberately deceived myself. It made it possible for me, for us both, to live.

I very quickly noticed that he was cheating, so the search for 'caches' began. The toilets, the lavatory cistern, in little waterproof bags, in tubes of toothpaste—I soon became an expert in the game of hunt-the-thimble for I had as much imagination as he did.

We quarrelled. One painful scene followed another: he was suffering terribly from the progressive withdrawal of the drug. The fine muscular body had shrivelled under the effect of the contractions, the muscles curled up. He begged me to stop the torture. What a temptation it was to let him pick up the syringe, to see his face relax for a moment at the idea that he was going to be able to prepare, with trembling hands, that terrible 'food', the powder you dilute in the spoon you heat. I resisted it, hoping that this actual stage would soon be replaced by an easier one, that we should be over the hump.

A less acute stage did make itself felt quite quickly: some-one had procured the drug for him! Everything had to be started again from scratch. In the end, inevitably, he had to go back into a clinic for any cure to have a chance of success. This was the pathetic part of his case, as it is with so many addicts: he wanted to 'kick the habit', to live normally again, to be happy as in the days at Rome. Those memories were to haunt him to the end.

Suddenly I heard that Bill and Micheline were separating, and getting a divorce. Olga told me she thought Bill was returning to the United States. 'Apparently he's talked about it to several people, even giving the date when he's going. It's only to be expected. He's always divided his time between the two countries, but his business is more over there.'

I didn't ask what business as it didn't interest me. But what would happen with Mike? I dashed off to see Mr Weill, who was not very encouraging. 'It's hard to know what your ex-husband may do.'

'Has he the right to take my son with him?'

'I don't see how he could be prevented from doing so. In fact, I really think you had better be prepared for this eventuality.'

But against all the probabilities, Bill entrusted Mike to me. 'Don't be under too many illusions. It's on a very precarious basis.' My realist lawyer had to put in his damper. Who cared? I installed Mike at home—in the room I had prepared over four years ago: *his* room. I could at last experience what I had always imagined: I would see him sit at his little desk, hear him laugh and play, and at night when he was asleep, go and listen to his regular soft breathing. It was the first time since his birth that he would be really mine.

My destiny seemed to be two-faced like Janus. It established a sort of balance: Mike was returning to me as Henri moved further away.

One evening I came home about six. Mike, back from school, was doing his homework in his room, directly above mine. I went through the sitting-room, feeling weary after dealing with various bits of business. I had had a long discussion with Olga about several parts which had been offered me, but I didn't like any of them. Some of my contracts had not been fulfilled yet, and I wanted to have a breather, to take my time over the next choice. I threw my bag and gloves on my bed, and took off my hat.

'Michèle!'

It was my husband's voice, but it sounded different, toneless. 'Yes, darling.' I turned round and went back into the sitting-room. He had just slumped into one of the armchairs; he was very pale, his nostrils were pinched, and he was having difficulty in breathing. I dashed over. His hand was cold. I seized his wrist and tried to take his pulse but couldn't find it. I took off his tie, ran to the 'phone, rang his doctor, and returned to him. He seemed almost unconscious, deathly white, his eyes closed, not stirring. It was in this state that the doctor found him.

After examining Henri, he told me it was not very serious. 'Not yet. Just a warning. A little heart trouble: between the drug, his cures and the rest, he's overworking his heart. But don't worry too much, it's still in fairly good shape.'

The rest! At the time we were in the manic phase. The last cure seemed to have been successful, or anyhow it had restored his vitality. He had an attitude towards this 'good health' which I now knew well; it involved all the masculine reactions needed to prove his fitness. He had grown fat. It was the period 'without', which meant without the drug but with a lot of whisky. This induced bursts of uninhibited energy in all fields, including sex. I reached the point of telling myself that at least he would have had that to enjoy. I had few illusions left for I knew that this period would be followed by the period 'with', which meant an amorphous creature, without desire, who had lost all his virility.

I led a see-saw existence which I found very draining: either I was with a sort of maniac who couldn't control himself and was believed to be an alcoholic (though in fact he was never that), or else with a zombie.

Parallel with this I was having a different struggle: to keep up appearances. It was equally exhausting, and called for vigilance at all times: no one must know. Mike had never noticed anything, and Henri for him had always been a big 'buddy';

when Henri was 'ill', he would stay in his room. Never in front of my son did he make a gesture or say anything which Mike would have found odd. But I trembled lest Bill should learn something; the professional background was the only one I couldn't quite cover—there were too many people who were in on the little 'fixes'. The proselytism of junkies is well known, but Henri, despite his condition, despised those who indulged in it.

The people I feared and shunned most were the journalists, more particularly the photographers. They mustn't see Henri in this state, above all if they worked for certain papers which in their sympathy for me would be likely to produce front-page headlines along the lines of MICHÈLE MORGAN'S CALVARY: MAN SHE LOVES IS HEROIN ADDICT ... HER LIFE A HELL, etc. Henri was already showing too many signs of wear and tear for me to be able to control things. As a matter of fact, I discovered afterwards that the press had been very understanding towards me in remaining silent. In giving credence to my white lies, they did me a great service; especially as at that time there was not the same freedom of speech on the subject as there is now. The use of drugs was still mainly confined to literary and artistic circles and it had not penetrated to the man-in-the-street. I had visits from the police, and the Superintendent of the Drug Squad boasted of the very small number of addicts. The word and the deed were still shocking; there was little attempt made to understand and to cure.

Such a completely unbalanced life inevitably had its effects on my career: from 1953 to the end of 1954 I was in eight films; in 1955 only three, *Marie-Antoinette*, *Si Paris m'était conté* and *Oasis*, a Franco-German co-production; and in the next two years it was down to one a year.

The exteriors of *Oasis* lasted for two months, during which we lived on the borders of the Sahara. The splendour of nights in the desert and the Southern Cross were far from making me forget my troubles; on the contrary, I had plenty of time to wallow in them. I did not stand up well to the heat, or the company of scorpions! Directly I was away from Henri, I was scared for him, and for us: any imprudence on his part, and the façade I was so painfully keeping up would collapse. How long was this life going to last? I still loved Henri, but I was going to leave him. If he realised this, if he knew I meant it, perhaps that would make him resist temptation.

It was in this state of mind that I returned, very tired. I arrived in Paris to learn that Papa was seriously ill. I dashed over to them, and Maman told me there had been a mistake in diagnosis: for years my father had been treated for his heart, and he had just gone into a uraemic coma.

Papa desperately ill—the memory of receiving this news is succeeded in my mind by a series of images: he comes out of the coma but is in terrible pain; he gets up for the last time and talks to me of the prophet Ezekiel; in his delirium he thinks there are a whole lot of people round him—'Why's everybody crowding round me, Simone?' There is nothing I can do for him, nothing. Is there anyone I *can* do something for? I can't for Henri, either. But perhaps for Mike? It was the sort of time when you ask yourself questions to which there are no answers.

Oh, if only I had come back sooner. Would it have helped? 'No,' said a doctor friend, 'it was already too late, it was irreversible.' A few hours later Maman and I were weeping in each other's arms. Papa was dead. He was only sixty-nine.

The weeks and months and years did not bring any change. Exhausted, constantly feeling at the end of my tether, completely aware of my inability to help Henri, to get him out of the vicious circle, I decided to send him away. I thought this might force him to make the effort needed for a final and lasting cure, such as his doctor friend had suggested: 'The only thing which might save you is to go away. If you really want to finish with it, there's a simple method: when you come out of the clinic, go off to the Far North, a Canadian forest, say, and cut down trees, amidst folk who don't know about drugs. If you stay here, you won't get clear of it.'

He couldn't have spoken a truer word. How often had I seen a determined Henri giving in yet again because of the drug people round him, who wouldn't allow him to desert like that. Before we had been at a restaurant or a nightclub five minutes, Henri would get up and go to the 'phone and men would furtively slip him messages. These whisperings in corners, his feigned casualness—'a friend of mine wanted me to find something out for him'—I pretended to be taken in, but nothing escaped me, and I knew that after a more or less brief interval he would relapse again.

Anyhow, it was done—and he had gone. A few days of relative peace followed, even though I couldn't stop thinking of him, having sudden memories breaking in on me, worrying about what would happen to him when left to his own resources. Then Olga came to see me: 'I had a visit from him. He was crying. He sobbed in my office like a child. I promised him I'd talk to you. One can't leave him like that. He said that this time...' All the arguments regurgitated over a hundred times came up again; and I gave in. A week later Henri presented the very image of decline, a worn-out rag. Everything had started again, but this time I knew that something had finished: an indispensable little spring, the one that never fails to set things in motion again, had snapped. After this it would never be quite the same.

Henri still worked periodically in between cures; he managed to keep going in the 'with' periods. In 1957 he was in a film with Romy Schneider which was being shot in Nice. The unit stayed at the Negresco, but I took refuge at the Hôtel du Cap in Antibes. I had no wish to be with Henri. I needed to recover my strength. I couldn't go on, and asked myself for the hundredth time what was left of our marriage. Two years of marvellous memories, two years of passionate love. We no longer had a life together, and heroin was responsible for the break-up. What had I become for him? I often felt he was afraid of me. The transformation from the rôle of mistress and wife to that of delinquent child's mother, or else nurse, had made things very different between us. I nagged him and got annoyed with him, and he couldn't stand my surveillance. He would react with equal fury, we would have a terrible scene, then he would ask my forgiveness and say he loved me. But perhaps the fear of losing me was a stronger force than love. I was the last solid element in his disintegrating life.

I was at this point in my reflections one day, when I was brought my coffee on the big terrace of the Eden-Roc, a place to dream, to love, to be happy . . .

'Madame, you're wanted on the 'phone.'

It was André Cayatte. 'Dear Michèle, I've a part to offer you, that of an ugly woman, very plain indeed . . .'

This was fairly unexpected. I had been offered dumbness and blindness, but not ugliness.

Cayatte burst out laughing, content with the effect produced. 'I believe you know Gérard Oury?' he went on.

'Yes, we were in *La belle que voilà* together.'

'We're at Saint-Paul-de-Vence, in my house, writing a script together called *Le miroir à deux faces*. We'd like to tell you the story-line. Gérard has had a very amusing idea, but I'll leave you with the surprise to come. There are three main parts: you, Bourvil, who will play your husband, and Gérard, the surgeon. A very special kind of surgeon. I'm not telling you any more. Are you free tomorrow evening? Come and have dinner with us at Les Corses, a restaurant above the Grande Corniche.'

It was months since I had seen Gérard Oury. The last time must have been with Jacqueline, his wife, at the Elysée Club, when we happened to meet at a première. Henri and I had dinner with them afterwards. An amusing recollection of Gérard remained in my memory.

La belle que voilà was in '49, six years before, just after Rome. Lydia and Joseph Bercholz had had the idea of re-teaming the stars of *Fabiola*. They looked for a story, and agreed on a novel by Vicki Baum, *Doris Hart's Career*, from which Françoise Giroud, our scriptwriter in *La loi du nord*, had produced a scenario for *La belle que voilà*. She was doing the adaptation and dialogue; the director was Paul le Chanois, a young man who looked middle-aged owing to his premature baldness. After he had read us the scenario, and we had passed the stage of collective enthusiasm, I had my doubts about our choice: Françoise Giroud and Le Chanois would need a lot of talent to give any authenticity to this sombre drama.

The role of Bruno, nicknamed The Beast—an impresario who abuses his power—had not yet been allocated, and over dinner one evening Le Chanois talked to us very warmly about a young actor, Gérard Oury, whom he had just seen in a play. 'He's got great presence, talent and charm, and he's such a nice chap, too.' We burst out laughing. 'That's not exactly called for in the part,' observed Lydia drily. Slightly vexed, Le Chanois defended his candidate. 'He has a flair for characterisation ... Right, just to prove it, shall we get him to do a screen test?'

I had forgotten about this discussion when Le Chanois insisted on my coming to see the dresses designed by Max Douy. In between two fittings, Olga and I went to the studios. 'Let's have a look at Gérard Oury,' she suggested. 'He's having his screen test.' I remember having thought: 'Poor chap, he must be having stage-fright just now.' He had come on, a slight young man with black hair and green eyes, and was going through his scene, with my understudy standing in for me. He had a good, deep, well-placed voice. Nobody had seen us come in, but when we walked towards the set, everything stopped. There was a hubbub of 'hello's' and introductions. The young man reminded me that we had already seen each other at the Simon School, about a dozen years earlier. 'You'd come back to the school just after *Gribouille*,' he recalled with an accuracy which slightly surprised me.

The shooting started. At the end of the scene Oury seized my understudy in his arms and kissed her violently on the mouth. The realism of his action made her choke. 'Oh, you, well, really ...'

'Sorry, but it's in the part. I am called The Beast.'

After a week of suspense, as Gérard told me later, he rang Le Chanois, who told him: 'Before we engage you, we must have Michèle Morgan's agreement.'

The rushes were excellent: they showed real vigour and authority. I gave my agreement, and Gérard signed his contract with Joseph Bercholz. We began the shooting, and came to the scene with the kiss. We were alone together in a lift, and after some rapid exchanges between us, The Beast had to seize me and give me that violent sensual kiss which had made such a big impact in the tests.

'Camera!' ordered Le Chanois.

The dialogue came to an end. What was he waiting for? He drew me to him, but without the authority which I had appreciated so much in the rushes. Worse, he was trembling. I cheated, and to help him, extended my mouth, half closing my eyes. Gérard Oury took me delicately by the waist, and planted on my lips the most tender, delicate kiss in the world.

'No!' yelled Le Chanois. 'That's not it at all! That's a romantic kiss! Start the scene again, will you, and do it for real this time.'

I looked at Gérard. He didn't seem the kind of man to be scared by women. 'Come on, don't hesitate. What's the matter? Have you got stage-fright? Are you afraid of me?'

'Not at all,' he protested, his face very pale.

We started again. When the time came, he took me in his arms and gave me a very nice film kiss. But it wasn't a Beast's kiss—we never managed one of those!

On 13 June, 1957—Gérard remembers dates—I met Cayatte, bright-eyed, aquiline, and a bronzed, smiling Gérard, at Les Corses. After an enormous steak, grilled over the wood fire, I listened to them narrating the scenario.

'The strange thing is,' said Cayatte, 'that Oury and I had the same idea at the same time quite independently: to find a story concerning the social rôle of the plastic surgeon in the world of today. All we had to do was to write it together.' They narrated it to me together, too, each taking over from the other at a suitable moment. I have never had a scenario so well 'acted' for me in duet.

Cayatte introduced the characters: 'Marie-José, a dull, dowdy young woman, a real plain Jane, is convinced no man will ever want her. When Bourvil, a school-teacher, asks for her hand, she melts with gratitude, and confuses this feeling with love. The honeymoon in Venice, on a shoestring, is a disaster. The man proves mean in every way, almost miserly. She is resigned, believing that with her appearance she is extremely lucky to have found a husband. So she holds her peace. But besides her husband, she has to put up with a formidable and malicious mother-in-law. Her life develops into a series of minor miseries with some fragile moments of happiness.'

Now Gérard came in. 'I'm Dr Bosc, a plastic surgeon. I am to blame for a car accident in which Bourvil is hurt. I have him taken to my clinic, and you are informed. In my office I stare at you, you interest me. I ask you: "Do you want to become beautiful?" The question throws you, you blush, and ask if I'm making fun of you. But all the same you're excited.'

Cayatte resumed the narrative. 'He knows what he's saying and what he can do. Bosc is one of the best-known plastic surgeons, and Marie-José's case is a pleasant challenge for him. He is sure he can transform her. Naturally, after hesitating, she accepts. The schoolmaster goes back home, and life resumes its course. With some difficulty Marie-José succeeds in leaving home, on the pretext of spending a month at an aunt's. In reality she goes into Bosc's private clinic—and the miracle is performed. One morning, when the last dressings are removed, and she contemplates herself in the mirror, she can't recognise herself. That woman in front of her, scrutinising her face with astonished, almost stupefied eyes—is it really her?'

Gérard: 'Imagine the scene, Michèle. First of all you feel nothing but amazement. It's incredible! You, the ugly duckling, have become radiantly beautiful. As you, Michèle, are, in fact. Then you're apprehensive: what is your husband going to say?'

Cayatte again: 'Your return home is disastrous. The marriage has been suddenly thrown off balance. You can picture the school-teacher staring at Marie-José, stunned, incredulous, furious. She is no longer the woman he married, carefully choosing her for her plainness so that he can reign over her, dominate her, crush her, and still feel sure she will never deceive him. He has been robbed of her ugliness, that guarantee of fidelity. Frantic with rage, he turns his hatred onto the surgeon.'

It was Gérard who finished the tale. 'I pay dearly for my mistake—introducing beauty into a marriage which can't stand up to it. In a fit of mad jealousy, convinced I've only done this to take advantage of her, which is untrue, Bourvil kills me. He has a loaded revolver. He fires—bang, bang ...' With a lavish gesture he upset his glass of Beaujolais onto my dress.

Superimposed on my memory was an identical gesture in Rome—with Henri's glass of port spreading over my dress.

When we left Les Corses, it was pelting, like the torrential rain which had made Henri and me take refuge in his car. Such analogies were dangerous.

'Shall I take you back to your hotel, Michèle?'

'No, to the Negresco, please.'

The first hairpin bends were taken in silence. Gérard drove well, and I felt safe in his Lancia; he too, it seemed, had a passion for Italian cars. The rain lashed against the windows, and the headlights turned it into a silver curtain the car was drawing apart. I looked at his profile, with which yesterday I had been quite unconcerned. Even on the way to the res-taurant I hadn't felt any special curiosity over him. Had it come when I heard him presenting his scenario with such pleasing force and authority? Probably. I was too shy myself to like shy men. And to think I had retained the memory of a young man nervous about kissing me. We began chat-ting, and enjoyed finding out how far our opinions and feelings agreed. We talked shop too, of course, and a little of everything. When Gérard stopped the car outside the Negresco, the rain was beating down just as hard, rebound-ing on the bodywork, and on the deserted Promenade des Anglais.

'Good-night.'

'Good-night.' I opened the car door. The porter with his umbrella was waiting for me. Gérard detained me for a moment. 'I'm going back to Paris in three days. Would you be free for dinner one evening?'

'Yes, perhaps.' I hesitated. 'I shall be back at Cap d'Antibes tomorrow. Ring me there. We'll see ...'

'What time?'

'I have a tennis lesson between eleven and twelve. Apart from that, I shall be in my hotel all the time.'

A slight wave, and I went into the foyer of the Negresco. The night-porter handed me the key. 'Good-night, Madame Morgan.'

'Monsieur Vidal isn't back?' I asked in surprise.

'No, madame. Not yet.'

I had promised to come and tell him how we had got on at Les Corses. It was now one o'clock, and if they had been shooting during the night, he would have left me a message. If it hadn't been so late, I should have left. I had long stopped trying to imagine what he might be doing or to find out where he might be. I went to sleep in one of the twin beds.

The noise of the door opening woke me. Through the blinds the sun seemed to be already high. Henri lumbered in. I had closed my eyes and I heard him undress, slump into the other bed, and fall into a heavy sleep, breathing noisily. I had experienced this kind of return so many times. Resignation and total discouragement had only come after over six years of a struggle which this morning I had no desire to carry on; and probably no strength, either.

I left the Negresco and returned to Cap d'Antibes in time for my tennis lesson.

It was past twelve when I came off the court.

'A message for you, Madame Morgan.' There was a pink sheet of paper in a telegram-shaped envelope which said: 'Monsieur Gérard Oury telephoned at 11.30.'

But I'd told him I was playing tennis between eleven and twelve! He must have made a muddle. I would ring him at the Colombe d'Or, Saint-Paul. But why 'phone? Why should I have dinner with him? No real reason. We should be meeting in Paris again anyhow to discuss the film. Best leave things like that.

I was driving my brother Paul to Nice, from where he was taking the boat to Corsica. It was a slow drive, and there was a hold-up near Cros-de-Cagnes. 'They must be shooting a film,' said my brother. 'I can see trucks with a lot of equipment.'

'Yes, it's *Tamango*, a grim story about a slave-trader, with Curt Jurgens. There's the frigate, right by the beach.'

The row of cars started moving again, and I gently accelerated.

'Michèle, Michèle!' Jurgens, an 1830 gentleman in top-hat, frock-coat and top-boots, was signalling to me frantically. 'Got a few minutes to come on board?'

We were in plenty of time for Paul's boat, and I always enjoyed watching others filming, so we accepted the invitation, and followed Jurgens up the accommodation ladder on to the 'set'.

'How long before I'm on?' Jurgens asked the director. 'I'm out of fags.'

'You can go and get some,' was the answer, 'but make it quick. I'd like you back in ten minutes.'

In about that time Jurgens returned—with Gérard Oury. 'You know each other?' he asked.

'Of course,' we answered together.

'I seem to be stopping all my friends today. Gérard was passing, I raised my arm, and here we are!'

'I'm going back to Paris tomorrow,' said Gérard. 'I was off to Nice to buy my ticket.'

'And I'm driving my brother there.'

'Then we're taking the same road—separately. That's a pity.' Gérard paused again and looked down. 'Did they give you my message at your hotel?'

'Yes.'

He looked straight at me again. 'I 'phoned when I knew you were at tennis.' His green eyes were fixed on mine. 'Deliberately,' he added.

I laughed. Was this another male ruse? I knew he was a good actor, but all the same there was a sincerity in his tone which made me give him the benefit of the doubt.

'So that was on purpose?'

'Yes. I rang hoping you wouldn't be there.'

'Well, you were satisfied.'

'In a way, but . . .' He suddenly became very positive, 'Let's have dinner tomorrow evening. I've lots to tell you.'

'About what?'

When he smiled, his whole face crinkled. 'About—work.'
He spoke the word lovingly, so that it sounded incongruous
and funny. 'We'll meet at Saint-Paul-de-Vence, right?' (He
didn't leave me time to say 'yes'.) 'In a restaurant called Les
Oliviers at nine o'clock.'

Destiny had given the signal, like the starting pistol for a
race. It was to be a long, hard race, with many hurdles before
we reached the winning-post.

The evening fell on that delicate Provence countryside.
It rather resembled Tuscany with the dark flame-shaped
cypresses, its chapels, its valleys, the beauty of its evenings.
The sun took its time setting; an orange glow lit up the restaurant terrace and the grey foliage of the olive trees, the light
divided the leaves into vibrant little brush-strokes—van
Gogh's!

'You see,' said Gérard, talking to me about 'work', 'to
uglify you, we'll have to shrink your eyes, eliminate the
beautiful way they tilt gently towards the temples, and then,
above all, disfigure your nose. It's so small and delightful,
we'll have to lengthen it. The curve in the nostrils is too perfect, that must be changed. And your mouth, and your
teeth—all that will have to be got rid of.'

It was hard not to feel flattered by this description of how
he was going to 'uglify' me.

After a brief pause he went on, with a sort of fervour:
'Only we shan't be changing anything but appearances. Your
inner beauty will remain, that's what counts. Any man
could love you as an ugly woman, because you'll still be
beautiful.'

He talked about me, and I listened. Then he talked about
himself, and I still listened. He told me of the tenderness he
felt for his wife, and strangely enough, she became a token
of his sincerity and honesty. Especially as he went on: 'Sometimes during the past years I've told her jokingly: "You see,
apart from you, there's only one woman in the world I could
love, Michèle Morgan."'

That was the moment when I ought to have stopped him.
But I didn't, and he continued, and the air seemed to grow
dense around us. 'That remark is certainly the reason why

yesterday, before leaving for Paris, she asked me, oh, very nicely: "Promise me not to have dinner with Michèle ... outside work." I promised. And as I've told you, I honoured my promise—more or less.'

More or less indeed: it was a sheer gamble! He had rung up at a time when he thought I wouldn't be there. But I might just as well have been there after all; fate can be very accommodating sometimes.

A smile, a change of subject, and the atmosphere relaxed. We talked plays and films and painting and music, and I found I was laughing a good deal. Since my meeting with Henri, Gérard was one of the first men who really made me laugh. I felt, too, how much I liked him, and this was a pleasant feeling. We are all easily attracted by those attracted to us. He talked like a man with plenty to say, and he said it well; the evening with him was becoming 'as good as a play'. We talked about the film and his ambitions. He told me how important it was for him that his first script should come off, and he confided that although he loved acting, it did not completely fulfil him or satisfy his creative urge. I still listened. When a man tells you about his life, it's because he wants to come into yours.

This thought neither shocked nor displeased me. I felt at once fancy-free and unable to commit myself.

The dinner finished, we lingered over our coffee. From the foot of the hotel terrace the hill sloped gently down into the olive-trees and vines, noisy with the first cicadas.

It was a long, long time since I had felt so good. Gradually, I, too, began to talk; and Gérard listened to me as any woman would like to have a man listen to her—quietly, attentively, understandingly. I began by telling him my worries over Mike, and soon came to what my marriage with Bill had been like, letting myself slip into the present, my obsession. It isn't easy to admit that you are not happy, still less to say it without accusing your marriage partner; to run Henri down would have been for me an unpardonable betrayal, worse than infidelity. I took refuge in the blanks of unfinished sentences—which did not deceive Gérard. It was our first collusion.

The night was soft and clear. 'Let's go for a walk,' said Gérard.

We walked reflectively through the tortuous little streets of Saint-Paul, then out on the road for a bit, turning off it for a footpath which led through vineyards. And under the olive-trees, all silvery beneath the moon, Gérard kissed me; gently yet fervently. At that instant I wanted to believe it was a mild flirtation, a delicious moment I badly needed, but without importance or possible sequel.

The next day I found this idea very satisfactory: a pleasant memory, a brief diversion beneath the olive-trees.

Charlie Parker, a well-known make-up artist, had been brought over from Hollywood to 'break up' my face. 'Beauty depends on harmony,' observed André Cayatte, who had come to watch the demolition work. 'We want to make each of your features just too big or too small.' Charlie Parker began his assault on the harmony, while the director continued to expound his ideas enthusiastically.

'The difference between beauty and ugliness is often only a matter of millimetres. Many beautiful women only just miss being ugly, and the converse is equally true—how many ugly ducklings are almost swans! With you we have to work by small touches. We're not trying to make you grotesque—only plain, without charm. Everything Charlie's going to add to your face will be such that it can be taken away or improved through a simple surgical operation. You'll see.'

For a time I didn't see much, though Charlie was very busy. A prosthesis, which took days to perfect, gave me a projecting jaw. With the aid of a thin piece of skin the shape of my eyes was narrowed. Shaggy eyebrows going down at the corners seemed to close the eyes up. A false nose, slightly too long, was put over mine. To change the oval shape of the face and to make it heavier at the bottom, big balls of cotton wool were stuck onto my cheeks. They also changed my diction, as they forced me to speak more slowly and carefully.

Two hours were needed every morning to fix this artificial ugliness. The first time Charlie said, 'Look at yourself,' I was stupefied. I couldn't possibly be this woman staring at me with a stunned expression, opening her mouth when I spoke.

What a shock to my vanity! An object lesson in the fragility of beauty.

Behind me in the mirror André and Gérard were examining me with critical eyes.

'Am I ugly enough?' I asked.

They seemed to be in doubt.

'Too much so, perhaps?' I suggested.

'No, it's fine for looks,' said André, 'but psychologically ...'

'Your eyes betray you,' Gérard explained, finishing the sentence. 'They're the confident eyes of a woman men turn to look at and women envy. Who's interested in Marie-José? No one. You have to learn the humility of people that no one looks at.'

This happened quite naturally and very quickly, without any effort from me: not being able to remove my make-up, etc., before the evening, I carried Marie-José's face round with me. It was with that face that I went into a restaurant, it was her that people passed in the street unseeing. It was a novel sensation for me. The problem was solved; nobody turned to look at Marie-José, or if they did, only to think things like: 'Good Lord, they're shooting a film with *her*! She really is plain.'

I didn't mind the anonymity imposed on me by my new face: you can look at the world more clearly when it doesn't see you; and I discovered that ugliness, like old age, often makes you invisible. I had never understood more clearly how far a woman's magic mirrors were the eyes of others! The experience was very useful for my interpretation; it helped me to present the character from inside. This unknown actress, who caused surprise by being in a film, was me; I therefore had the chance of giving life to a character when none of the credit was attributable to the shape of my eyes or a photogenic face. I enjoyed being liberated from all that. I won't go so far as to say that it was an encumbrance, but the present metamorphosis allowed me for once to act a part without the aid of the good looks which had been a main attraction right from my first film.

The make-up was so successful that on one of the first afternoons, when Henri came to the set, he passed by me without
looking at me. He searched about, and asked La Miche where
I was.

'I'm here, behind you!'

He turned round, looked at me incredulously, and burst
out laughing. 'It's marvellous—but don't forget to take your
make-up off before you come home.'

Yet a strange thing happened that evening when I abandoned my false nose: I almost missed it. I no longer recognised my real face. I passed my finger over the end of my
nose, which had become incredibly small again; in the end
I had become used to Marie-José's sad long nose. I began
wondering about my real face—was it so harmonious after
all? I found this reaction extremely consoling. Many ideas
I had had about ugliness, about the conditions of life and
thoughts of those afflicted with it, crumbled away. They
could take comfort from the grace which is given us to
become ourselves, to accept even our plainness, and better
still, to find satisfactions in it. As a matter of fact, very few
women are really aware of what they look like. They all have
something which satisfies them, and quite often, strangely
enough, it is one of their less attractive features: one will criti-
cise her quite average nose and be pleased with a graceless
mouth; another will be sad about her very nice breasts and
take delight in her skinny legs.

Indeed both ugliness and beauty are highly subjective—
I could say this after being artificially ugly for a few weeks.
Was I beautiful in 'real life'? So people said; but one day the
word had overcome me because of the circumstances and
the man who uttered it—the apparently misanthropic
Michel Simon. This was in Rome, while we were shooting
Fabiola. Henri was waiting for me. We were going out to
dinner. He was talking to Michel, and they both watched
me come towards them. I was astonished to see big tears
flowing over Michel's cheeks. 'What's the matter?' I asked
anxiously.

'I'm crying because you're beautiful,' he answered.

I can still hardly believe that I affected him of all people

in this way; but it has remained in my memory as a shattering, wonderful statement.

The shooting of *Le miroir à deux faces* was at once a transition
between two phases of my life, a link between them, and
an alibi.

I had returned to Paris in some dismay, for I could no
longer delude myself about my feelings towards Gérard. I
was frightened of those feelings and at the same time welcomed them. The thought of not seeing him any more was
already intolerable to me. I was probably being selfish, but
I needed his strength, his equilibrium, his interest, his love.

Physically, I was very detached towards Henri, but I
suffered emotionally from watching him destroy himself.
Knowing how it had started, I couldn't despise him; and
although I hated the role of nurse which he forced me to play,
nothing would make me give that role up.

I did see Gérard, regularly, and every second spent with
him gave me new courage to face the painful hours when
both Henri and I waited for the onslaught of the monster—
heroin. I fought it with the only weapons I had: love, tenderness, vigilance. But the times when I was with Gérard wove
indissoluble bonds between us. The flame of his passion
kindled mine, confronting me with a decision which couldn't
be avoided: which of the two men should I choose? I couldn't
lose one or desert the other. I was constantly tormenting my
brain with a cruel game of dice in which a new aspect of
the dilemma kept turning up at each throw.

Gérard wanted me—as much as Henri did—and was
always telling me how indispensable I was to him. His professional life was developing fast in its new direction: he was
still acting, but also writing scripts. He would tell me their
story-lines, imagining these with a power and dynamism
which was later to produce *Le corniaud*, *La grande vadrouille*,
and other great successes. As in all love affairs, every moment
counted for us. I vividly remember our secret meetings,
usually in his car or mine. Few people can have become more
familiar with some of the side-streets of Paris, where we
would stop the car for a while, never long enough, feeling

we had become a tiny island in the middle of the city. It was in these moments that our lasting partnership was born, fragile and yet so strong.

During the shooting of *Le miroir* we experienced our first separation. I had to go to Venice for the exteriors of the honeymoon. Gérard said he wouldn't be able to start off with us.

'Can't you really?'

'I'm afraid not, Michèle. I have to watch the plastic surgery which we're using as a model for the film, and that's being done at the end of the week. I'll join you as soon as possible.'

'You'll come quickly?'

'Very quickly.'

He did join us, and we had reached the last day of the shooting at Venice; Bourvil was about to play his big 'drunk' scene. André explained his 'positions', which were fairly complex: the schoolmaster is returning home full of drink and resentment; his wife's beauty has broken up their marriage. He hates her for it, and yet still loves her. Bourvil has to go round bumping against the furniture—a precise and complicated circuit—insulting Marie-José, half crying, half sneering. Although we knew Bourvil as an outstanding actor with a tremendous range of expression, the technical difficulties made a scene of this kind very difficult to bring off successfully, even with many takes.

For once there was an almost religious silence on the set, like the roll of drums before a new circus number. From cameraman to producer we were all conscious of the concentration such a sequence demanded.

'Camera! Take 1!'

The scene went through, 'Cut!' cried André.

Then something exceptional happened. From the gangways at the back of the set came a burst of enthusiastic clapping.

Bourvil saluted, laughed, did a pirouette, struck up the silly little song he was so fond of, 'It's we who are the bees, buzz buzz', then whirled me round in a crazy waltz.

It was irresistible. Gérard and I caught each other's eye, aware as usual of shared feelings. We were both moved by

Bourvil's reaction to the applause, and appreciated the genuine modesty it revealed, characteristic of this honest, sensitive, spontaneous man.

The end of *Le miroir* left us rather at a loss. Gérard and I had been happy on the set. There was an amused connivance in André's eyes when he directed us. We had mixed feelings about this: we were glad to have his approval, but worried that our secret should be so easily guessed despite all the trouble we took to act the part of good friends working together. A production team is perceptive and hard to deceive; between shooting sessions they have plenty of time to observe you. What the dresser has failed to notice, the make-up man will have spotted; and someone else may have registered your whispered arrangements for a meeting. Yet these undercover meetings were the breath of life to us. We couldn't have kept going without them.

Gérard was about to start work in *Le dos au mur* with Jeanne Moreau, under a new young director, Edouard Molinaro—directing his first film. Meanwhile I was preparing for *Maxime* with Charles Boyer. These films would mean days and days of not seeing each other.

I had got into a sort of insoluble situation you think only happens to other people: I really did love two men at once, though they were different sorts of love.

When Henri and I were together in the evening, he at his desk in the drawing-room, calm, almost too calm, writing a poem, then getting up and stretching out on the sofa, smoking cigarette after cigarette, while I read a script by the fire—it seemed to me that anyone seeing us would have taken us for a happy couple. But we were no longer happy or a couple. Henri knew he had in some way lost me, that every day made the loss more irretrievable. I didn't lie to him, but he realised there was another man in my life. All I kept from him was the man's name. He didn't try to find out, nor did he ask questions—he was past all that. What he still wanted from me was my tenderness, care, affection—my love, even if it was not love as we had known it before.

Except for short periods, I couldn't even be happy with

Gérard any more. He would come and take me out to a pleasant restaurant on the outskirts of Paris, and when we got there, I would have to apologise and rush off to 'phone home to see if Henri was all right before I could enjoy our dinner. Gérard accepted this situation with infinite kindness and understanding; but could I expect this kind of sacrifice much longer, take so much love from a man and in return give him my presence only in dribs and drabs? Suppose he got tired of it, should I relapse into the monotony of an existence where I was no longer fully a woman?

When with Henri, I tormented myself by thinking of the complete liberty which our affair allowed Gérard, who had meanwhile got a divorce. Since then he had been waiting for me, seeing me very little, in a working environment which contained plenty of attractive women, and friends to introduce him to them. But he remained wonderfully faithful, often ringing up under a false name, evading journalists' questions and, above all, reassuring me. An hour with me, he said, gave him the courage to work, the will to create. How sweet these words sounded in my ear!

I had another subject for anxiety at this time: Mike. For a year he had been at school in Paris, and he and I spent some idyllic holidays together. But I was not the only parent in the picture: Bill, having acquired a taste for France, was now visiting it often for quite long stays, during which he saw a great deal of our son. After these visits I had to listen for days on end to Mike expatiating on his father's virtues. At fourteen he was the age where you need to have a father who is an archetypal male, and Bill did everything possible to give him the image of one. War hero and Darryl Zanuck-style producer, he threw in for good measure a few highly appreciated James Bond touches. These largely fictitious exploits lent him a seductiveness which seemed very formidable to me; I didn't know where they were going to lead us, but felt sure I should be the one to pay. Once again I was powerless, for Bill had retained the custody of his son: the fact that he had left Mike with me had not made any difference to the legal terms. I sensed there was a threat hanging over me, but did not know how the danger would strike.

It did so sooner than I could have foreseen, and more dramatically. I was getting ready to go out when the 'phone rang. Rolande, my faithful Rolande, who with her husband, Etienne, had shown me so much kindness during my trials, said: 'It's the headmaster of Mike's school, Madame.'

'I have to inform you,' said the headmaster, 'that your husband has just taken your son away.'

I understood, and tried to pretend I hadn't. 'It's a weekday. How can he do that?'

'He has withdrawn him from our school.'

'But—but to go where?'

'They were leaving for California. I gathered they were going directly to the airport.'

The headmaster went on talking, but I scarcely listened to him. What did I care about the apparent legality of this abduction? For that was what it was in my eyes, and a pathologically brutal one at that. It was also the collapse of another whole part of my existence.

Long afterwards I learnt that Bill had dazzled Mike with all sorts of attractions—claiming, for instance, to be the owner of a ranch. What boy could have resisted the mirages of the Wild West? Owning a horse, riding in the prairies, campfires, rifle in the saddle-holster—he put all the panoply of a Hollywood western at Mike's disposal.

I was beaten.

The letters I received were friendly but a little distant. 'I'm well', 'I'm enjoying myself', 'America's marvellous'.

I had no alternative but to resume my trips to California, which I did—to start further legal action. This involved a lot of negotiations, which seemed quite hopeful at one time but ended in disappointment. Mike belonged to Bill till his coming of age.

The weeks and months passed, and I could not settle down in my life. I felt rather as if I were on a deck-chair in the park from which, for reasons unknown to me, I might be chased away at any moment. This was an image from one of my dreams, but it defines pretty well the feelings of insecurity I had.

I went back to Italy for the shooting of *Vacances d'hiver*, and felt like sighing: 'Oh dear, one more film!' Professionally, I was no longer satisfied by my films. I wasn't being rigorous enough in choosing those I would appear in; and though there were actually fewer than before, as I have mentioned, they seemed too many for my weary spirit.

On my return, Henri was not at the station to meet me, but Tanine was. When we got home, I was horrified by his appearance: deathly pale, his eyes without lustre, his manner distraught. The look he gave me was a cry for help. He seemed to collapse before my eyes. I realised he was having a stroke. Tanine and I hastily did what we could for him, and he regained consciousness quite soon.

I was very frightened, sitting there with him. Choking and close to tears, I gazed at him, taking in all the ravages on that emaciated face. I felt once more that I was fighting against hopeless odds, and this time I refrained from saying all the comforting things I had said a hundred times before.

But now he spoke. 'I've made up my mind to go into the clinic again—for my final, definitive cure. This time I'll stick it out'—he smiled wryly—'to the bitter end. I'll be a brave boy.'

He was brave all right. It needed a lot of courage to face the suffering he knew was awaiting him. 'I've fixed it up. They'll take me in three days.'

'Shall we go to Montigny? The air will do you good.'

He agreed, and in that house, which belonged to him, we spent three peaceful days. On the last morning—I shall always see him, coming out of the dining-room into the garden; it was a fine winter morning, a bit cold, and the light made him stand out against a misty background—he turned to me and said: 'I don't know what it is, but—I've got a nasty sort of presentiment.'

'In that case don't go. You're going to be in there for some time. We can put it off for a few days.'

A day or two seemed to matter very little—because I didn't believe in a lasting cure. I had long given up that hope.

But he looked me straight in the eye, and in a firm voice, with new energy, a kind of vehemence, he answered: 'No. This time it's finished. I'm forty, and my follies are over.'

He went into the clinic that day, 9 December, and wouldn't even let me come with him. 'You'll see, my darling, this time I'll get free of it.'

Our parting this time was unbearably sad.

Twenty-four hours after Henri had left the house, I woke up as if by some special prompting. I shut my eyes in a refusal to enter that day which felt fraught with disaster. Images formed behind my closed eyes, and yet I was not asleep: I could see myself at a funeral in a cemetery which was unknown to me. With me were Olga and Bob Dallan, Henri's best friend, who like me had fought with all his might against the drug. He was sobbing desperately. I knew that the funeral was Henri's.

I opened my eyes on the familiar surroundings of my little almond-green room. Behind the window there was a tiny terrace looking out onto the Seine. A barge passed, all was peaceful. What had just happened to me? Why that vision—or was it one? I shook myself. I had to forget my terrors very quickly. I 'phoned the clinic. 'Everything's all right,' said the nurse, 'he's calm and cheerful.' I told her I would 'phone again during the day—and rang off, much relieved.

The day had all the heaviness of my forebodings. When I 'phoned, he was asleep and I decided not to have him woken. Tired and extremely depressed, I returned home early and managed to drop off to sleep. I was woken by the telephone, imperious, insistent. At this time of night—a bad joke by some stranger, or an obscene call? An old friend who had suddenly arrived in town? A wrong number? As I lifted the receiver, I looked at my watch: two o'clock.

'I'm putting you through to the doctor, Madame,' said an impersonal voice.

Then, through a haze, incredible phrases reached me: '... you must be very brave ... I'm afraid your husband ... heart attack ... robust constitution, but his tenth drug cure ... too much for him ...'

Forty-eight hours later I was in Auvergne, in a small

unfamiliar cemetery, with Olga and Bob. It was cold and fine. The December light brought out images sharply. Bob was sobbing his heart out. I was at the setting of my premonitory vision.

In the church, just when the coffin was being blessed, a cock crowed. I don't know what it ought to symbolise, but for me the sound is still associated with grief and tragedy.

For a long time, I hesitated before reporting this extended, painful episode in my private life. In the end I made up my mind to do so for the sake of all the young people today who are attracted to drugs, and who, like Henri, believe they can kick the habit when they want to. If some of them read this account, I shall be satisfied, hoping my testimony may help them to understand just what risks they are taking if they, too, yield to the terrible temptation.

Henri's death left me in an unbalanced state of mind. For eleven years he had been at my side. We had known two years of exceptional love, and for nine years I had been fighting with him against the drug, only to reach this result.

I had been well aware that it was the only possible outcome, yet it surprised me. These last months Henri had been a mere shadow of his old self, but I had remained deeply attached to him. Every day I had worried about what he might have done; I dreaded his appearance in the doorway, when I would judge his condition at a glance. All that was true and terrible and intolerable, but he had been alive. I could rage at him, be sorry for him, lecture him, quarrel with him, slam the door, leave, return—everything then was still possible. Now nothing was.

I began brooding about him, and realised that he had always been an enigma for me: he was one of the people who destroy everything around them, quite at random, without even sparing themselves. I confided my doubts and questionings to Olga and Tanine, who told me I had nothing to reproach myself with. 'I'm not reproaching myself,' I said. 'I just want to understand.'

I avoided thinking about the short pieces of happiness I had enjoyed with Gérard. I felt Henri's death had made everything impossible. 'You're punishing yourself for having been happy. But take care,' Olga warned me. 'You're also punishing Gérard. Do you think he deserves it?'

No, he didn't. Obviously he was even less guilty than I was. Still, it had happened, and I couldn't throw all the guilt onto a dead man. Naturally, in retrospect I see things differently and more objectively. But I had been too shaken by the tragedy to be capable of reasoned judgment.

I felt emotionally drained, and wanted to be alone—except that I missed Mike; his absence was a cruel blow for me just then. I went to see him in California, and found a perfect American teenager. He presented me with the image his father wanted me to receive, and Bill refused to understand that there couldn't be any national rivalry between us. I was not in opposition, trying to make a French boy out of Mike. There was nothing offensive or disagreeable to me in my son having his origins in two different worlds. On the contrary, I could see only advantages: he would possess two cultures, would be bilingual and a wider life would thus be open to him.

Only one thing counted for me, that he should be happy—and he was. California was bound to seem a paradise for a fifteen-year-old in his circumstances, with sun, swimming pool, horse, and vast spaces available to him, dimensions France could not offer, I hoped that in the short term that was enough for him. He was nice to me, but talked about America as if I had never lived there. Without exactly rejecting me, he clearly wanted a man. I could sense that. He was his father's son.

Directly I got back, I became absorbed in two films, for in time of trouble nothing helps like work. One was a re-make of *Grand Hotel*, in which I took over Greta Garbo's role, the dream of the girl I had been; the other was *Les scélerats* with Robert Hossein. Before they were finished, Olga was already talking to me about a prospective film called *Fortunat*, in which I should play opposite Bourvil. She knew that name had a double resonance for me: when I heard it, it conjured up not only my close friendship with Bourvil, but Gérard too. For me they were inseparably linked and would remain so.

Gérard! Olga, as sensitive a friend as ever, kept slipping in little remarks about him with a 'by the way' or 'did you hear that . . .'; following his life from a distance was a bitter-sweet satisfaction in which I allowed myself to indulge. When she declared that he was constantly thinking about me and talking about me, that he was unhappy—I didn't shut her up. I merely didn't respond positively, and left the allusions to him floating in the air, just between the two of us.

I hadn't seen him for six months. One evening I was having dinner with Olga. As we finished the meal I felt relaxed and cheerful for the first time for ages. I felt back in the world again.

'Did you know Gérard has just finished *La main chaude*, his first film as director?'

I heard myself answer: 'I'm very happy for him, I'm really pleased about that.'

'Can I tell him so?'

'No, Olga.'

Perhaps my tone was less firm than usual. She may have sensed a crack in my resolution of which I was not yet conscious.

'Listen, Michèle, I've understood your attitude very well. At the time it may have seemed justified, but now ... You really ought to see him again. Such patience and faithfulness, such sincere love. Why should you have to make yourself unhappy, *and* him?'

'Don't press me—not yet.'

'Give him a date. Meeting him will help you to see yourself more clearly, and realise your true feelings.'

I changed the subject, and talked of Mike, of film plans, of her, of everything except Gérard—whose name was not mentioned again.

On leaving her house, I decided to walk for a bit. I made for the Trocadéro. It was a soft June night; a light breeze stirred the trees in the avenue du President Wilson. I went down towards the Alma. Two years ago I had been at Saint-Paul-de-Vence, dining on the terrace of Les Oliviers with Gérard ...

Why had I said 'no' in answer to Olga's question? 'He's unhappy,' she had said, 'Give him a date. You're going on hurting yourself and him for no reason.'

It was true. That evening there suddenly seemed no reason for it, even though a slow change of mood had been necessary for me. Gérard had given me so much joy—why had I imposed this test on him, on us?

I stopped a taxi. I had to call Olga, I hadn't a minute to lose. She was right: I mustn't make him wait any longer.

So I rediscovered my love; but I hadn't yet rediscovered my son. It did seem to me, however, that Mike's letters, although not so frequent, were less distant. I read between their lines a need to draw closer to me. Bill had put his son in a university near Los Angeles. Mike referred to it little and rather evasively. As to his new stepmother, Ginger Rogers—Bill had just married her—Mike did not mention her in his letters.

At this point Gérard went off to do a film in America. Knowing my anxieties, of course, he made it his business to see Mike. A few days after his arrival, during a telephone conversation, he told me succinctly: 'I've seen Mike. He's splendid! He sends lots of love.' The next week or two he wrote that he often met Mike in Beverly Hills. 'We talk a great deal about you,' he told me. 'By the way, I've straightened up a few wrong ideas he'd got in his head. But he's a man now, you know. No one can dictate to him what he should think.' The phrase sounded a bit cryptic, so Gérard amplified it. 'One has to let him take decisions alone. It's for him to decide what his choice will be ... I think this will be important in the future for your relationship. I gather, too, that he's not enjoying his studies. His father made him do law, and he's only interested in filming and literature.'

In this way I learnt a little more every day about my son. When Gérard returned, he told me the same things again, with one additional item: 'I think he now very much wants to come back over here. "Just to see" is how he put it. That "just to see" is a precaution Mike takes with himself, with life. We have to wait.'

The boy I went to meet at Orly in 1961 was a strapping blond giant, a head taller than me, with a chubby face, blue eyes and a man's voice.

This time he had really returned of his free choice. I was happy, but knew there was still a long way to go before he would rejoin us for good. Mike had never had his father and mother at home together, a partnership essential to his equilibrium. I imagine that a reason why he married very young was because he wanted to achieve the real home and family life he had missed as a boy. He and his wife, Catherine, had a little girl, Samantha, but soon afterwards agreed to a divorce, although, as mentioned earlier, they remained on friendly terms. Seeing for himself how these things can happen, he gained a better understanding of his parents' divorce, and this no doubt helped him to take the last step needed towards me!

From 1960 to 1965 I appeared in many films. Too many—fifteen in five years. This brings me back to a subject I referred to before, on which I must now linger a little. I had been caught up in a system which could not bring much satisfaction. You commit yourself to it the day you accept a scenario which does not really suit you—in order to pay your taxes. This happens insidiously, almost without your knowledge, through a simple mechanism: you become a box-office star, you are paid big fees, and the following year you pay taxes as a result—all very normal. Your name is then thought to represent for producers the guarantee of good takings, which isn't always justified. From these premises things will invariably develop in the same way: a producer offers you a film for which, he tells you, he has obtained the services of X as director, always a prestigious and highly respected name. You read a scenario which you find fairly mediocre. Still, since very often the bare plot is nothing very much—the content of the greatest masterpieces could be summed up in a few trite lines—you take reassurance from the thought that talent can change lead into gold, and that if X accepts the idea, he knows what he's doing.

It is at this precise point that misunderstandings creep in. All too often X is in the same state as you—his predominant interest is to pay his taxes. Having his name advanced has been a guarantee for you, so you do not at once turn down the offer made to you. The producer, armed with what he considers an acceptance in principle, tells the director whose name has been advanced, often before that director has even been approached: Michèle Morgan, say, or Jean Gabin, has agreed to appear in a film with this scenario. X reads it, and goes through the same sort of reasoning as you. If Michèle, or Jean, has accepted it ... So both are taken in, needing the money, and you all come together to make a film it might have been better not to make, because talent can't be forced.

After this first stage, the second aggravates your situation so that it is beyond curing. The fee for the film having increased your income, your taxes will also be heavier. The following year, to pay them, you will have to accept a plot which doesn't quite suit you—and so the knot tightens.

I am simplifying a bit, of course: the process is sometimes more complex. But it is still basically the same, and a good many mediocre films, despite fine cast lists and excellent production teams, have come about like this.

It's a dangerous system, but as Olga observed: 'If you want to finish with it, it will mean big financial sacrifices.' I realised that. I was quite clear-sighted, and knew perfectly well that such a decision was going to transform my existence. But I not only accepted the decision, I welcomed it: I would make fewer films, but have more time to live.

Directly I had made up my mind, I began by eliminating the films and television appearances where there was a story I didn't believe in, a poor part which was out of character for me, or to which the public wouldn't give credence if played by me. For instance, the only time I agreed to play the part of a 'bitch', in *Retour de manivelle*, no one found it convincing!

It is not only producers who shut you off in a particular category; you are type cast, of course, by the public as well. Some are naturals for acting 'goodies', others are doomed to play bastards. I was assigned victim parts, women with unhappy fates, who are generally crying and/or dying. This is ironical for someone like me who loves cheerfulness and laughter, and we have always in my family had a vocation for happiness.

No producer or director had dared move away from the model in which I had been cast from the age of sixteen to the age of forty. It took the advent of *Benjamin* for me to be offered a character which, without being quite the real me, no longer conformed to the Michèle Morgan stereotype. I very much enjoyed interpreting this role and felt at ease in it. With a confidence justified by the film's success, I awaited offers of similar parts; but none came. There were plenty of other offers, but none had the qualities I was looking for.

Had I become too 'choosey'? I didn't think so, but I was at an age when one has reached a turning-point. It was nice that newspaper articles hailed 'the still beautiful Michèle Morgan', very gratifying that the polls still proclaimed me 'the most popular actress'; but this did not alter the facts— that I needed a different choice, and was not being offered one. The New Wave came up. These young directors were not without talent, only money. They hadn't the resources to pay for stars, and this contributed to the birth of a new generation of leading film directors, actors and actresses, who were and are remarkable enough. To one director, Claude Lelouch, I owe much—for it was he, eight years later, who offered me the female lead in *Le chat et la souris*. This film must take a big place in my professional life, for without it I might have finally succumbed to the wear and tear of thirty years of stardom.

It was a revelation to me. After thirty-five years in my career, a director was using me as I was: a real-life character. This film technique, less static, in direct contact, delighted me. No more dialogue learnt by heart, no more marks to set out the course you had to cover. The lines you spoke arose out of the situation and the actor could modify them in accordance with the feeling of the moment; a camera on the shoulder allowed an exceptional freedom of movement, in which I immediately felt at home. In my fifties I was discovering a new liberty!

This was not only professional. Before that I had experienced a different liberty, the sort which lets you take holidays. Suddenly time had changed its dimensions. I felt I was going to be able to put everything I wanted into it: reading, exhibitions, travel, painting. Since my first lesson with Kisling, I had never stopped painting. Whenever it was possible, I had taken my brushes to try to re-create faces or landscapes. It was like a thirst; it became almost a necessity of life as more and more images accumulated within me. I had passed the stage of the quick sketch that gives you fair satisfaction; I wanted something else. I was looking for a way of expressing myself, realising my deep need for shapes and colours.

It was through doing linear exercises that I began to produce abstract compositions which were displayed in an exhibition. Through them, in contrast to the way artists generally develop, I came to the figurative, in the form of cut-outs—which were also exhibited. But now I have gone on to something else: large profiles, above all of Samantha, my favourite model, more than life-size, in which pen and wash occupy a preponderant place, bordering on the decorative.

Painting, in fact, is a way for me to communicate with others, with life. But of course nothing would have been the same if I had not had Gérard at my side.

When we found each other again, we knew it was for good—in both senses. Deliberately, to safeguard our love, we have chosen to remain 'lovers'. Why should we marry? As a married woman, though no doubt my career was partly responsible, I had never known what a married couple's life could be like. Today, paradoxically, I really do lead a wife's existence. I am Madame Oury in all but name. Whether it's a matter of excursions or his work, we stay together. It's another way of continuing in this profession, which I have never ceased to love. Film projects, scenarios, ideas—we discuss them together. He reads me his dialogue, his gags; I am his 'test bench' and my spontaneous laugh makes me, he says, his best audience!

With *La folie des grandeurs* we went to Spain together. *Le Corniaud* took us to Italy. For *Rabbi Jacob* I returned to the United States. I had lived in that country for six years, and had travelled in it a lot, but there were some parts and some sides of it that I did not like or did not know. Gérard has completely changed my view of things. He has a different way of looking at the world, wide and comprehensive, which draws me to new horizons.

The only thing we have never achieved together is a film. But, then, Gérard is above all an author and director of comedy films, which, alas, are evidently not for me. For years I may have been rather 'difficult' when offered parts. If so, it is because I don't want to be separated from him, and very often turn them down so that I can stay in his company. With Gérard I have found happiness.

You don't tell a story you are in the process of living, even if it has already lasted for twenty years.

Les Oliviers, 1977

550